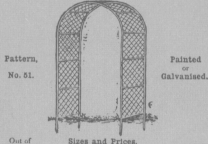

GLASS HOUSES

May Woods and Arete Swartz Warren

GLASS HOUSES

A History of Greenhouses, Orangeries and Conservatories

RIZZOLI
NEW YORK

For Gil, James, Hattie and Simon Woods
&

William Bradford Warren and James W. C. Swartz

First published in the United States of America in 1988 by
Rizzoli International Publications, Inc.
597 Fifth Avenue, New York, NY 10017

Library of Congress Cataloging-in-Publication Data

Woods, May.
    Glass houses / May Woods and Arete Swartz Warren.
        p.   cm.
    Bibliography: p.
    Includes index.
    ISBN 0-8478-0906-4 : $45.00
    1. Glass construction.   2. Conservatories.   3. Greenhouses.
I. Warren, Arete Swartz.   II. Title.
NA4140.W66 1988
728'.9—dc19   87-32048
                                                CIP

Designed by Derek Birdsall RDI

Printed and bound in Hong Kong

Contents

Introduction

Acknowledgements

The friendly helpfulness of the people from whom we have sought assistance in the task of writing this book has been a source of unexpected pleasure. Not only have staff in libraries and record offices helped in finding information, but owners of old greenhouses and conservatories, gardeners, garden historians, architects and manufacturers of conservatories have often gone far beyond a quick reply, and enriched the book with their thoughtful answers. In an effort to ensure as much accuracy as possible, many people have read paragraphs about specific buildings; to all those who contributed in this and other myriad ways, our gratitude is far from perfunctory. Particular thanks are due to Mr Leo Pemberton, Head of the School of Horticulture at the Royal Botanic Gardens, Kew, who corrected and added to the chapter 'The Conservatory Today'.

We are most grateful for information, ideas or permission to photograph from the following people in Britain and Europe: Mr Bruce Bailey, Mr Paul Barker, Mrs Mavis Batey, the Marquess of Bath, the Duke of Beaufort, Signora Benelli, Mrs Jinty Blanckenhagen, Viscount Boyne, the Marquis de Breteuil, Miss Juliet Brightmore, Mr Aafke Brunt, Mr Julius Bryant, M. Jean-Noel Burte, Mr T.H. Byers, Mr J.R. Chichester-Constable, Professor Ferdinand Chiostri, Mrs H. Clifford, Mr Thomas Cook, Mrs Rosemary Dee, the Duke of Devonshire, Madame Jean-Claude Dewavrin, Mr John Dinkel, Lady Dodds-Parker, Mrs A. Dundas-Bekker, Mr Paul Edwards, Lord Egremont, Lord Eliot, Sir Edmund Fairfax-Lucy, Lord Faringdon, Mr J. Faulkner, Mrs Charles Foster, Mrs James Franks, Mr Jeffrey Gold, Lady Graham, Col. Tom Hall, the Earl of Harrowby, Col. J.B. Hickson, Mrs M. Houliston, Mr Norman Hudson, Lord Hylton, Sir Thomas Ingilby, Mr F.C. Jolly, Miss Fiona Laird, Mrs Ian Laird, Madame Emanuel La Roche, Miss Helen Littledale, Signor Marchi, the Duke of Marlborough, Mr and Mrs Peter Marston, Mrs Eve Molesworth, Mrs Patricia Moore, Mr Charles Morris, Mrs P.M. Nicholson, the Marquess of Northampton, the Comtesse d'Oultremont, Mr Frank Owen, Mr A.E. Pattison, Mrs D. Peake, Mr M.A. Pearman, M. René Pechère, Signora Petropoulo, Mr John Phillips, Mr T.R. Robertson, Mr John Martin Robinson, Lord Romsey, Mrs Kay Sanecki, Mr Kurt Schwarz, Vicomte de Sigalas, Lord Somerleyton, Mrs Charmian Stirling, Mr H.R. Tempest, Mr M. Thoroton Hildyard, Dr Eric Till, Mr Maurice Tomlin, Mr Michael Verweij, Comte de Vogüé, Mrs G. Waud, Mrs Roger Wethered, Dr D.O. Wijnands, Mr G.D. Wilson, Madame Charles de Yturbe.

In the United States of America, we greatly appreciated the assistance of the following: Emilio Ambasz, Dwight Ashdown, David Bates, Edward Larabee Barnes, Alistair Bevington, Paul Doguereau, Emily Monk Davidson, Jane B. Davies, Rudy J. Favretti, Joel Fry, Michael Jantzen, Francisca Paine Irwin, Thomas Martin, Melinda Florian Papp, Patrick Pinnell, G. Bland Platt, Michelle Plaut, Paul Rudolph, Mrs Morgan Schiller, Mrs H. Gwynne Tayloe, Peggy Wiseman.

The staff of many institutions have also been most helpful, and we would like in particular to thank: Berkshire Record Office; British Library; Chelsea Physic Garden, Mr Duncan Donald; Cheshire County Council; English Heritage; Fairlawne Estate; Glasgow Botanic Gardens, Mr E.W. Curtis; Hampton Court Palace, Mr G.W. Cooke; Landmark Trust; Lord Chamberlain's Office, Mr M.E. Bishop; National Library of Wales; National Trust, Miss B. Cousens, Mr Tom Garnon, Mr J.P. Haworth, Mr Martin Knebel, Dr John Maddison,

Mr A. Mitchell, Mr Christopher Rowell, Major H.N. Williams; National Trust for Scotland, Mr J.E. Robson, Mr Michael Tebbutt; Northamptonshire Record Office; Nottingham University Library; Oxfordshire County Record Office; Royal Botanic Gardens, Kew, Mr John Simmons, Mr Hans Fliegner and several members of staff in the Library; Royal Commission on the Ancient and Historical Monuments of Scotland; Royal Commission on the Historical Monuments of England; Royal Horticultural Society, Dr Brent Elliot and his assistants; Royal Institute of British Architects, Drawings Collection and Library; Scottish Record Office; Somerset Fire Brigade; Surrey County Record Office; Victoria and Albert Museum; Warwickshire County Record Office.

The staff of American institutions whose assistance has been invaluable include: The Avery Architectural and Fine Arts Library, Janet Park and Lisa Rosenthal; Biltmore Estate, Susan Ward; Canadian Centre for Architecture; City of Baltimore, Horticultural Division; Commonwealth of Virginia, Division of Historic Landmarks, Calder Loth; Connecticut Historial Society; Cooper-Hewitt Museum of Design, The Smithsonian Institution; The Historical Society of Pennsylvania; The Horticultural Society of New York, Vicki Moeser and Charles Anzalone; *House and Garden*, Diana Edkins; John Bartram Association, Ruth Wett; The Library of Congress, C. Ford Peatross; Longwood Gardens, Colvin Randall; Lord and Burnham; Lyndhurst, The National Trust for Historic Preservation, Barbara Hammond; Mark Twain Memorial, Wynn Lee; The Maryland Historical Society, Barbara Wells Sarudy; The Metropolitan Museum of Art; The Missouri Botanical Garden, William Wagner; Mount Vernon Ladies Association, Dean Norton; Municipal Archives, Evelyn Gonzalez; The New York Botanical Garden, Susan Fraser; The New-York Historical Society; The New York Public Library; The New York Yacht Club; The Redwood Library and Athenaeum, Richard L. Champlin; Society for the Preservation of Long Island Antiquities, Robert B. MacKay and Carol Traynor; Society for the Preservation of New England Antiquities, Laura Condon; Stevens Institute of Technology, Jane G. Hartye; Historic Hudson Valley, Jacquetta Haley; Walpole (New Hampshire) Historical Society, Ruth Lepovsky.

We are indebted to the former art editor, Alison Rivett, and to the editor, Angela Dyer, for advice, encouragement and answered queries. We also thank Hugh Palmer, for originally introducing us to Aurum Press, and for his photographs which capture magic, fragility and tranquillity. To the designer, Derek Birdsall, who turned a thick manuscript and bundles of photographs into an elegant book with breathtaking skill, we are profoundly grateful.

Many friends, too numerous to list, have helped in locating yet more glass houses, and in countless other ways. But to all the members of our families go the greatest thanks. Their ability to teach computer skills, to tolerate neglected domestic tasks, to advise on the text, and to maintain (apparent) enthusiasm has been magnificent. We thank them all, particularly our husbands, Gil Woods and William Warren.

M.W. & A.S.W.

Preface

The idea for this book arose during a conversation in 1984 with Peter Marston, of Marston and Langinger, a company which was building a new conservatory for my husband and me in London. When Peter confirmed that a 'how to' book on conservatories did not exist, the challenge of writing one became irresistible. The book therefore started as a practical guide, with a summary of the modern conservatory's antecedents. But old orangeries and Victorian conservatories were found to be so appealing that the book turned rapidly into a history, embracing architecture, horticultural experiment, and the people who brought the buildings to life. The scope expanded still further as research revealed the fascination with exotic plants of gardeners, master and servant alike, in the sixteenth and seventeenth centuries, and the close contact between gardeners in the countries of northern Europe. It then seemed logical to describe the influential buildings of Europe, and to carry the tale across the Atlantic to North America; and so I asked Arete Swartz Warren, a good friend for many years and an art historian, to write about American glass houses.

One of the early problems was in deciding how to handle a basic discrepancy in terminology: a building now commonly called an orangery in Britain was called a greenhouse until the early nineteenth century. The reader may be surprised to read about 'the greenhouse at Kensington Palace', rather than 'the orangery at Kensington Palace', but it was impossible to sustain use of the term 'orangery' when all contemporary quotations referred to a 'greenhouse'. For this reason, the buildings in this book are called as they were by their owners at the time of construction.

The main challenge has been in selecting examples from the wealth of material uncovered, and in having to omit many names and places. The book has been written for the general reader, not purely as a thesis for plant, garden and architecture historians who might have found a longer catalogue of references useful. Equally, the enormous volume of engravings, architectural drawings and photographs has led to the exclusion of much material, so that the illustrations, like the buildings, are but a representative sample.

This is the first historical survey of greenhouses, orangeries and conservatories in Britain since Kenneth Lemmon's *The Covered Garden* in 1962, and the first ever study about their counterparts in America; since there is still much to be researched and much to be written, it is hoped that the book will stimulate others to explore this fascinating subject further.

May Woods
London 1987

Introduction

The history of orangeries, greenhouses and conservatories is a study of architecture, but architecture influenced by man's perception of the needs of tender plants, and his desire to enjoy them. When delicate plants from the East, such as citrus trees, reached the centre of the Roman Empire, primitive arrangements were made to protect them in winter. As the citrus were taken northwards and as tropical plants were added to the old sub-tropical favourites, so perceptions of their requirements changed, and the buildings changed too. Gardeners theorized on heat and light, and architects made plans accordingly, within aesthetic limits. From the plain masonry house with large windows of the mid-seventeenth century, the eighteenth-century greenhouse evolved gradually into an elegant temple for orange and lemon trees, oleanders and geraniums, usually emptied in summer so that the plants could benefit from maximum light.

The era of rapid change came in the first forty years of the nineteenth century, stimulated by a flood of tropical plants, reaching a climax at Chatsworth. With the introduction of glass roofs, the old decorative greenhouses were transformed from empty halls in summer to permanent landscaped displays, gleaming with flowers and glinting in the sunlight. Then followed the proliferation of conservatories, large and small, public and private, but ablaze with blooms under a canopy of tapering palm leaves, until many were shattered by war in the twentieth century.

Glass buildings have a certain irresistible fascination. The system of construction is apparent even to the layman, and inside, the brightness of the environment is particularly appealing. Recent books[1] have stimulated an interest in the glass houses of the nineteenth century, while today's architects use glass for dramatic and subtle effect in commercial buildings and in the new botanic houses at Missouri, Frankfurt and Kew.

With the exception of the twentieth-century commercial buildings, glass houses have come about through the curiosity of man the gardener. Gardeners are inventive, taking great pleasure in growing a superb rose or succulent peach, while botanists delight in examining and classifying a new plant, discovering its habits, its needs, its flowers and its fruit, its means of propagation and, nowadays, in saving it from extinction.

A page from a volume of illustrations of plants, birds and animals, written and illuminated in northern Italy in the late fourteenth century. The volume is thought to relate to the Secreta Salernitana, a manuscript about plants with medicinal properties which was compiled in Salerno during the twelfth century.

The Gardens of the Ancient World

Nothing much changes under the sun, and gardeners today are much like their predecessors. While gardeners of ancient times would have been preoccupied with food production, time would still have been found for trees and flowers; insatiable intellectual curiosity caused any novel seed or seedling, pip or kernel, bulb or root to be cherished with devoted care. Plants have crossed frontiers and seas by design and accident. Sometimes seeds would be brought by traders dealing in grain, in fruit and in vegetable produce. Sometimes seedling trees or small plants would be dug up and transported. And sometimes strange seeds would simply be blown on the wind.

Clues about the native climate of the newly arrived plant would be sought by the gardener, but luck and good judgement would probably determine its chances of survival, within the parameters of conventional wisdom. The Greeks and the Romans were well aware that warm soil promotes root development, especially important in the early stage of a plant's life, and encourages growth generally. Its efficacy is particularly apparent in the spring when combined with slowly strengthening rays of sunshine; a combination of the two together produces earlier flowering, which in turn produces an earlier crop of fruit or vegetables. This technique is known as forcing. And what was the heating agent? It was dung from the stables. Known to farmers as an excellent fertilizer when spread liberally on fields, manure when piled up generates considerable heat, which it retains for two or three months.

Villa gardens around Rome and other major cities of the Empire were planned as pleasant retreats. Shady walks of cypresses, groves of olive trees, hedges of bay and laurel, clipped box, fountains and marble basins, pools of water and statues were the principal features, but the kitchen garden was important too. Using all the techniques at their disposal, Roman gardeners employed the principle of forcing growth by making hot-beds, either by digging pits in the ground, or by constructing raised beds surrounded by a low brick wall and filling them up with manure. A third option was to make a bed on wheels, a giant wooden wheelbarrow that could be trundled in and out. The outdoor beds would often be covered at night with wooden boards to keep the heat in and protect emerging plants from late frosts.

Thoughtful gardeners realized that if warmth and daylight were available for longer they could produce even earlier crops. However, although Roman glassmakers produced plenty of beautiful beads and fine drinking vessels, they were not very adept at making flat glass. Their attempts, by pouring molten glass into trays, were largely unsuccessful because the finished product was scarcely transparent at all; transparency could only be achieved if the cast pane was then ground and polished, a very expensive process.

The alternative was mica, which was used in house windows. Mica is a type of rock which, when split into thin sheets, is surprisingly transparent. By covering hot-beds with sheets of mica, melons and cucumbers were forced to crop early and to crop late, thus extending the season considerably. By the second century AD, the gardeners' expertise was sufficiently reliable for Emperor Tiberius Caesar's doctor to prescribe a cucumber a day to cure an imperial illness. History does not relate if the gardeners fulfilled this order or not, but Tiberius Caesar's penchant for throwing unpopular guests and disgraced servants over a cliff top must certainly have concentrated the minds of his gardeners!

Other techniques for advancing growth were also used, such as pouring hot water into a trench surrounding rose roots or covering plants with bell jars, and building fires in between vines on frosty nights. There were experiments too with stoves within a little house with a mica wall. Archaeologists have found the remains of just such a building in Pompeii, which obviously predates the destruction of that city in 79 AD. It has a wall with flues, to allow heat from the stove to warm the bricks and thus the air, and tiers of masonry on which plants would be displayed. There are also indications of the existence of a screen of rough glass or mica.[1] This may seem a far cry from the greenhouses and winter gardens of northern Europe, but nonetheless it is the glass house in embryo.

Apart from forcing vegetables, gardeners of the ancient world lavished care on orange trees. The sweet fragrance of orange flowers, the colour of the fruit, the quality of the flesh and the versatility of the juice all combine to make an orange tree beguiling. The fruit had been immortalized, too, in Greek mythology, in the legend of Hesperides. Hesperides owned a magnificent garden that abounded in ornamental trees and exquisite fruit; amongst its greatest treasures were trees bearing golden apples, since assumed to mean oranges. This enchanted place, where Hesperides' daughters played, was forbidden to gods and mortals alike and was guarded by a fearsome dragon that never slept. However, the golden apples were so tempting that Hercules devised a plan to outwit the dragon and steal the golden apples. He succeeded, but Minerva returned them to the garden, fearful of the dragon's revenge. The legend of Hesperides was well known in Renaissance days, and resulted in his name being associated with the culture of orange trees.

Different varieties of citrus fruit reached Italy over many centuries from south-east Asia. Oranges, lemons and limes grew wild on the southern slopes of the Himalayas and in southern China. The fruit and its blossoms were praised in poems and commemorated in paintings. But they were also sought after for medicinal purposes, as the astute Chinese had found that eating the fruit was beneficial. For the Japanese, the flower was a symbol of romantic love.

From China and Japan, citrus trees had spread to India, and it was from India that Portuguese traders were said to have brought more orange trees to Europe in the later Middle Ages. The name also came from India, the Sanskrit word for orange, *naranga,* being modified into *auranja* in Old Provençal, into *orange* in French and *arancia* in Italian.

Italian Gardens in the Renaissance

Italian decorative gardens of the fifteenth century contained only a limited number of plants and trees, a concentration which must have heightened the effect of massed blossom and the power of fragrance. From the Romans, Renaissance gardeners had inherited orange trees, myrtles, oleanders and pomegranates. Medieval introductions included maidenhair fern and the Italian arum lily. The fruit of the early orange trees was very bitter, but in the fifteenth and sixteenth centuries came a less bitter orange, *Citrus aurantium,* the Seville orange, *Citrus aurantium bigardia*, and the lemon, *Citrus limonum*, plus the citron tree, *Citrus medica*. Another welcome arrival was white jasmine from Persia, *Jasminum officinale*, with its enchanting scent, and two new lilies, *Amaryllis belladonna* and *Amaryllis blanda*.

In the gardens and groves of Naples and southwards citrus trees grow outside in the ground, but further north they need to be protected. They can tolerate a short spell of near freezing temperatures, and some soggy snow, particularly the bitter orange, which is hardier than sweeter varieties. Around Rome, many centuries ago, trees would have been moved indoors or covered with wood or

The garden at the Villa Aldobrandini, laid out between 1598 and 1603, is dominated by potted trees raised on every available wall. They would all have to be watered twice daily in summer.

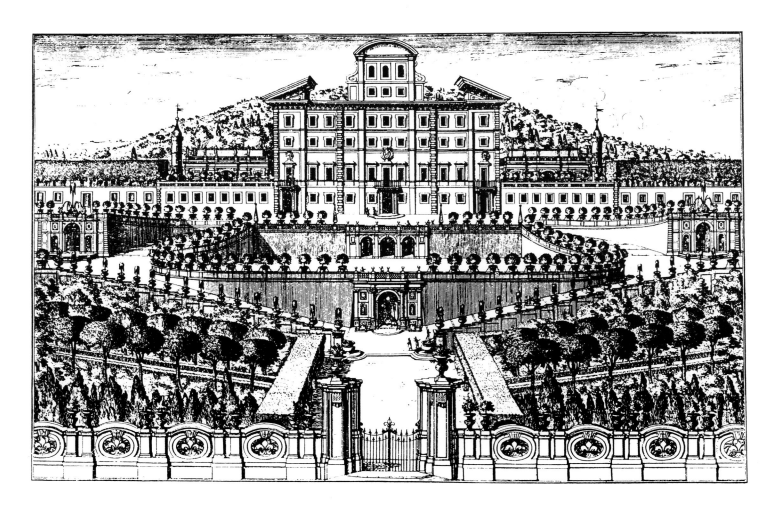

canvas. In central Italy, the Po valley and Tuscany, wooden houses were built up around them from October to April. An alternative was to move the trees to a stone building, which required heating only in long periods of exceptional cold. Another practice was to place the trees in dry underground caves, or grottoes. Plentiful daylight is not an important factor in winter months; much more important is keeping the trees in a dry atmosphere.

While there are still many villas that date from the fifteenth century, few gardens can be proved to have remained unchanged over five centuries. In Tuscany, the Villa Palmieri, which is on the old road from Florence to Fiesole, has a lemon garden which is said to date from the middle of the fifteenth century. There has been a house and a garden on this site since the middle of the fourteenth century, for Boccaccio so fell in love with it that he immortalized it in *The Decameron,* written in about 1350. Boccaccio's idyllic garden was filled with *a thousand different kinds of gaily coloured flowers, and surrounded by a line of flourishing bright green orange and lemon trees, which, with their mature and unripe fruit and lingering shreds of blossom, offered agreable shade to the eyes and a delightful aroma to the nostrils.*[2]

In 1454 Palmiero Palmieri bought the villa, and tradition asserts that he created a lemon garden. The villa has been rebuilt, and the garden altered over the centuries according to prevailing fashions, but the citrus trees are still there. In the middle is a fountain with a wide circular bowl, surrounded by eight stately lemon trees. More lemons are arranged in the four quarters of the oval garden, placed between neatly clipped box hedges. Behind is the *limonaia,* or lemon house, where the trees are taken in winter. Of simple, pleasing proportions, it is decorated with a balustrade and urns, and the terraced roof provides a good prospect of the lemon garden, the countryside and the city of Florence. The lemon house is thought to date from about 1700, when much of the villa was rebuilt.

Another Italian, Pasello da Mercogliano of Naples, grew orange trees for the kings of France at the end of the fifteenth and early in the sixteenth century. Mercogliano may have been engaged by Charles VIII, who conducted a triumphant campaign in Italy in 1495. The French king, his generals and his knights were all immensely impressed by the achievements of the early Italian Renaissance; they returned to France bursting with new ideas on architecture and gardens. With the aid of Italian artists, craftsmen and gardeners, Charles VIII set about turning his castle at Amboise on the Loire into an earthly paradise *à l'Italien.* Mercogliano made an orange garden surrounded by a wooden gallery, partly made of trellis, and probably including the building where the trees passed the winter. Charles VIII died in 1498 before it was completed, but his successors continued the project, and helped to spread the Italian concepts of garden design throughout northern Europe.

The Flowering of the Renaissance

In the midst of the crescendo of artistic activity in Renaissance Italy, the garden was not forgotten. Major architects, such as Giuliano da Sangallo, Niccolo Tribolo and Michelozzo, produced drawings for a garden when making plans for a new palace or a new villa. The garden was treated as a visual extension of the house, and architectural features were incorporated into it to unite the two in a single concept. Terraces, balustrades, stairways, statues, fountains, cascades, shaded pools, grottoes, mazes and long walks were all typical features of sixteenth-century gardens.

The architectural treatment of the garden also extended to trees and plants. Cypress, box, bay and citruses were popular because they could be made to play a part in the great scheme. They could be planted in handsome terracotta pots and clipped to a variety of shapes – conical or ball-shaped, standard with a round head or espaliered – and could therefore give height to a flat terrace. Of all the delicate foreign plants grown in Italy at the time, citrus trees became the most important precisely because they responded to the need for sculpted form. They achieved a significance greater than blossom and fruit alone could justify.

Two methods of culture had evolved. The first was in response to architectural demands, with trees being grown in pots to adorn terraces and stairways. Apart from the aesthetic satisfaction of this method, there was the further advantage that the trees could be grown in the best possible compost, superior to natural soil in the ground. These had, however, to be moved away in winter, for to protect individual trees in situ would have been unsightly. Winter accommodation was either indoors in a stone building, in a purpose-built house in the larger gardens, or in a dry cave.

In creating the famous gardens of the Villa d'Este at Tivoli, near Rome, from 1550 onwards, Pirro Ligorio insisted on movable trees. The theatrical effect of rows of trees was vital, and a garden bare of orange trees in winter was preferable to one dotted with ramshackle little sheds or canvas shrouds. The same approach was found at Frascati, another celebrated garden. It had been laid out for Cardinal Aldobrandini when Giacomo designed the villa between 1598 and 1603. Here, orange trees in pots were packed on to every wall and balustrade to accentuate the divisions between one part of the garden and another.

The other method was to plant the trees in rows together in the ground and build up temporary shelter around them in winter. This principle was in widespread use, as ground-planted trees are taller and bushier with more flowers and fruit, and in many ways are easier to grow for they do not need constant watering. The disadvantage was that erecting the winter house every year must have been a major performance; the structure was bound, by definition, to be draughty, making heating much more difficult; and the sheds were very plain. However, in many eyes, the size and quality of the fruit outweighed such considerations.

The gardens at the Villa Pratolino, painted by
Giusto Utens in 1599. Elaborate waterworks
were the most spectacular feature of this garden,
which also boasted a wooden frame for winter
protection of orange trees in a prominent position
near the villa.

The gardens of the Villa Pratolino in Tuscany, famed for their water-works, had just such a wintering shed around a small plantation of citrus trees. As shown in Giusto Utens's painting, it is in a prominent position close to the house, and the frame of the shed appears to be a permanent fixture. Another example of a movable wooden structure was at Ferrara, on the banks of the Po. A German traveller, by the name of Schickhardt, visited it in 1599, and described how orange trees covered an area fifty yards long by thirteen yards wide. The trees were sheltered from north winds by a high wall, and boards were erected every winter. This type of construction was copied further north, at Heidelberg in Germany and Beddington in England.

Villas and gardens were a major interest for the Medici family, the bankers and rulers of Florence. They owned several villas outside the city, which they used as hunting lodges, as a retreat from the heat of the city, or as a bolthole when the political climate became too hot, such as the Villa Reale di Castello. This villa became the favourite residence of Duke Cosimo I and his wife, Eleonora of Toledo, whom he married in 1538. Cosimo and Eleonora created a spectacular garden, with stone and bronze statues, a fountain and a superb grotto. There were also orange and lemon trees which Eleonora had brought with her from Naples, as she considered them superior to those in Tuscany. A simple stone orange house, an *aranciera*, was built to the west of the garden; this was replaced in 1815 by the large building which now houses some four hundred citrus trees in winter, many of which may be Eleonora's trees and their offspring. Some of them are many, many years old, with thick and twisted trunks, and some are in pots bearing the Medici coat of arms so they must have been made before the disintegration of the ruling family in 1730.

Duchess Eleonora was largely responsible for creating another splendid garden at the Pitti Palace, now known as the Boboli Gardens. The citrus collection was, and still is, summered on a round island, called the *isolotto*, set within an oval pond. The centrepiece is an enormous fountain by Giovanni da Bologna, and the island is now planted with box and roses and studded with orange and lemon trees. There is a very large early nineteenth-century *aranciera* nearby, with an immense doorway, which houses the trees in winter.

The beauty and riches of the Italian Renaissance had a profound influence beyond the Alps; garden design was just one shining facet of cultural brilliance that astounded travellers from the north. Sixteenth-century visitors found the gardens of Italy infinitely superior to their counterparts in Germany, France, the Low Countries and England. When they journeyed back they took with them not only the Italian concept of design and technical expertise, but also some of the basic ingredients: myrtles, pomegranates, oleanders, oranges and lemons.

The Neapolitan gardener, Pasello da Mercogliano, whom Charles VIII had brought to France from Italy in 1495, became the most influential garden designer in France. He undertook major commissions at Blois for Louis XII and at Gaillon for Cardinal Amboise, and many others, although it is not known where, other than at Amboise, he introduced exotic plants. The impact of Italian tastes in the arts was continually fostered too by young French architects returning from the cities of Florence and Rome, and Florence also provided Henri II with his bride, Catherine de' Medici, in 1533. She would have been reminded of home by the garden at Fontainebleau, where orange trees in tubs surrounded a fountain to Diana. The garden at Fontainebleau had been laid out for François I in the 1520s when citrus trees would still have been a great novelty. In addition to Italian stock, the Portuguese are known to have brought a cargo of orange trees from India to France in 1520, and also planted them in the Canary Islands and Madeira about the same time. By 1566, there was a large orange grove at Hyères, near the port of Toulon in the south of France. This and other orchards in Provence supplied the market around Paris with citrus trees, which were becoming extremely fashionable.

Most large collections of citruses were probably covered with timber in winter, but some would have been moved indoors, per-

The orange garden, or orangerie, *at Fontainebleau*

haps into *orangeries*. Such was the one at the château of Anet. The château and *orangerie* had been designed by Philibert de l'Orme for Diane de Poitiers, Henri II's mistress, and built in 1555. There was a walled orange garden, complete with stone *orangerie*, outside the private garden. The orange garden is quite small, surrounded on three sides by protective walls, with a house standing on the north side. The orange trees were kept in the centre section of the ground floor, behind three arched windows which provided light and winter sun. The château and its gardens were illustrated by Androuet du Cerceau in *Les Plus Excellents Bastiments de la France,* published in 1576, but the Renaissance garden and *orangerie* have long since gone.

From the middle of the sixteenth century, the famous five – orange and lemon trees, myrtles, pomegranates and oleanders – were novelties within the reach of nobles and merchants as well as kings. They could be bought in the horticultural markets of France and the Low Countries. From simple winter quarters they were brought out to grace the parterres in summer, an important feature of the formal Renaissance garden.

The château of Anet, built in 1555 for Diane de Poitiers, illustrated by Androuet du Cerceau. Above the château and its walled garden is the orangerie, *with three arched windows and turreted towers.*

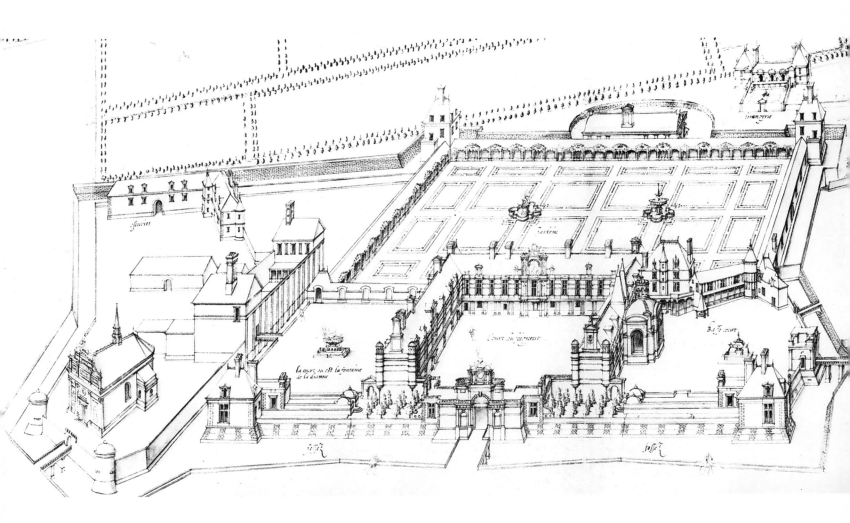

If delight may provoke men's labour, what greater delight is there than to behold the earth apparelled with plants, as with a robe of embroidered worke, set with Orient pearles and garnished with great diversitie of rare and costly jewels?

From the dedication to Lord Burghley in John Gerard's *Herbal*, 1597

John Gerard's vision of the earth as a robe fit for the Faerie Queen, gleaming with pearls and dazzling with jewels, shows how ambitious garden design had become by the end of the sixteenth century. The inference is that the native plants of England alone could not have produced such a shining panoply, and they had indeed been supplemented by new foreign species during the course of the century.

Every monarch and courtier in Europe vied with his or her foreign counterparts in pomp and pageant, fashion and learning, and delighted in displaying signs of civilized achievement. News of Renaissance Rome, Florence, Venice, Padua, Vicenza and other Italian cities had filtered steadily northwards, brought by travellers, soldiers of fortune and envoys. There was immense curiosity too about the world beyond Europe and the Mediterranean; explorers and adventurers risked their lives searching for knowledge, ancient civilizations and treasures of gold and silver. Novelties of every sort were brought back to Europe and carefully examined for information that could expand the sum of human knowledge. People liked to make collections of rare items, which they would show to friends and visiting travellers. This enthusiasm for rarities spilled into the garden.

One Englishman whose interests reached beyond the Channel was Sir William Cecil, later Lord Burghley, who became Queen Elizabeth I's Secretary of State on her accession in 1558. Apart from directing affairs of state, he was one of the foremost architects of his day, building no less than three prestigious mansions: Burghley in Northamptonshire, and two which have been demolished, Cecil House in The Strand, London, and Theobalds in Hertfordshire. Although nothing remains of the Tudor garden at Burghley, some of Cecil's correspondence reveals an inquisitive interest in exotic plants and the art of gardening.

William Cecil's elder son, Thomas, was a wild young man, whom his father sent to Paris in 1561 in the charge of Sir Thomas Windebank. Correspondence between the two knights shows that young Thomas had no intention of denying himself any of the pleasures that Paris had to offer. While writing about Thomas's behaviour, Cecil asked Windebank to find a French gardener for him, and also any novel plants. On 25 March the following year Cecil wrote to Windebank again about gardening matters, saying that he had heard that *Mr Caroo* [Francis Carew of Beddington] *meaneth to send home certen orege pomgranat lymon and myrt trees. I have alredy an orrege tree, and if ye price be not much, I pray you procure for me a lymon, a pomgranat, and a myrt tree, and help that they may be sent home to London with Mr Caroo's trees, and before hand send me in wryting a perfect declaration how they ought to be used kept and ordered.*[3]

Sir Thomas lost no time in carrying out these orders, and replied at some length on 8 April, slightly worried about the cost of his purchases. *According to your commandement, I have sent unto you by*

William Cecil, Lord Burghley, attributed to Marcus Gheeraerts the younger

Mr Curo's man with his master's trees, a lymmon tree and 2 myrte trees in 2 pottes, which cost me bothe a crowne, and the lymmon tree 15 crownes, wherein Sir, if I have bestowed more than perhaps you will at the first like, yet it is the best chepe that we colde get it. And better chepe than other noble men in France have bought of the same man. You will not thinke your monny lost if it doo not prosperre, it shall take awaye your desire of loesing any more monny in like sorte. My Lord [?] and Mr Caroo weare the choosers of it.[4] Windebank gave full instructions on how to look after the trees, and was particularly pleased to point out that there would be no freight charges, since they were to go with Mr Carew's trees.

Where Cecil kept these trees is unknown. He is thought to have preferred the country to life in town, but his official duties would have kept him near the court, and it is therefore more likely that he installed his exotic treasures at Cecil House, where he could watch for evidence of flower buds and fruit. Shrewd as always, Cecil had picked one of the best gardeners of the day to look after both Theobalds and Cecil House. He was John Gerard, who was already working for Lord Burghley by 1577, and had established a good friendship with Jean Robin, the celebrated French gardener who was appointed Keeper of the King's Garden in Paris in 1597. Gerard was a collector of rare plants and seeds, some of which were sent by Robin. As well as caring for Lord Burghley's gardens, Gerard also maintained his own garden in London, in the area of Holborn or Fetter Lane. In 1599 a catalogue[5] of plants that grew in his garden was published, a document that is still a principal authority for dating the importation of many species into England. Amongst those which he described are various tender plants which he grew from seed each year. They included oleander, abutilon, yucca and hibiscus. Of this hibiscus, he says, rather sorely, *I had with great industrie nourished up some plants from the seede, and kept them unto the middest of Maie; notwithstanding one colde night chauncing among many, hath destroied them all.*

Was Gerard surprised when these foreign plants succumbed to the rigours of an English winter? He was obviously aware that their chances of survival were slight if they had come from a warmer climate, but found it interesting to see which ones would prove tough enough to withstand cold, wet, windy England. His other well-known publication was his famous *Herbal*, which appeared in 1597, and was dedicated to Lord Burghley. It contains fanciful descriptions of exotic plants, all of which were started from seed every year.

Although Gerard did not mention any plants that he over-wintered indoors, an earlier writer, William Harrison, Dean of Windsor, wrote *The Description of England* in 1577, which does refer to imported plants. *Strange hearbs, plants and annuall fruits are dailie brought unto us from the Indies, Americas, Taprobane [Ceylon], Canary Iles, and all parts of the world: ... for delectation sake unto the eye, and their odoriferous savours unto the nose, they are to be cherished, and God to be glorified also in them, bicause they are his good gifts, and created to doo man helpe and service.*[6] He added that he had seen *capers, orenges and lemmons, and heard of wild olives growing here, besides other strange trees, brought here from afar, whose names I know not.*

How and where were these plants kept in winter? They were probably grown in tubs, and simply moved into frost-free out-houses or else indoors, into halls or long galleries, where foliage and fruit could be appreciated. There is no evidence to suggest that there were any purpose-built masonry orange houses in Tudor England; and glass was still very expensive. Although the Countess of Shrewsbury stunned everybody with the sheer size of the windows in her Derbyshire mansion, Hardwick Hall, *more glass than wall*, nobody thought that tender plants needed or deserved similar treatment.

Curious foreign plants were propagated by seeds and cuttings and shared amongst enthusiasts. Since they were not available from nurserymen in England, keen gardeners sent abroad for them. Citrus plants seem usually to have been bought in France or Holland.

That swashbuckling Elizabethan sailor hero, Sir Walter Ralegh, is credited with having brought orange pips to England. There was a tradition in the Ralegh family that Sir Walter imported the first oranges into England,[7] and that from the pips were grown the trees of the orange garden at Beddington. The first part of the claim is certainly fallacious, and the second part may or may not be true, but it leads us to the most famous orange garden of the Elizabethan age, Sir Francis Carew's garden at Beddington in Surrey.

Francis Carew was nine years old in 1539 when he inherited his ancestral estates in Surrey. As a young man he travelled in Europe, living in Paris for about a year from 1561 to 1562, and possibly visiting Italy, as John Aubrey maintained. His daily activities in Paris remain a mystery, but one reason for his stay was to see his sister Anne, who had married Sir Nicholas Throckmorton, English Ambassador in Paris. Francis and Anne seem to have been very close, and Anne spent much time at Beddington.

It is clear from the already quoted correspondence between Sir William Cecil and Sir Thomas Windebank that Francis Carew was making purchases in Paris for his garden in the spring of 1562. In his letter of 25 March to Windebank in Paris, Cecil wrote, *When this messenger was redy to depart my La Throckmorton* [née Anne Carew] *gave me a line fro Tho Cecill wherein he maketh mention that Mr Caroo meaneth to send home certen orege pomgranat lymon and myrt trees.*[8] Then followed Cecil's request for a lemon, a pomegranate and a myrtle. While Cecil was buying individual specimens, it would seem that Carew was buying in quantity, certainly in the plural. When Windebank managed to slip Cecil's

An illustration from Hesperides *by J. B. Ferrarius, 1646, shows a permanent framework built round Duke Farnese's orange trees, with a roof tiled in the winter months. At Beddington wooden boards were used in preference to terracotta tiles, but both systems were extremely labour intensive.*

three trees in with Carew's for shipment to England, it may have been that three extra made no difference to the cost, because Carew had bought so many. Or perhaps Carew was simply pleased to do the Secretary of State a favour.

Francis Carew now had a good nucleus of citrus trees, pomegranates and myrtles, the same species that he and other travellers may have seen when visiting the great gardens of Italy. The oranges were of a bitter type which would be used for flavouring, but not eaten as dessert fruit. Bitter as they were, Carew's collection must have been well known, since the Earl of Dorset wrote to him asking for specimen plants of myrtle and orange trees. He may have expanded his collection by careful husbandry and by growing more trees from pips given him by Sir Walter Ralegh. Carew and Ralegh certainly knew each other by 1592, since Sir Walter had married Bess Throckmorton, Francis's niece, in 1591 or the following year, so oranges or pips may have come back from Spain or Portugal in his trunk.

John Aubrey asserts, in his *History of Surrey* (begun in 1673 and published in 1718), that the orange trees were *transplanted from the Warmer Breezes of Italian Air, into our more inclement Climate,* and brought from Italy by Francis himself. This is also possible. His enthusiasm for all these tender plants might derive from having admired them first-hand in the gardens of Genoa, Florence, Rome or Naples, rather than in the French version of an Italian garden in Paris. He could also have studied the means by which they were protected in winter, and copied the timber framework which was boarded over in the cold months.

The diarist John Evelyn wrote that these were the first orange trees grown in England. However, he made this particular claim in 1658, nearly a century after the event, so whether Francis Carew actually had a horticultural first with his orange trees from Italy is debatable, but he certainly was one of the earliest to grow citrus fruit successfully in England.

Once at Beddington, how did they fare? Very well indeed, according to later accounts. Unfortunately, very little is known of Francis's garden in detail, but the orange trees certainly flourished, as is evident from several seventeenth- and eighteenth-century sources. The trees were planted in the ground, and a wooden shelter, most likely with windows, was built up round them each winter, with the main supporting posts probably left permanently in the ground. Some of the side sections may have been easy to remove, to let in light and sunshine on mild winter days. There were two iron stoves, which would be lit during cold spells, but would not need to be fired continuously from October to April.

The only contemporary reference to the building during Sir Francis's lifetime is in an account book, where there is an entry dated 10 January 1608 as follows: *Paid to Sadler for half a daye sweepinge Downe the sknowe of the orringe howse iiijd* [four pence].[9] Perhaps the structure was a little shaky, and could not support a great weight of snow, so snow clearing was imperative. There is also

Another illustration by Ferrarius shows the elevation and groundplan of Duke Farnese's orange garden. Sir Francis Carew's orange garden and wintering sheds at Beddington were built on the same principle.

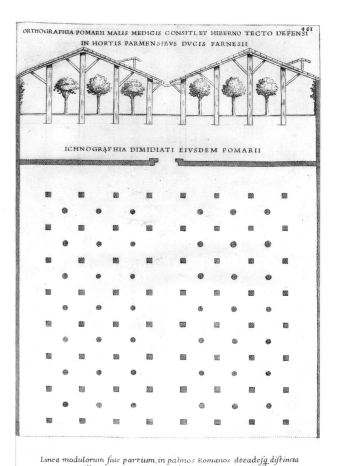

an item in William Blake's accounts of 1609 of fifty-five shillings being paid to a Mr Samuell Hare for a 'stoove', almost certainly for the orange house.[10] The origin of the word stove is Dutch, and the Dutch were equally interested in protecting orange trees in winter, and passed their technology across the Channel. The stove would have been made of iron, and would have given out considerable heat when the fire was lit. The cost of fifty-five shillings is greater than the advertised rate, in *Rates of Merchandize* of 1618, where iron stoves were listed at forty shillings. Francis Carew probably wanted a large version. Account books also show significant expenditure on coal and wood, but there is no breakdown between fuel for the manor house and fuel for the orange house. The location of the orange house can only be guessed, but it was probably south-east of the house, and south of the later greenhouse wall.

Apart from the orange house, Francis was also famed for another great horticultural achievement, that of producing ripe cherries in August 1599 for Queen Elizabeth's visit. The words of Sir Hugh Platt, from the *Garden of Eden*, describe the ingenuity of Carew and his gardener, William Joanes: *Here I will conclude with a conceit of that delicate knight Sir Francis Carew, who for the better accomplishment of his royal entertainment of our late Queen Eliz, of happie memorie, at his house at Beddington, led her majestie to a cherry tree, whose fruit he had of purpose kept back from ripening, at the least one month after all cherries had taken their farewell of England. This secret he performed by straining a tent or cover of canvas over the whole tree, and wetting the same now and then with a scoop or horn, as the heat of the weather required, and so by withholding the sunbeams from reflecting upon the berries, they grew both great and were very long before they had gotten their perfect cherrie colour; and when he was assured of her majestie's coming, he removed the tent, and a few sunny days brought them to their full maturity.*

'That delicate knight' died in 1611 at the age of eighty-one and left Beddington to his nephew, Anne Throckmorton's son Nicholas, who changed his name to Carew. The Civil War was disastrous for Carew fortunes and another Nicholas, aged fourteen, inherited a bankrupt estate in 1649. The Ralegh connection came to the rescue, as Sir Walter Ralegh's son, Carew Ralegh, became the boy's guardian. Carew Ralegh had arranged that Beddington should be leased to the Earl of Warwick, and he was responsible for overseeing the affairs of the estate and for collecting rent. Warwick

repaired the fabric of Beddington, which had probably suffered much from recent neglect, and account books[11] show that in January 1652 he paid £7 for *repairs to the old stoves in the orange house and repairs of the fountain house.* He laid out the very considerable sum of £60, also in January 1652, to *Constable ye Carpenter for building of a new orange house.* This structure was similar to the old one, but larger, and it needed two new iron stoves, since *the old stoves would not serve the turn.* They cost £7. 10s. each, but were not very effective, for a note in the margin of the accounts says *New stoves sett up by my ld. but of little use.* Carew Ralegh must have been anxious to preserve the estate and its famous orange garden, since he allowed Lord Warwick's rent to be reduced by the sum of £60, the cost of the new orange house.

This orange house was the one that John Evelyn saw on 27 September 1658. *To Beddington, that antient Seate of the Carews, a faire old hall, but a scambling house: famous for the first orange garden of England being now over-growne trees, & planted in the ground, & secured in winter with a wooden tabernacle and stoves: This Seate is rarely [well] watered, & lying low invirond with sweete pastures &c. The pomogranads beare here: here is also a fine park.* By 1691, Gibson recorded that Beddington garden had *the best orangery in England. The orange and lemon trees grow in the ground, and have done so near one hundred years,* as the gardener, an aged man, said he believed. Gibson said that there were *a great number of them, the house wherein they are being above two hundred feet long.* This house, he said, had been built that year. Repairs and replacements would have to be done regularly, as the wood rotted. Most of the trees were thirteen feet high, *and very full of fruit, the gardener not having taken off so many flowers this last summer as usually others do. He said, he gathered off them at least ten thousand oranges this last year.*[12] An astonishing crop for the south of England! Doubtless many of them would have been given away, for the accounts do not record any revenue from the sale of oranges. The rest of the garden was neglected, as the gardener spent all his time looking after the orange trees.

In the eighteenth century the wooden orange house was replaced by another with a removable roof,[13] and probably with three wood and glass walls; all that remains now is the fourth wall, built of brick, long and high and complete with flues. Carew's orange trees have long since gone.

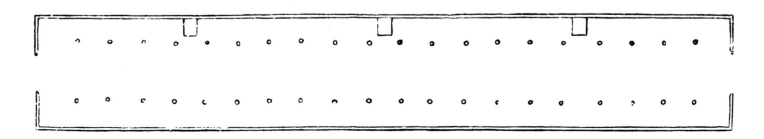

Oh that I were an orange-tree,
   That busy plant!
Then I should ever laden be,
   And never want
Some fruit for Him that dressed me.

George Herbert, 1593–1633

Lord Burghley's second son Robert, later Lord Salisbury, inherited his father's offices of state, and also his delight in creating houses and gardens. Having exchanged Theobalds for Hatfield House to please James I, Robert Cecil set about building a great house at Hatfield, with gardens laid out in the very latest Italian fashion. By 1610 John Tradescant was in charge; his salary was £50 per annum. The gardens at Hatfield were planned on a large scale, and were to be stocked with the best flowers, trees, fruit and vegetables that could be found. The nursery gardens of England simply did not carry the variety that Lord Salisbury and Tradescant desired, so Tradescant set off to search for them in France. In Paris he made many purchases, including year-old orange trees at ten shillings each, oleanders at two shillings and sixpence, and a pomegranate, while in Rouen on the way home he added three pomegranates and two more orange trees. Salisbury must have been delighted with this rich and varied haul. However, as seems too often the case, he can hardly have tasted the produce of the first crop, nor enjoyed watching the garden take shape, for he died in 1612. Tradescant stayed on for two more years.

In 1609, King James I and his wife, Anne of Denmark, decided to renovate and expand Somerset House in London. The plans, rich in architecture and allegorical symbols, included an orange house and a banqueting house, and it is likely that walks were lined with tubs of orange and lemon trees.

No trace of the Somerset House garden remains, but the plans were the first known instance of a grand new garden in England where specific provision was made for over-wintering tender plants. Its creator, Salomon de Caus, was born in Normandy in 1576, but was familiar with the greatest Italian gardens, including Pratolino in Tuscany and the Villa d'Este at Frascati, which he visited when he was about twenty years old.

By 1614 de Caus had found his way to Heidelberg, where James I's daughter, Princess Elizabeth, had recently married Frederick, the Elector Palatine. Frederick and Elizabeth were young, enthusiastic, and rich enough to give de Caus the huge job of making a new princely garden beside the Nechar River. This was to become known as the 'Hortus Palatinus'.

Salomon de Caus's first design for a temporary winter orange house, thought to date from 1619.

The garden at Heidelberg was already famous for its orange trees. Here, the removable shed principle was used. Olivier de Serres, the French garden expert, wrote about this orange garden in the widely distributed first edition of *Le Théâtre d'Agriculture,* published in 1600. He described it as having large windows which could be opened *pour réjour les arbres,* and being heated by pans of charcoal. The trees were wonderfully healthy, glowingly described by him as examples of *magnifiques sumptuosités.*

De Caus must have examined the old orangery carefully, and decided to make some improvements in the design, perhaps influenced by de Serres's ideas in *Le Théâtre d'Agriculture.* His plan, never quite completed, was to make a long narrow orange garden and build round it a permanent framework of stone, so that only the roof and windows would be removed in summer. This would reduce spring and autumn labour, and provide the orange trees with more airtight quarters. It sounds like a good compromise, given the existence of venerable old orange trees, so the trees were moved with the greatest difficulty to their new position on one of the terraces. Much of the great work was finished, including elaborate parterres, a labyrinth and a celebrated grotto, when Frederick and Elizabeth became King and Queen of Bohemia. Their accession was quickly

Salomon de Caus's second design for an Orangerie *at Heidelberg, published in* Les Raisons des Forces Mouvants *in Paris in 1624. The groundplan has windows in both north and south elevations, showing de Caus's determination, albeit misguided, to admit as much light as possible in winter when the roof was covered. North-facing windows were never widely used, however, since light gain proved insignificant compared with heat loss.*
The detail opposite shows the ivy-twined rustic columns which betray the romantic within the architect-engineer. De Caus's many talents ranged from hydraulic engineering to architecture to garden design, all of which were dominated by a flamboyant yet aesthetic imagination.

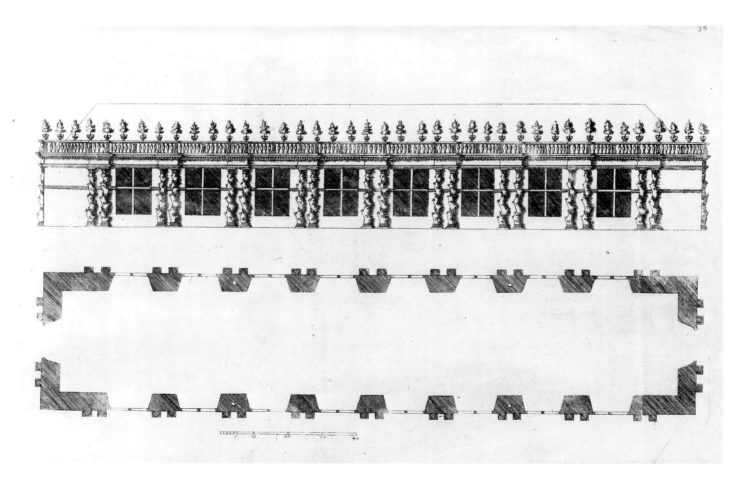

followed by the outbreak of the Thirty Years War; de Caus departed for France and the gardens fell into ruins.

Olivier de Serres's contribution to horticulture (and agriculture) was immense. It is a fitting tribute that his name is commemorated in the French word for greenhouse – *serre* – which had passed into the language by the middle of the seventeenth century. De Serres gave a detailed description of how to build a protective house in the sixth section of *Le Théâtre d'Agriculture*. The trees, he said, should be planted in the ground in front of a wall. About 12 feet in front of the wall there should be a row of columns in wood or stone, these being 13 feet high and 8 feet apart. Rafters stretching from the columns should be attached to the wall some 16 feet above the ground, making a lean-to roof with a shallow angle. The roof should be thatched, and should have opening skylights. In colder, northerly areas, the house must be made airtight, ideally with well-fitting glass windows, but as glass was very expensive, the economy version could have canvas, waxed so that light could pass through it. The interior should be heated with charcoal or dry wood; although de Serres does not suggest how warm it should be, it was probably intended to be just above freezing. In summer, the windows or frames would be removed but, by inference, the roof was fixed.

Four sorts of citrus trees were recommended by de Serres – *Oranges, Citroniers, Limoniers et Limones* – but he also suggested growing a few exotic novelties, namely date palms, sugar cane and cotton. All three need more heat than citrus trees, so may not have long survived. De Serres was quite clear that every *homme d'esprit* must have his collection of tender plants with which to beautify his garden, and he testified to the abundance of citrus trees, which he said were transported everywhere throughout the kingdom, and to Paris by the boatload.

De Serres's description of his early model greenhouse was a distinct improvement on the removable wooden shed. Having a permanent roof and frame would reduce labour and draughts. As understanding of plants' light requirements developed, and as glass-making techniques improved, this little thatched house with removable walls changed gradually into what we think of today as the greenhouse.

Meanwhile, the fashion for architectural gardens was developing, and developing faster in the grander gardens of France and Germany, where aesthetic demands predominated. Amongst the finest princely gardens were those in Paris. In 1600, the marriage of Henri IV of France to Maria de' Medici brought a further infusion

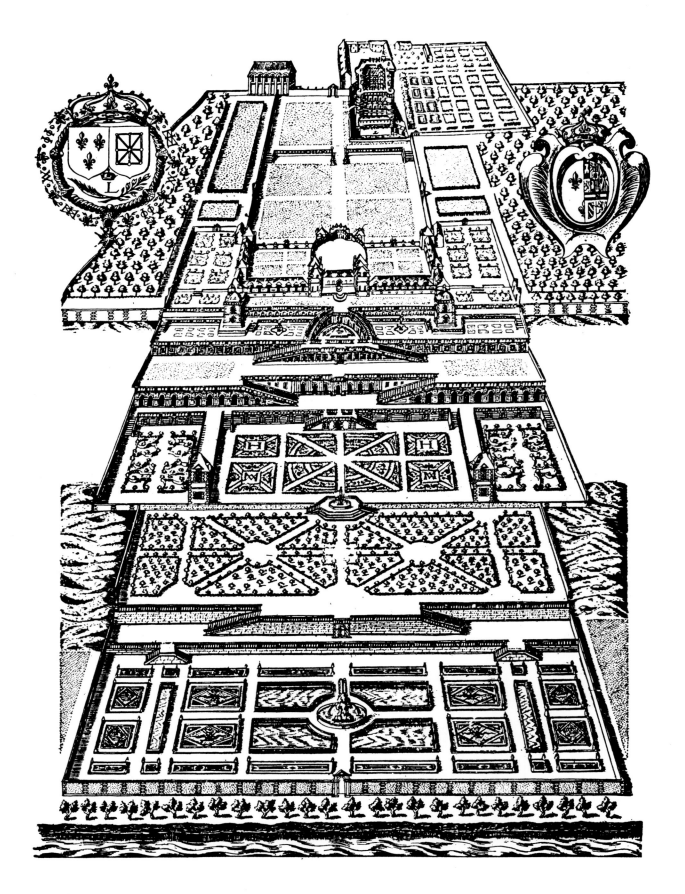

of Italian taste to Paris. Queen Maria introduced many Italian customs and artists into the court, including the garden designer, Francini, who was employed to remake the gardens of the renovated palace of St Germain-en-Laye. The result was a splendid Italian garden descending to the Seine in a series of six terraces, with one especially for decorative citrus fruit complete with *orangerie*. There were *orangeries* in the Tuileries Gardens, at Fontainebleau, and in the gardens of the Palais du Luxembourg. There is to this day a fine collection of citrus trees in the Luxembourg Gardens; some of these are known to be at least 350 years old, and have survived thanks to tender loving care and a secret mixture of compost. This recipe, as ancient as the trees and still in use, is based on sheep dung mixed with other ingredients, and kept for a year before application. It works well.

Across the Channel, at Oatlands Palace, Walton-on-Thames, Surrey, was another royal residence where exotic plants were grown. It was part of the jointure of Charles I's wife, Queen Henrietta Maria, who was the daughter of Henri IV of France and Maria de' Medici. Henrietta Maria's ideas of what was right and proper for kings and queens therefore had a distinct French and Italian air. When she was giving orders for the refurbishment of the palace, and planning the gardens with the help of John Tradescant, she wrote to her mother asking for rare plants to be sent. An orange garden was made, and a 262-foot-long *shedd* was built, complete with *a Colehouse adjoyning thereunto*.[14]

The palace and gardens at Oatlands were, however, quite overshadowed by Henrietta Maria's other great building project at Wimbledon Manor House, bought for her by Charles I in 1639. As far as the garden was concerned, the Queen turned again to France, and sent for André Mollet. Mollet was part of a family of gardeners, his father, Claude, being head gardener at the Tuileries in Paris. André Mollet worked in Holland and Sweden, as well as England and France, and later in his career published books on garden design. His work spread the French taste far and wide.

Mollet's plan was for a large, regular garden on various levels, with baroque stairways, a delightful birdcage, two banqueting houses, a maze, a wilderness, a vineyard and a sprinkling of summer-houses. The orange garden was beside the house to the east, and was overlooked by some of the principal apartments. It was sheltered by high walls and against the east wall was *a garden or shadow house*, where Henrietta Maria might have meant to sit in the shade, enjoying the garden.

The Queen's improvements to house and garden are known through an inventory of the fabric and contents of various royal properties made after Charles I's death in 1649. This document, the Parliamentary Survey, describes the orange house: *In the North side of which sayd oringe garden there stands one large garden house ...fitted for the keepinge of Oringe trees*. The walls were made of brick and the ridge roof was covered with blue slate; it was valued at £66. 13s. 4d.; curiously, much the same as the cost of rebuilding the wooden

The remarkable royal gardens of St Germain-en-Laye near Paris, designed by Francini in the first years of the seventeenth century. The influence of gardens like those at the Villa Aldobrandini is obvious.

orange house at Beddington. The winter contents of the orange house were, however, much, much more valuable than the building. At the time of the survey there were *fortie two Oringe trees bearing fayre and large Oringes* standing in squared boxes in the garden. The parliamentary officers worked out that the value of orange, lemon and pomegranate trees reached the grand total of £558. This was a large sum, especially for a minor palace, and was a quarter of the total value of the entire contents of the garden: flowers, trees, roots, garden buildings and walls. It appears that the Queen was prepared to spend lavishly at Wimbledon, using the best advice and acquiring the finest specimens.

André Mollet probably started work in 1640, but the remaining accounts and papers[15] for this and the following year are fragmentary. In April 1642 he was paid £50 for half a year's salary. After the main construction work was completed, he left other French gardeners in charge. By May, some orange trees had arrived, or were about to arrive, for Erasmus Armstrong, a joiner, supplied *20 Cases for ye orrenge trees*.[16] Also in May came the first of several deliveries of sacks of charcoal, suggesting that the garden house was heated with

Wynstanley's etching, dated 1678, of Wimbledon Manor House; the orange house on the right was built in the early 1640s for Queen Henrietta Maria, and well stocked with a variety of citrus trees.

open trays, rather than a furnace. Orange tubs or boxes were supplied regularly until March 1648, and there was also a record of payment *for 24 hoops for the orring trees tubbs*.[17] The gardeners were clearly training the trees in particular shapes.

Wimbledon Manor House and the gardens were well maintained throughout the Civil War, since the Queen's Treasurer, Sir Richard Wynn of Wynnstay, lived there; the Survey records that it was all in very good condition.

After the Restoration of Charles II, Henrietta Maria sold Wimbledon Manor House to the Earl of Bristol. John Evelyn first saw it in 1662, and was a regular visitor until 1678. The orange house must have been of interest to him, and may well have helped him develop his ideas for building a conservatory or greenhouse. In 1678, the house was sold to Sir Thomas Osborne, Earl of Danby and later Duke of Leeds, and it was he who commissioned Wynstanley to make engravings of his new property. In 1717, the Tudor and Carolinean house and gardens were completely demolished to make way for a new mansion for Sarah, Duchess of Marlborough.

The story of the orange tree in the early Stuart years is a tale of the rich and rare, a tale of people who knew each other and employed the same garden designers and gardeners. Monarchs and powerful men played at growing frivolous, pretty flowers and curious fruits, as ideas and plants crossed frontiers with ease. However, the citrus culture seems to have spread to more modest gardens too. In France, Olivier de Serres gave the impression that the trade in citrus trees was so significant that French roads and rivers were a forest of moving trees. In England, Francis Bacon mentioned them in his essay *Of Gardens*, published in 1625, as if they were quite familiar to his readers; they were an accepted part of the horticultural scene.

A further sign that tender plants were more widely cultivated after the turn of the century comes from a book published in 1629, John Parkinson's *Paradisi in Sole Paradisus Terrestris*. This is the first publication in English to write with convincing authority on how to grow them. Parkinson wrote of *Out-landish flowers* that had been introduced from overseas, describing first the oleander, which needed winter protection. He delighted in the strong, sweet smell of jasmine, wrote of pomegranates and said he had had much pain and trouble with myrtles. He waxed quite lyrical about the orange trees, and suggested that they should be planted in square boxes and placed in a *close gallerie* in winter. The alternative was to plant them against a brick wall and protect them with boards covered with *seare-cloth* and warm them with a stove. He warned that *no tent or mean provision will preserve them,* but his proposal sounds very primitive compared with de Serres's version.

Interest in the design and content of gardens increased steadily in the first few decades of the seventeenth century. Queen Elizabeth had been loth to spend money on anything other than her wardrobe, and thus royal gardens were low on her list of priorities. She preferred to watch her subjects spend their own money, and entertain her with myriad delights. By contrast, the Stuart kings in England and the Bourbon kings in France stimulated the arts by patronage and example, a movement which was only temporarily suspended in England during the Civil War.

The Sun King

Following the execution of Charles I in 1649, Cromwell's England was not a land where display of wealth was wise. Royalist supporters were intent on repairing their fortunes and certainly not embarking on ambitious garden projects. To the Puritan Roundheads, fanciful schemes for embellishing their properties would have verged on immorality; they preferred to invest in trade. A pall of gloom hung over German gardens too. The Treaty of Westphalia brought the Thirty Years War to an end in 1648, but Germany had been devastated by the conflict, and took many years to recover. France was in a better position, but still beset with domestic religious troubles, and government coffers were often disastrously empty. However, the power and prestige of the French monarchy were immense and this suited that flamboyant monarch, Louis XIV, perfectly.

Louis XIV established personal rule at the age of twenty-three on the death of the regent, Cardinal Mazarin, in 1661. Louis was a compulsive builder of palaces and gardens and regarded the two as equally important. The significance he gave the latter may have stemmed from his love of the outdoors, as he hunted nearly every day and enjoyed walking, hence the need for large, private gardens and parks. One of his first building projects was at his father's hunting box, to the south-west of Paris at Versailles. The house itself was modest for a royal residence, but it did have a moat and two parterres. Louis XIV started his lifetime *chef d'œuvre* not by rebuilding the château but by concentrating on the gardens and the park, where there was plenty of space to expand. The garden designer chosen to invent and implement the plans was André Le Nôtre.

How Louis came to employ Le Nôtre is an interesting tale that starts with a man of great ambition, Nicolas Fouquet, and the château he created at Vaux-le-Vicomte. Fouquet was appointed Financial Secretary in 1653 by Cardinal Mazarin, and, through lending his own money and borrowing from others to lend to the Crown, he succeeded in replenishing the royal coffers. At the same time, he lived a life of extravagance and luxury, surpassing even that of the young king.

As a mark of his power, he decided to replace an old house at his estate at Vaux-le-Vicomte, between Paris and Fontainebleau, and chose men from the rising generation of talented artists to implement his ideas. Among them were the architect, Louis Le Vau, the painter and interior designer, Charles Le Brun, and the garden designer, André Le Nôtre, who had worked at the Tuileries Gardens in Paris. These three combined to produce a jewel of a château, moated, set within elegant parterres, shimmering pools and canals. It took only five years to build, and, at the king's instigation, Fouquet gave a tremendous *fête* to celebrate its completion in August 1661. His guests were entertained in the most lavish manner, with a magnificent dinner, masques and fireworks, and showered with expensive gifts.

A capriccio of an imaginary formal garden,
in which an allée with stylized orange trees
and tall cypresses is the only major feature.
The painting is attributed to Robert Robinson,
c.1700.

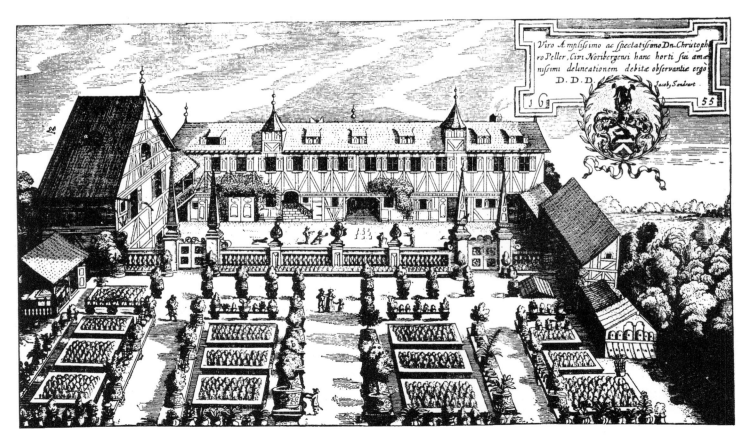

Viro Amplissimo ac spectatissimo Dn.Christoph
ro Peller,Civi Noribergensi hanc horti sui ame
nissimi delineationem debitæ observantiæ ergo
D.D.D.   Jacob,Sandrart.
16   55

The vast royal orangerie at Versailles designed by Mansart in 1685, illustrated in a book written by the royal gardener, Jean de la Quintinye.

The garden of Dr Christopher Peller at Nuremberg. Tender foreign plants were often grown for medicinal purposes by doctors as well as for pleasure.

Three weeks later Fouquet was arrested on Louis's orders, on charges of financial irregularity; however, the young king's jealousy of Fouquet's ostentatious château, and Fouquet's attentions to the king's mistress, were thought to have been the principal causes of his downfall. The magistrates who tried Fouquet condemned him to banishment from France, a sentence which Louis overruled, and changed to imprisonment for life. Fouquet died in gaol in 1680. As Nancy Mitford observed dryly in *The Sun King,* few people gave lavish parties for the king after that, nor made advances to his mistresses.

Louis was clearly enchanted by the château and the gardens at Vaux-le-Vicomte, as are visitors more than three hundred years later. For the new royal palaces, he resolved to employ the same artists as Fouquet had used, as well as taking from Vaux anything that was movable. Gradually, Vaux was stripped of its treasures: furniture, pictures, tapestries, marble statues – and orange trees. Estimates of the number of orange trees vary between 190 and over a thousand, but in any case the quantity was considerable, and the trees were distributed around several royal establishments.

After the Vaux episode, Le Nôtre was commissioned to create a garden at Versailles that would be the wonder of the world. At Vaux he and Fouquet had developed a new concept, an all-French style which overtook the Italian tradition. The garden was no longer divided into separate self-contained units, where terraces were enclosed by walls and balustrades. Instead, the château was to be integrated with the garden and from it there should be pleasing prospects in every direction, with nothing to interrupt the view. The individual features should be modified to unite them in a single composition, so that the garden could be seen as an entire work of art, in harmony with the surrounding park. This unity was achieved at Vaux and it was what Louis sought at Versailles.

From 1661 Le Nôtre worked for years on a scheme of breathtaking magnitude. At that time, the château had not been enlarged, so the grandeur of Le Nôtre's plan was totally out of proportion to the smallish house, but Le Nôtre would have been aware of the king's intentions to create a palace on the same scale as the gardens. King and servant always had an excellent relationship, and Le Nôtre enjoyed the total confidence of his master. There were, however, some areas of disagreement, such as flowers. The king loved brightly coloured flower beds, which Le Nôtre abhorred, declaring that they were only fit to be seen by nursery maids. Le Nôtre won the argument, certainly in the early years, as the main parterres near the château had wonderfully intricate patterns, all in shades of green.[1]

Louis was also passionately fond of orange trees. Although it was the custom to place the trees outside in summer and in the *orangerie* in winter, Louis had them brought indoors at any season and placed in silver tubs. From the time the Hall of Mirrors, the Galerie des Glaces, was completed in the 1680s, orange trees were part of the decoration. The vision of the Galerie des Glaces in Louis's day, with the orange trees in their silver tubs, silver consoles,

silver chandeliers and candelabra, gilded woodwork, ceiling paint‑
ings, all lit by a thousand candles and reflected in the mirrored wall,
still dazzles the imagination. From mid‑summer to late winter,
when blossoms are rare, glossy green leaves and ripening fruit would
have looked very fine, and their scented blossoms in spring must
have been a true delight in the stuffy atmosphere of the court.

Gardeners would be up very early in the morning to remove
flagging trees and replace them with fresh ones. Under the supervi‑
sion of Jean de la Quintinye, the head gardener in charge of all fruit
and vegetables, the trees were clipped into different shapes according
to where they were to be placed: smaller ones were for the salons
indoors and large ones for the parterres. Often, the trees were tall
with a round head, so the main stem was trained upright, straight as
a die, to a height of six or eight feet before it was allowed to bush out.

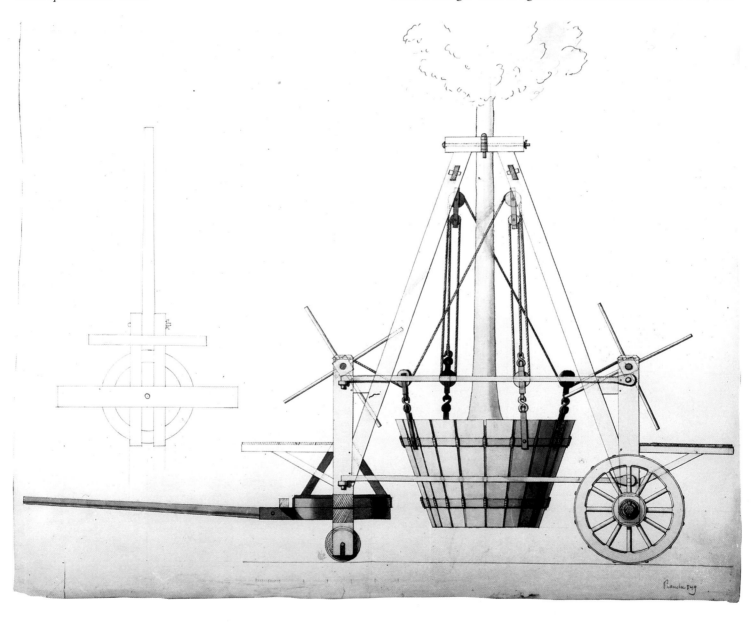

*A machine for moving orange trees,
drawn by Nicodemus Tessin*

Meticulous care and patience were needed to achieve this, so large trees were extremely valuable.

Louis's orange trees symbolized his power, his ability to dominate everything, just as nature had been dominated by man shaping the delicate foreign orange tree to his will. Orange trees also demonstrated the gulf between the ruling élite and the common man, whose survival depended on growing lettuces and onions, not luxurious fruit.

The Sun King's first *orangerie* was designed by Le Vau and built by 1664. Within five years of its completion there were plans to double its size, but these were not carried out. The second *orangerie,* built by Jules Hardouin-Mansart in 1685, was even more impressive and is still magnificent. It is twice the length of Le Vau's building, much deeper and with long projecting wings on either side, at the end of which are flights of one hundred steps. This *orangerie* was also infinitely more lofty than the earlier version, involving the removal of vast amounts of earth to lower the level of the garden in front. Its huge capacity must have reflected royal demands.

The stonework is rusticated and plain, with no decoration to enliven the façade. The doorways are recessed, and the wooden doors, still the original ones, are quite enormous, and very thick; the upper part is double-glazed, with several inches separating the two layers of wood and glass. No heating system was built into the design, and to this day the *orangerie* remains unheated. Its situation, with a roof two metres deep, only one outside wall, and double-glazed windows, is thermally very efficient, making heating unnecessary.

The *orangerie* parterre was also enlarged, and here palm trees, oleanders, myrtles, pomegranates (*grenadines* in French), daturas and many varieties of citrus trees spent, and still spend, the summer. Several of the citrus trees there today date from Louis XIV's time, and can be identified by the metal supports now necessary to hold them upright.

Autocratic Louis insisted that important visitors to Versailles should view the gardens following a particular route, and he took the trouble to write down the itinerary.[2] As far as the *orangerie* was concerned, visitors should descend the right hand (west) flight of steps into the orange garden and go to the fountain, from where the building should be viewed. Then they should walk along the *allées* of tall orange trees, and enter the vaulted *orangerie couverte,* leaving it by a door leading to the labyrinth.

For the twentieth-century visitor, free to wander at will, the design of the cases in which all these trees are planted deserves mention. They are large, sometimes very large, and square, and the interesting feature is that the sides are hinged, and can be opened like a door. This means that the tree does not have to be removed from the case for repotting; the roots can be trimmed back and fresh compost added before the side is replaced. This design is common to many old French gardens, and is more practical for large trees than the Italian terracotta pot.

Louis started major rebuilding of the château at Versailles in 1666, and work continued for over twenty years. Within the park he made the Trianon de Porcelaine, a charming little tea house. It was made of wood, designed as a perfumed bower for the display of newly arrived blue and white porcelain from China. Every sort of scented flower was planted there. Oranges and citron trees were grown in the ground, surrounded by myrtle and jasmine, and protected in winter by a wooden house, while outside were daffodils and tulips, hyacinths, wallflowers, tuberoses and sweet-scented stocks. Everybody found it enchanting, but Louis eventually had it pulled down, to build instead another exquisite summer-house in pink marble for Madame de Maintenon. This was known as the Grand Trianon; the garden was filled with flowers of all sorts and colours, and an *orangerie* was included for the citrus trees.

Louis's palaces and gardens were viewed by diplomats and travellers, and accounts of them were published in journals. Engravings showing bird's-eye views of each entire garden, plus the individual features, were printed in Paris and widely distributed. To say that Versailles was famous throughout Europe is an absurd understatement. All eyes were fixed on the legendary Sun King and on everything he did, and his influence spread to the very edge of the civilized world and beyond.

The England of John Evelyn

Architectural tastes in England had undergone a major revolution since the days of Queen Elizabeth and King James I. Inigo Jones's Banqueting House in Whitehall, built in 1620, had been a flash of the future for its time, compared with the designs of Jacobean town houses and country mansions. By the time the monarchy was restored in 1660, fascination with the architecture of ancient Rome and distant classical Greece had spread to northern Europe, and in Italy the restrained lines of Renaissance buildings had been overtaken by the flamboyant baroque of Bernini. This had filtered north too, and became the dominating influence on English architecture. The national psyche had also changed dramatically. Charles II's London was brimming with excited optimism. Everybody was busy and anything was possible. Trading companies were, literally, opening up the world, fascination with science gave birth to the Royal Society, theatres were packed, decorative arts flourished, and architecture and garden design were visible proof of the new ideas.

Materials were also changing. Bricks were increasing in size and stone was used more widely. Glass was cheaper, thinner and finer. The principle for making it had not altered: it was still blown and then spun on a disc until cold. But the size of the disc had increased, and it was possible to make discs five feet in diameter, although large sizes were very difficult to handle. Panes were cut between the edge of the circle and the thick eye in the middle, so were restricted to about eighteen inches.

As glass production improved, perceptions of its value in protecting plants were evolving too. The phenomenon known as 'the greenhouse effect' was being steadily exploited. The principle is that glass allows heat from the sun to pass quickly through it to warm the air inside a building; as this warm air is trapped, the heat builds up, disproportionately to the air temperature outside; and the greater the area of glass, the greater the heat. For flowering plants, light in winter, when they are dormant, is less important. The real value of large areas of glass comes from mid-February onwards, when a combination of heat and lengthening days stimulates plants to start growing earlier than they would in darker, cooler conditions. Seventeenth-century gardeners realized that winter and early spring sun must be captured. The sun is too low in the sky to warm east and west walls for long, so windows or glass walls had to be on the south side only. Since most of the plants and trees cultivated in the middle to late seventeenth century were all moved out in summer,

there was no need for the building to have a glass roof. Plants that need more heat than a northern European summer provides, and therefore require a glass roof as well as glass walls, arrived in greater numbers only towards the end of the seventeenth century. So the design principles that had been used at Anet for Henri II, at Wimbledon for Henrietta Maria, and at Versailles for Louis XIV, prevailed, with the main improvements occurring in the ratio of glass to wall and in heating methods.

Free-standing iron stoves had been used at Beddington, and were popular in Holland where the most skilful gardeners in Europe practised their art. Efficient as a means of heating, iron stoves could be fuelled to maintain various temperatures, including the levels needed for tropical plants in winter – about 70°F and 20°C. Thus the word 'stove' gave its name in England to the building where tropical plants were housed. The disadvantage of an iron stove was that some of the noxious fumes from the fire escaped the chimney to pollute the air and poison the plants; for this reason charcoal was often burned instead, as it was less damaging than coal, but still not entirely satisfactory. It is also doubtful if charcoal could maintain temperatures high enough for tropical plants.

In England, John Evelyn, the diarist, turned his mind to the

The interior of Jan Commelyn's Winter-plaats *at Leiden, illustrated in his own book, showing two metal stoves and a staircase to an upper floor.*

Pieter de Wolff's well-ordered orange house and citrus collection, here being tended by gardeners and admired by visitors. The illustration is from Commelyn's book Nederlantze Hesperides, *1683, which was translated into English two years later. This and other Dutch publications and practices had a profound influence on horticulture in neighbouring European countries; the Dutch were renowned for their cultivation of exotics.*

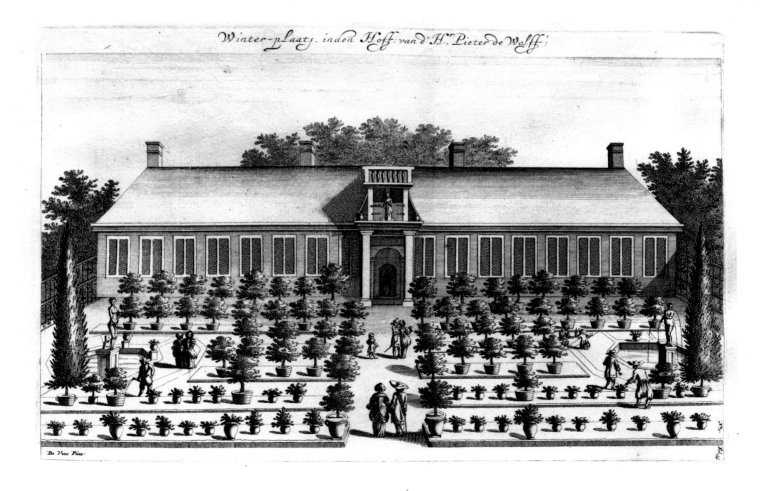

Winter-plaats, inden Hoff: van d'H.ᵉᵉ Pieter de Wolff:

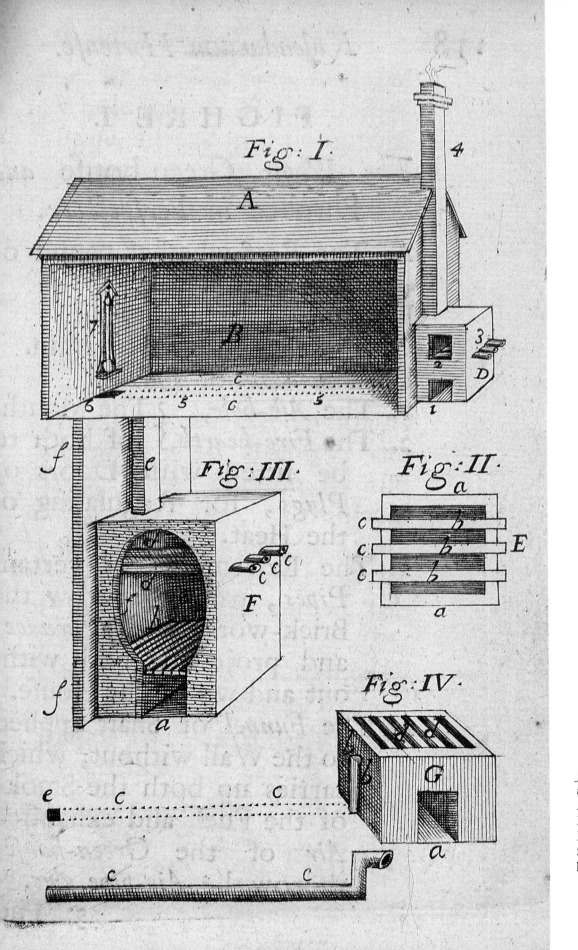

John Evelyn's greenhouse plan first published in the 1691 edition of Kalendarium Hortense. *Figure I:* The Whole Greenhouse and Furnace in Perspective. *Figure II:* The Furnace Air-pipes. *Figure III:* The whole Stove or Furnace. *Figure IV:* The Ash-hearth.

question of heating, and invented a new method which he described in a book called *Kalendarium Hortense*, published in 1664. This is a general gardening book, and has one chapter called 'A New Conservatory or Greenhouse'. Evelyn said that he proposed this new system because iron stoves and the newly introduced *Subterranean Caliducts* often left the plants *sick, langourous and tainted*. He thought that stoves and pans of charcoal made the air too dry and effete, and that plants needed a constant stream of fresh air. He was more or less right; but the plants needed copious supplies of fresh air because stoves and charcoal polluted it, rather than dried it out. In fact, the air ought to be as dry as possible in winter. Evelyn's stove was outside the house, and the heat was transferred inside by air passing through very hot pipes; cold air from the floor area was drawn through a ground pipe to fan the flames of the furnace. Natural convection would therefore ensure a continual supply of fresh, warm air. This ingenious scheme solved the author's passion for fresh air as well as heat, but was probably not very efficient in thermal terms.

As far as dimensions were concerned, it can be no coincidence that Evelyn chose exactly the same measurements as Olivier de Serres had advised in 1600 in *Le Théâtre d'Agriculture*; conventional wisdom had not altered in sixty-four years. The only difference lay in the roof: de Serres's version was lean-to and Evelyn's had a ridge. De Serres also put in a skylight, unnecessary in Evelyn's plan as his house was empty in summer. There were certainly no frills in the *Kalendarium Hortense* design; however, the author's intention was to put across the principle of the construction, leaving style to the architect. Evelyn's simple building could be left plain for the kitchen garden or enhanced to suit its position by the parterres. The windows should be large and ample *for Light itself, next to Air, is of wonderful importance*. There should also be a porch with a door, to prevent cold air rushing into the greenhouse when the gardener entered it, and an internal thermometer at the opposite end wall from the furnace.

Unfortunately for the curious reader, Evelyn could not specify the air temperature which his furnace maintained, since thermometers at that time were very primitive, with vague variations between cool and warm. Evelyn also had a theory[3] that the walls should be lined with cork; although not mentioned in *Kalendarium Hortense*, it seems it was common practice to put mattresses or reeds round the walls as insulation from cold and damp; cork, he thought, would be an improvement.

The *Oxford English Dictionary* credits Evelyn with being the first person to use the word 'conservatory', meaning a place for conserving delicate plants in winter; the word 'greenhouse', which he used much more frequently and in the same context without differentiation, meant a house for evergreens, or greens, as they were often called. An 'orangery' was an area in the garden for the display of orange trees. A certain confusion has arisen because Evelyn and other writers borrowed the French word, *orangerie*, which for them meant orange garden, but in the nineteenth century was used to describe the building, hence the reason why many seventeenth- and eighteenth-century greenhouses are called orangeries today.

John Evelyn, *the great virtuoso* as Aubrey described him, had travelled extensively through France and Italy. He was an expert on subjects from medicine to numismatism and sculpture; horticulture was but one facet of his vast wealth of knowledge. When he returned to England from Paris in 1652, he started creating a new garden at Sayes Court, Kent, imbued with what he had seen abroad. He certainly had a greenhouse, and grew citrus trees successfully, since he entertained Verrio, the artist, and others to dinner in September 1679 with *China oranges off my own tree, as good, I think, as were ever eaten*. Although later writers[4] suggested that Evelyn was better at the theory than the practice of gardening, the practice was obviously adequate.

In 1687 Evelyn made notes about gardening, *Directions for the Gardiner at Sayes-Court*, for an apprentice whom he had engaged, and these shed more light on horticultural techniques of the time. Fresh air was still an obsession – he sounded like a Victorian children's nurse – and light was also important. Both oranges and lemons should be sown from seed and grafted on to the rootstock of the bitter Seville orange at four years' growth, since grafted trees produce fruit earlier than those sown from seed. Experimental grafting was all the rage, and for fun, young seedlings could be grafted on to a quince root. The recommended fertilizer was a pungent mixture of sheep and pigeon dung infused in water, pigeon dung being readily available from the dovecote.

John Evelyn was also interested in food, and instructed that in the summer months orange pips should be sown purely to provide a source of fresh young leaves, which were excellent mixed with a salad. This is true, but the leaves must be very soft and very tender, otherwise they are bitter.

Evelyn was not the only devotee of foreign plants in the middle of the seventeenth century. A second John Tradescant, named after his father who had been gardener to Robert Cecil and Queen Henrietta Maria, had set up a museum of rarities in south London at Lambeth, and called it The Ark. Most of the exhibits such as fossils, birds' eggs and a dried pineapple, were indoors, but some grew in the garden. Tradescant's list of 1656 shows that many new exotic species had been brought to England since Parkinson had written *Paradisi in Sole Paradisus Terrestris* some twenty-six years before. The familiar list of citrus, oleander, pomegranate and myrtle now had all sorts of additions: hibiscuses and passion flowers, mimosas, canna lilies, plumbago, geraniums and a pelargonium, three kinds of tender jasmine, asplenium, solanum and daturas, amongst others. These would all have been grown in pots, and treated in much the same way as the citruses. It is hard to tell how widely the new types were grown, but there was a nucleus of activity in and around London.

Decorative plants were prized, but another factor in the quest for

Oranje-boom met Gekrulde bladeren van Ferrarius.

'Exoticks' was the search for medicines. Rare plants from abroad were grown in the Physic Gardens of Chelsea and Oxford and in private collections. Physicians and apothecaries were particularly anxious to find a cure for malaria, and experimented with any new foreign plant they could find.

Curiosity, aesthetic satisfaction and discernment were still the reasons that made the nobly born and educated collect foreign plants. *Persons of quality and ingenuity have in all ages delighted themselves with beautiful gardens, whose chiefest ornaments are choice flowers, trees and plants,* wrote Sir Thomas Hanmer in his *Garden Book* of 1659.

One *person of quality and ingenuity* who delighted in his garden was Philip Stanhope, 2nd Earl of Chesterfield. He was born in 1633 and had toured around Europe, like many of his contemporaries, before inheriting his father's estate of Bretby in Derbyshire. The 1st Earl had built a large mansion, and the 2nd Earl surrounded it with a huge garden, an arrangement of fountains, labyrinths, groves, greenhouses, grottoes, aviaries, orange trees and water-works and a marble summer-house.[5] Versailles was the inspiration for the entire plan, and the finished version was said to be the finest in Europe after Versailles itself.

Work started in 1669, and three years later Chesterfield was an authority on preserving tender plants through freezing Derbyshire winters. He wrote a chapter about how to care for citruses in a book called *Glasford on Fruit Trees,* by William Glasford.[6] Who Glasford was, or how he was associated with Chesterfield, is a mystery, but the small handwritten volume contains Chesterfield's advice on citruses and *other winter greens as are to be housed in winter.* Deeply enamoured of his orange trees, Chesterfield wrote in colour-ful prose: *Some of these plants where with we adorne our Gardens and Perfume our houses beare so beautifull fruit that many have thought it was ye tree forbidden to our first Parents.* The orange tree, he con-tinued, with flowers like orient pearls, *Gratifies all at once both the sent and sight ... The cittron tree may be compared to the blush of a ruby the continuall* [foliage] *has the Emrolds perpetuall Shining Green and ye ripe fruit in ye midst of all these apeares by its Luster like Apples of ye Purest Gold.*

Chesterfield had a wide variety of citruses. In those pre-Linnaean days when names were up to the individual, Chesterfield listed them for their characteristics: out of seventeen types of lemon he grew, there was *the ordinary cittron, the sweet and sharpe cittron, the long cittron of St Benedict, the midle sised cittron.* His collection of orange trees numbered twenty-three varieties, including *the civil* [Seville] *orange, the sweet orange, the sweet orange of Caserta which bites, the sweet orange of Gaetta which always has a star by ye stalke, the hermophodite orange* [that] *has one quarter of the same fruit Lemmon ye other orange* and so on. Chesterfield was beguiled by their scent. Dwarf oranges should be taken indoors *into a Ladys Chamber, where being sett on a table they Perfume the whole room,* he advised, and sweet-smelling bracelets should also be made from tiny fruit.

The Earl recommended having *both a summer and a winter Green-house exposed to ye Sun or South.* The summer one was a transitional stage *to acquaint* [the plants] *with ye air by degrees,* from March to May and in October and November. By inference, this greenhouse had much more glass than the winter version.

As far as the orange trees were concerned, some were in cases in a very prominent position near the marble summer-house. Celia Fiennes admired them and the summer-house in 1698, and, a few years after the 2nd Earl's death, Cassandra Willoughby, Duchess of Chandos, gave a glowing description of them. *From ye Great Fountain to a Sumer House floored and sided with Marble, is a Walk set on each side with Orange Trees and between every Tree a Bason which throws an arch of water which you walk dry under to another Fountain at the foot of the Sumer House.*[7] Chesterfield also had orange trees grow-ing in the ground, a good six feet high, full of flowers and some large fruit, and protected in winter by a wintering shed. Perhaps the movable orange trees spent the winter in the marble summer-house, which faced south; with considerable heating to counteract the iciness of marble, it would have been suited to the purpose. Unfor-tunately the summer-house, greenhouses, gardens and mansion of Bretby were all demolished in 1780.

The Earl of Chesterfield's seat at Bretby, drawn by Knyff and engraved by Kip in 1707. The seven-bay pedimented greenhouse to the north of the house is one of several main features in this huge and impressive scheme, which was said to be second only to Versailles.

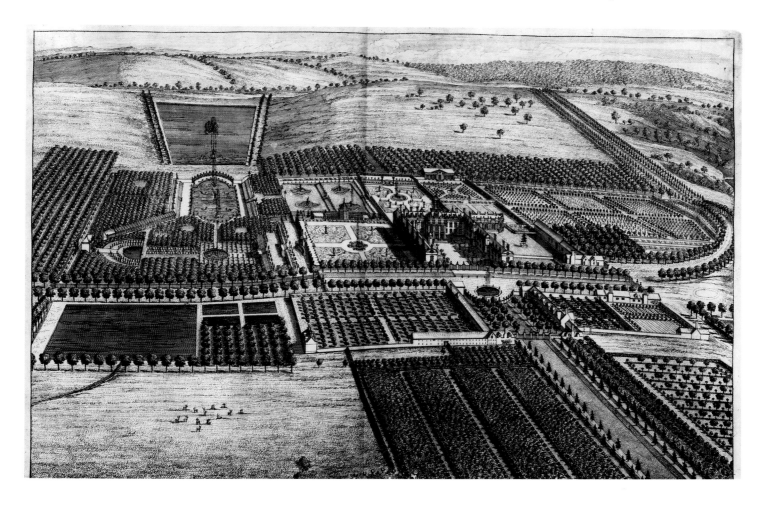

By the 1680s there were several good nursery gardens close to the centre of London. Brompton Park in Kensington was one of the best, and its owners, George London and Henry Wise, enjoyed the highest reputation as garden designers and suppliers of rare trees and plants. They had a huge greenhouse, whose south-facing wall was entirely made of glass framed in wood. It was big enough to house King William's collection of greens (tender evergreens, of course, not cabbages), which were moved there in winter from the gardens of Kensington Palace, as well as the many trees, seedlings and cuttings that London and Wise required for their regular stock. Descriptions of other London gardens and nurseries were given in a paper written in 1691 by J. Gibson[8] who listed twenty-four private gardens, twenty-two of which have greenhouses, and five nurseries, including Brompton Park, which all sold tender plants. No longer did the English have to go abroad to buy 'Exoticks'.

John Aubrey also recorded the influx of new plants: *In the time of Charles 11d, Gardening was much improved and became common: I doe beleeve, I may modestly affirm, that there is now [1691] ten times as much gardning about London as there was in AD 1660: and we have been since that time much improved in foreign plants: especially since about 1683, there have been exotick Plants brought into England, no lesse than seven thousand.*[9]

Earlier in the century, both John Tradescants had gone on plant-hunting expeditions; but now many new exciting specimens were being brought by merchant traders and sea captains from the shores of Africa, particularly the Cape, and from Persia, India and beyond. The discovery of new plants from America also captured the excitement and imagination of London collectors. One of these was Henry Compton, Bishop of London. Compton and his young protégé, the Reverend John Banister, an Anglican missionary, were compulsive botanists. From 1678 when he first landed in the West Indies and soon thereafter settled in Charles County, Virginia, until his untimely death in 1692, John Banister collected, described, and sent to Compton approximately 340 species of plants. They were kept in a range of stove houses in the bishop's garden at Fulham Palace, and formed the most significant private collection in England.

Compton and Banister between them imparted the greatest knowledge of America's natural history to English gardening enthusiasts at the end of the seventeenth century. Banister's work was published posthumously, under a number of authorships, but during his lifetime he was recognized as a virtuoso in the colony of Virginia as well as in Britain. He was well acquainted with all the major landowners of the time, having lived at William Byrd I's plantation, The Falls, intermittently for fourteen years. The results of his studies encouraged a number of naturalists and botanists throughout the eighteenth century, including John Clayton, Mark Catesby and John Bartram of Philadelphia, whose own findings continued to challenge collectors across the Atlantic.

At the end of the seventeenth century, there was little published information about the particular needs of these new arrivals. Presented with a new species, gardeners would err on the side of caution in their treatment of it, for details of its natural habitat and climate may not have travelled with the plant. The gardeners' grapevine would have been the main source of information on what to do with what.

Garden enthusiasts in London seem to have taken the horticultural challenge by the horns. Dr Uvedale, Sir Anthony Vesprit and Sir Dudley Cullum were all experimenting with 'Exoticks'. The Archbishop of Canterbury had a greenhouse at Lambeth Palace, about which Evelyn had been consulted. It was of a new design, which had recently become very popular, being divided into three sections, with a stove and flues underneath. The centre room would have been heated to a higher temperature than the two adjoining ones, and was designed to accommodate the new arrivals from hotter countries.

Many keen gardeners lived to the west of London. Communication by the river Thames was one good reason, and fresh air was another. The capital was a forest of chimney stacks, disgorging filthy smoke from quantities of coal fires and furnaces. Pollution in winter was often intolerable; plants as well as people suffered from the smutty air, and those who could afford it moved out, often westwards. Chelsea was fashionable, and there were many famous gardens there, including the Chelsea Physic Garden, or the Apothecaries Garden of Simples, as it was also known. This had been founded in 1673 for the purpose of growing and studying plants for medicinal use. Some of these plants came from warm climates, so a conservatory was built near the river in 1680. John Watts, the keeper of the garden, experimented with different methods of heating, and by 1684 had *a new contrivance, at least in this country; viz. he makes under the floor of his greenhouse a great fire-plate, with grate, ash-hole, etc., and conveys the warmth through the whole house by tunnels; so that he hopes, by the help of the weather-glasses within, to bring or keep the air at whatever degree of warmth he pleases.*[10] The technology was Dutch, and Mr Watts was over-optimistic about its performance. However, Evelyn found it impressive when he went to visit the Physic Garden in August 1685. *What was very ingenious,* he wrote in his diary, was *the subterranean heat, conveyed by a stove under the Conserveatory, which was all Vaulted with brick; so as he leaves the doores and windowes open in the hardest frosts, secludeing only the snow.* It must have had some merit to impress Evelyn, and may have served as a model for others, including Lambeth Palace and Powis Castle.

A few steps along the banks of the Thames was the most important mansion in Chelsea, Beaufort House. Its history is extremely confusing, since it changed hands and names so many times, but in the sixteenth century it had been the home of Sir Thomas More, and by 1674 was owned by the Earl of Bristol. An anecdote, quite irrelevant, forges a bond between this distant garden and today.

Beaufort House gardens stretched from the river bank northwards as far as a little farm track; this track ran east—west along the north side of the garden, and turned down the west side for a short distance, before resuming its original direction. The track continued westwards to Putney Bridge, and eastwards to Westminster and St James's Palace. King Charles II persuaded all the farmers and landowners who owned it to let him use it in preference to busy Fulham Road. They agreed, and it became known as 'The King's Road', the name it still bears; the sharp bend round the edge of the garden is still there, the 'kink' in King's Road.[11]

Inside the garden walls, the Countess of Bristol must have had a substantial greenhouse, as she cherished a large collection of tender plants; possibly some had come from Wimbledon Manor House, which was also owned by the Bristols. Like most gardeners, she was

Ham House, Surrey. To the west, or left, of the house is a small hipped roof greenhouse with three large windows and a chimney, built, according to John Evelyn, by 1677. Although much altered, it is possibly the oldest existing greenhouse in Britain.

HAM-HOUSE in the
County of Surry One of the Seats of The Right Honorable the Earl of Dysart

generous with cuttings and plants for friends. The Countess of Sunderland, of Althorp, Northamptonshire, knew of Lady Bristol's orange trees and asked John Evelyn to buy some for her. A low, conspiratorial voice can be heard in her letter of July 1679 to Evelyn. She wrote: *I should be mighty glad to have 6 of ye best curld orange trees [that] my lady Mordent had if you will be pleased to make them and agree for them; let me know ye price, ye money shall be sent you and Ile send a wagon for them.*[12] So the trees were trundled off to Northamptonshire to join an already established display there.

Across the river, in Surrey, lived various distinguished gentlemen who collected rare plants. First and foremost was the ex-Ambassador to Holland, Sir William Temple, who owned The Priory in West Shene. Temple's diplomatic career had been fraught with difficulty and anxiety, and gardening was his solace. The contrast between his career and his private pleasures was described most vividly by Stephen Switzer the agricultural writer: *The greatest Consolation of his whole Life being, in the lucid Intervals he had from Publick Employs, in his beloved Gardens at Sheen.*[13] He had a greenhouse with a good stock of greens. Orange trees were placed on Portland stone pedestals in summer; he also had a movable shed for ground-planted trees, but these did not grow well there, perhaps because of poor soil. In 1680 Temple bought a house near Farnham, which he renamed Moor Park. Here he made a very Dutch sort of garden, to which he moved his orange trees. He was so devoted to this garden that when he died he gave instructions that his heart was to be buried in a silver box under the sundial. This was duly done.

Sir Henry Capel, later Lord Capel of Tewksbury, was another pioneer in gardening. He lived at Kew, and started the great greenhouse tradition continued to this day on the same site by the Royal Botanic Gardens. Capel had two greenhouses adjoining the house. Just as Evelyn was obsessed with fresh air, Capel was obsessed with shade. *He was contriving very high palisadoes of reeds to shade his oranges during summer, and painting those reeds in oil,* according to Evelyn, who called on Capel in March 1688; the orange trees and myrtles were apparently *very beautiful and perfectly well kept.* Gibson's account in 1691 described how Capel's *orange trees and other choicer greens stand out in summer in two walks about fourteen feet wide, enclosed with a timber frame about seven feet high, and set with silver firs hedge-wise, which are as high as the frame, and this to secure them from wind and tempest, and sometimes from the scorching sun.*

Nearby, the Earl and Countess of Lauderdale had a greenhouse at Ham House by 1677; it still exists, though in altered form. Sir Robert Clayton of Marden, banker and Lord Mayor of London, also collected foreign plants and built a greenhouse, but he had not taken good advice about its position; the greenhouse did not catch the winter sun because it was too close to a hill. This was quite a common error: the greenhouse at Lambeth Palace was shaded by the church, Lord Fauconberg's greenhouse at Sutton Place and Mr Watts's at Enfield both had no sun at all in winter, according to Gibson.

Royal Greenhouses

Charles II's interest in gardens was slight compared to his cousin Louis XIV's passion for them. There was, however, a royal greenhouse in St James's Park, and Samuel Pepys said that he saw orange trees for the first time in the park. The King also had a conservatory at Euston in Suffolk, a house he bought for its proximity to Newmarket and the races. The conservatory was sizeable, about a hundred feet long, and decorated with statues and maps, and there was a fine orange garden, according to Evelyn. But Charles's interest in exotic plants, if he had any, hardly leaps out from the pages of history. His association with oranges is rather via his mistress, Nell Gwyn the orange seller, than through clipped orange trees. In 1681, Charles installed Nell in a house in Windsor, just beside the castle. A Kip engraving of the house, called Burford House and later St Albans House after her son's titles, shows a fifteen-bay greenhouse facing south beside the house. Nell, who loved a joke and poked fun at everyone and everything, would have enjoyed the humour of an orange seller finally owning her own orange trees.

The first royal greenhouse that has survived is at Hampton Court Palace. After their accession in 1688, King William of Orange and Queen Mary engaged Sir Christopher Wren to make major alterations to Hampton Court, and add a greenhouse, which was a regular feature of all significant Dutch gardens of that time. Amongst the baroque façades and elaborate gardens of the palace, Wren's greenhouse is quite plain. The twenty large square-headed windows are edged with lighter coloured bricks than the rest of the walls, a simple enhancing technique much used by Wren, and the ridge roof is tiled. This practical building, light and with pleasing proportions, now houses the Mantegna cartoons.

Queen Mary took great interest in planning the gardens, with the assistance of a Dr Plunket, who was paid £200 per annum. Cultivation of exotics was taken seriously by royal gardeners; the greenhouse was for myrtles, orange trees and oleanders, which went outside it in summer and also ornamented the state rooms, as at Versailles, according to Celia Fiennes. There were other stove houses, which were *so artificially contrived that all foreign plants are there preserved in gradual heats, suitable to the climes of the respective countries whereof they are natives.*[14]

King William cast a blight on the building industry in general in 1695, when he imposed a very high duty on glass. The effect was instant and disastrous, and soon the tax was halved. In 1698, it was repealed because of continued unemployment in the glass industry. Non-essential garden buildings must have suffered more than any others during these three years, and it is probably not mere coincidence that there are no records of greenhouses being built until after the tax was removed.

The greenhouse at Kensington Palace was built for Queen Anne in 1704, probably by John Vanbrugh and Nicholas Hawksmoor, and is one of the best remaining examples of this type of

Kip's engraving of Nell Gwyn's house at Windsor, known as Burford House or St Albans House after the titles conferred on her royal son. The greenhouse, to the right of the house in the foreground, is plain but hardly small. Further up the hill is Windsor Castle and St George's Chapel, and beyond the castle, the river Thames twists round Eton College.

baroque building in England, and, without doubt, has the finest interior. Queen Anne took a considerable interest in the gardens of her palaces; she enjoyed rare plants from foreign lands, and had a significant greenhouse built for them. The Kensington greenhouse is a confident building, decorated with many different devices. The brickwork is an interesting feature, columns and pilasters on either side of the centre door being made entirely from bricks, and the door is further accentuated by a full entablature and carved cornice. The interior has been enhanced with architectural forms not found in other contemporary greenhouses; semi-circular columns interspersed with niches for statuary combine to make an elegant apartment. In front of the orangery, as it is now usually called, are walks bordered with bay trees. In Queen Anne's day, these would have been clipped into tidy shapes, round or conical. Now they are large and stately, and dominate the garden and even the greenhouse, but there is a curious harmony between building and bay trees.

Queen Anne used the greenhouse as a winter promenade and she also ate there. Daniel Defoe recorded that *the Queen oft was pleased to make the greenhouse, which is very beautiful, her summer supper house.*[15] Orangeries or greenhouses lend themselves happily to supper parties and banquets; although it is hard to find further evidence at this date, it is very likely that they were used for informal meals and formal entertaining. Banqueting houses had been a feature of most important gardens since late medieval days, particularly in the sixteenth and seventeenth centuries. Some were flimsy wooden affairs, with open sides, but others were airtight and watertight, built of stone. Summer-houses had become fashionable too, as garden retreats from the heat of the sun or chilly breezes; some were enclosed with windows.

The distinction between these three different types of building becomes blurred on close inspection. Was there much intrinsic difference between a banqueting house and a summer-house? No, possibly only in size. When could a banqueting or summer-house be used as a greenhouse? If it could be heated is the plain answer, even if orientation and design were not ideal. While sophisticated heating systems were being developed, pans of charcoal could easily be used to keep the frost out of the banqueting house. And the conservatory or greenhouse could be decorated with statues, swags and garlands of flowers and orange trees for summer banquets, or maybe for a concert of Mr Handel's music.

The greenhouse at Hampton Court Palace, built by Sir Christopher Wren for William and Mary, c.1690. Orange trees were placed in the state apartments as well as in front of the greenhouse.

The elaborate interior of the greenhouse at Kensington Palace, in which Queen Anne took her supper. Built in 1704, it now houses a permanent display of Ficus benjamina.

Country Seats

Many of the owners of London town houses also had large estates in the country. The first Duke of Beaufort had bought the Countess of Bristol's house in Chelsea, including her collection of exotics, but his principal residence was Badminton in Gloucestershire, where there was a greenhouse that looked much like a house, and also some stoves. The Duchess, a sister of Sir Henry Capel of Kew, loved her garden, and after her husband's death in 1700, spent nearly all her time in it. The Bishop of London, Henry Compton, and the Duchess of Beaufort shared the highest reputation in England as growers of 'Exoticks'. Her pleasure in growing things was described by Stephen Switzer in *Iconographia Rustica* in 1718. *Badminton in Glocestershire was the Seat where this noble Lady us'd to spend those Moments that many other Ladies devote to the tiresome Pleasures of the Town. What a Progress she made in Exoticks, and how much of her Time she virtuously and busily employed in her Garden is easily observable from the Thousands of those foreign Plants (by her as it were made familiar to this Clime) there regimented together, and kept in a wonderful deal of Health, Order and Decency.*

As the collection of seeds, cuttings and plants grew, more stove houses were built, with good light and effective heating systems. Not content with familiar citruses and oleanders, the Duchess branched into tropical fruit. Pawpaw, or papaya, was grown from seed, and the guavas produced perfect fruit, the first in England, according to John Cowell in *The Curious and Profitable Gardener*, published in 1730. Cowell described the guava achievement: *This Plant, in the Country where it grows, is a Shrub; but by her Grace's fine Greenhouses, grew to about sixteen Feet high, and bare several ripe Fruit at Christmas ... Her Grace had them brought to Table fresh from the Tree, and some others preserved in Sugar, but I have not heard of any since, of that Fruit, that have ripen'd in our Gardens, though several have blossom'd.*

The Duchess commissioned a Dutchman, named Kik, Kick or Kichious, and a footman-turned-artist, Daniel Frankcom, to illustrate her prize specimens; these included paintings of passion flowers, trailing geraniums, a castor oil plant, daturas, aloes, cacti, nerines, oranges, bananas, hibiscus and arum or calla lilies. The paintings were bound into two books and kept at Badminton.[16]

William Cavendish, 1st Duke of Devonshire, had a greenhouse at Arlington House in London, which later became Buckingham House and then Buckingham Palace. He built another one at Chatsworth in Derbyshire, while the house was under construction. This was the start of the great Chatsworth tradition of growing foreign plants with heat and glass. The greenhouse, dating from 1698, was probably designed by William Talman, the architect who was working on the house at that time. It is important because it was designed as an integral part of a new garden, the focal point behind a rectangular lake, facing south, with six windows on either side of a central door. The greenhouse has been moved to the south

A trailing geranium, now called Pelargonium peltatum, *from the Duchess of Beaufort's flower book. Everard Kick, the artist commissioned to illustrate the Duchess's flowers in 1703, was one of many talented flower artists in the Kick family of Amsterdam. The orange engraving on page 32 is by another member of the family. Botanical detail is accurately portrayed in all the Duchess's illustrations, both by Kick and by Daniel Frankcom whom he trained.*

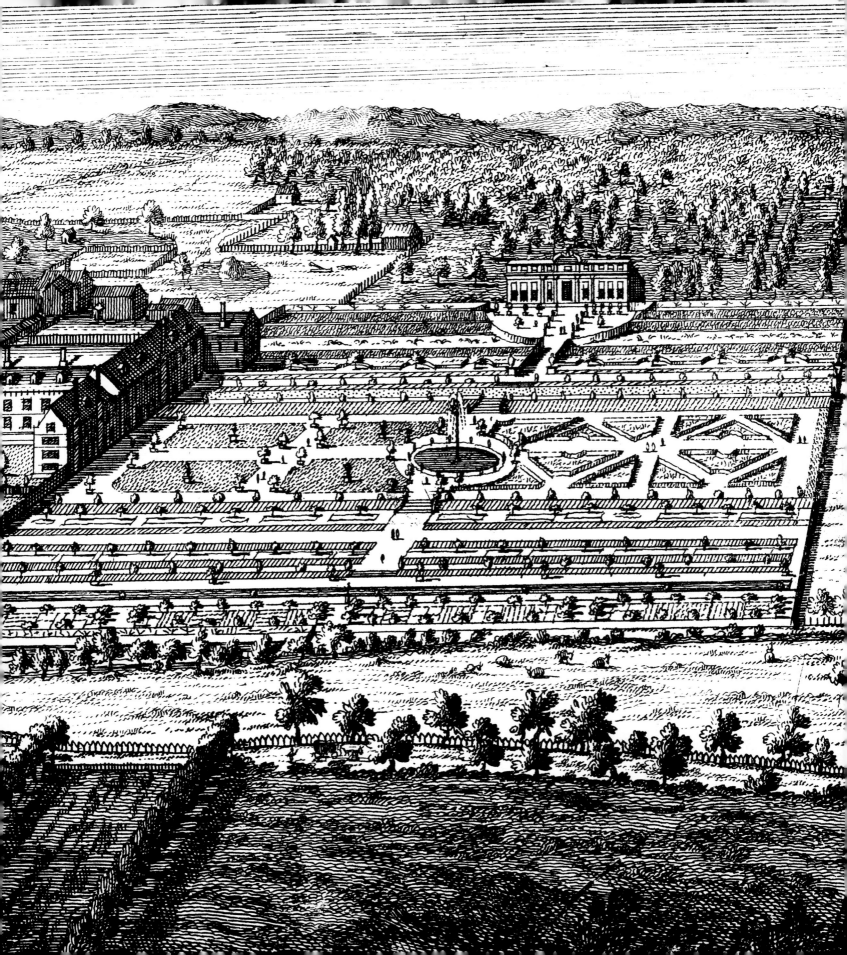

and slightly to the east and much altered, and is now known as the camellia house.

Talman's greenhouse at Chatsworth is recognizable only in length now, whereas the one at Dyrham, Avon, is much as he left it. Talman rebuilt the east front of Dyrham from 1698 for William Blathwayt. The greenhouse is decidedly grand compared with other contemporary English greenhouses, besides those in royal possession. There are four arched windows separated by coupled pilasters, and on either side of the arched door are massive coupled columns. Rusticated stonework round the windows is reminiscent of the *orangerie* at Versailles. A balustrade and urns hide the one feature that has changed since Talman's time, the roof. The original opaque roof was replaced with glass early in the nineteenth century, as the windows are too widely spaced and too small to be ideal for growing plants throughout the year. The house and gardens were much admired in their time, and minutely recorded by J. Kip in his engraving of 1712.

The significant feature of the gardens of Southwick, as engraved by Kip, is a two-storeyed greenhouse behind a semicircular orangery.

Talman's greenhouse at Chatsworth was built in 1698 behind a rectangular pond, but moved south-east some fifty years later. It was much altered by Joseph Paxton in the nineteenth century.

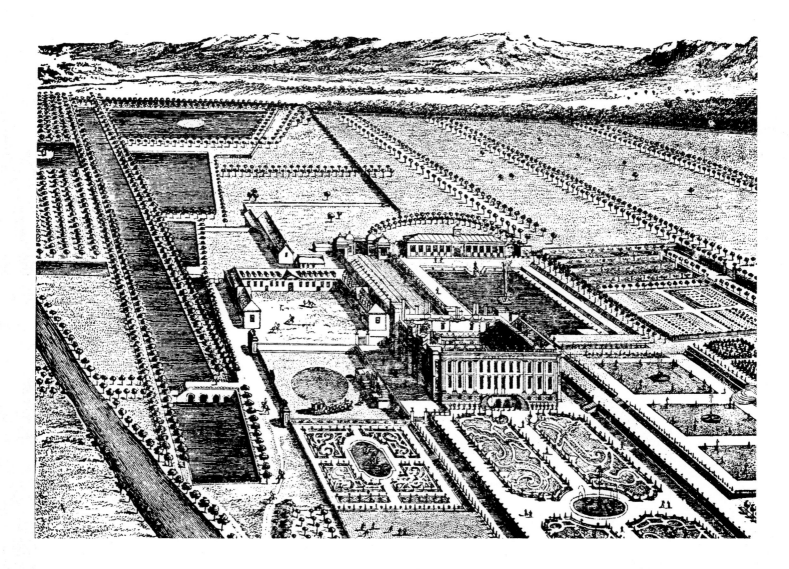

Part of the palazzo and garden of Sri. Conti Allegri in Cucciano, illustrated by J. C. Volkamer, 1714. Orange trees are grown in the ground under a framework, as in the gardens at Pratolino a century earlier. This Italian garden consists of statues and scrolled beds of coloured stones; ornamental trees are the only living feature.

The aranciera at the Villa Aldobrandini at Frascati, probably built at the beginning of the seventeenth century, illustrated by J. B. Ferrarius in Hesperides, 1646. The arrangement of a secondary row of windows above the principal level may have influenced the design of greenhouses in northern Europe throughout the seventeenth and into the eighteenth centuries.

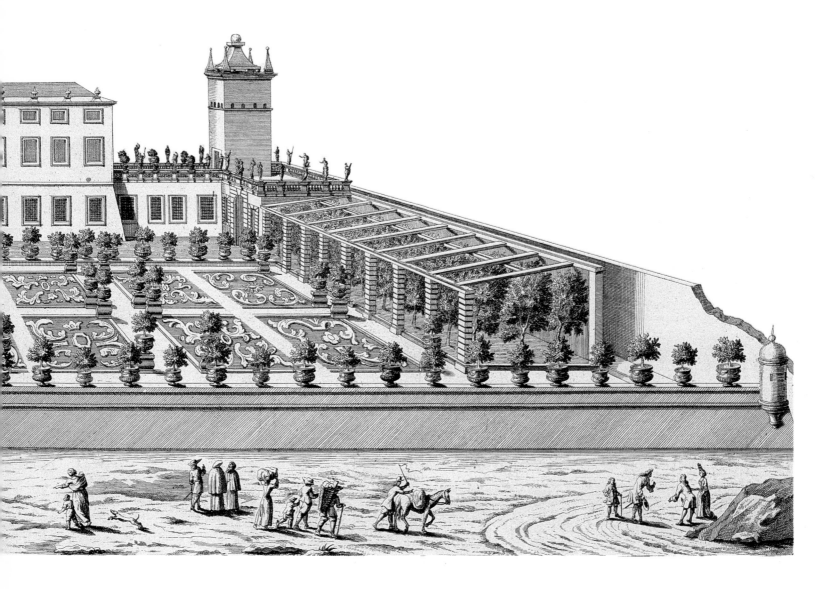

ALDOBRANDINORVM
CELLA TVSCVLANA
TVTANDIS PER HIEMEM
AVRANTIIS

Stephen Switzer described the greenhouse as *one of the most beautiful and commodious Piles for its Purpose.*[17] He continued: *This Green-house in the Winter is replete with all Manner of fine Greens, as Oranges, Lemons, Mirtles, &c set in the most beautiful order; several Rows of Scaffolds one above another, are erected for this Purpose, on the Topmost whereof are plac'd the most tender, but largest plants; and the Shrubs, Flowers, &c below, so as to make the Figure of a Slope with Walks between the whole Length, for the Gardener to examine into the Health and State of his numerous Vegetables.* The heating system was up to date and quite adequate. Below the floor were underground vaults with stoves, as well as a repository for garden tools, while internal shutters helped to insulate from wind and frost.

Switzer's description of the greenhouse in summer provides evidence that it was not intended just for plants, but was used by people as well: *when most of the hardiest Plants are expos'd Abroad, it is usual here to preserve two or three Rows of Oranges, &c the Length of the House, which make most beautiful and fragrant Walks within Doors; and the whole house is whitewash'd, and hung round with the most entertaining Maps, Sculptures, &c. And furnished with fine Chairs of Cane for the Summer.* The Blathwayts were able to make frequent use of this pleasant place, because it adjoined the house.

The idea of adjoining greenhouses was quite new. Hampton Court Palace was probably the first example in England; it is attached to the Palace, even though it was still quite a stride for the royal feet compared with the Blathwayts' quick step through a closet. Since royal activities have always had immense influence on the population, it is hardly surprising that the attached greenhouse was copied elsewhere. Switzer again provides proof of this influence. *The Nobility and Gentry of Great Britain ... were all this while very busie in Imitation of the Royal Examples of the then King and Queen.*[18]

Blenheim Palace in Oxfordshire has another fine example of a greenhouse, built between 1705 and 1716. John Vanbrugh's original design for the Duke and Duchess of Marlborough included two greenhouses, one to the west and one to the east of the mansion. The Duchess insisted that the western one should be omitted, despite Vanbrugh's plea that it was the identical symmetrical effect that mattered. For Vanbrugh, the greenhouse was there for architectural rather than horticultural reasons; his proposed buildings were not simply for *a parcel of foolish plants.*[19] This theme, of the greenhouse as an enhancing adjunct to a house or ornament for a landscape, recurs frequently in the eighteenth century. At Blenheim, however, the Duchess triumphed and there is only one greenhouse behind the Italian garden. All the usual tender plants were grown there for the Duchess, and orange flowers were sent to her in London by command.

Most early eighteenth-century greenhouses were free-standing; some were handsome and some quite plain. The Oxford Physic Garden, founded in 1621, had a large, impressive stone conservatory by 1675; here, the Bobarts, father and son, were both *very*

eminent in *Botanick Amusements,* according to Switzer in *Iconographia Rustica,* and studied any botanical specimens they could acquire. At Dunham Massie, in Cheshire, there was a simple building with leaded windows which was shown in Adrian van Diest's painting of 1696, but later demolished. In Norfolk, the orangery of 1705 at Felbrigg has survived. It is a startlingly plain building, by an unknown architect. Inside are some huge camellias, planted at about the turn of this century, feathery ferns and fragrant rhododendrons, and an attractive floor of square stone flags set diagonally.

There is one more greenhouse from this early period which can still be visited: remote, unique and enchanting, it is at Powis Castle in Wales. The castle, a bombastic fortress of red sandstone, commands a ridge which looks across the Severn valley towards the English Marches. Below the castle are the terrace gardens, facing south-east, on four narrow shelves carved out of the rock. A giant hedge of yew shelters the terraces from cold winds from the north-east, creating a micro-climate where half-hardy plants can survive, particularly on the upper level, nicknamed 'the tropical terrace'. The treatment of the various levels is strongly architectural, reminiscent of the Italian gardens of the Renaissance or the gardens at St Germain-en-Laye, but on a scale compressed by necessity. The top level has a niched wall for sculpture, and the second an aviary with six arches. Raised beds along the back wall of the aviary are now planted with scented rhododendrons and the climbing *Trachelospermum jasminoides.*

The orangerie *at Chevergny, Loir-et-Cher, built in 1701. Chevergny's most famous protégé was not a plant but a painting, Leonardo's Mona Lisa, which was stored inside the orangerie during the Second World War.*

A German Orangerie *in winter, with shutters closed and a gardener busily chopping wood to keep the furnaces ablaze.*
The fashionable German Orangerie at the turn of the century usually had a centre block of two floors, with single-storeyed wings terminating in end pavilions, which again had two floors. A prime example of this is the baroque building at Kassel, which dates from 1701. Curved wings were also favoured, as at Gaibach Castle and also in the Schlossgarten at Zerbst, both c.1700. German Orangerien *were often located at the furthest limit of the garden, only distantly visible from the house.*

The greenhouse is on the third terrace. The gentle warm tones of the brickwork, mottled with cream, are set off by the stone doorway, stone dressings round the window and the balustrade above. The columned doorcase, built about 1665, was originally at the gateway and was moved to the greenhouse early in the twentieth century. Lead figures of shepherds and shepherdesses, which seem to dance on the balustrade above, have recently been restored and painted white, as they were in the eighteenth century. Lead urns, unpainted, decorate either end, and the aviary above. Built into the rock, having no side or rear walls and a roof so thick that it forms the terrace above, the greenhouse does not need much heating. There was, however, a furnace room below, reached by a small brick staircase, and underfloor hot-air flues. By 1708, account books have entries for the purchase of *a myrtle and a pashion flower,* and a traveller, the antiquarian John Loveday, observed *a very large Aloe, one of its leaves four feet long*[20] in the greenhouse in 1732.

The architect was probably William Winde, who was employed by the Earl of Powis at Powis House in London and at the castle, and the greenhouse was most likely built during the decade of the 1680s. It remains one of the most attractive examples of this early period.

The greenhouse at Powis Castle, Wales, c.1685, is thought to be by William Winde. Inside are busts of Roman emperors and a small selection of plants, such as abutilons, that flourish in a relatively low level of light.

3 The Golden Age of the Greenhouse: 1715–1800

Whigs and Tories and Landscape Gardens

The years 1714 and 1715 marked several watersheds in Britain and Europe. George, the Elector of Hanover, succeeded Queen Anne as British monarch in 1714, the Treaty of Utrecht of 1714 brought peace in Europe, and the near-immortal Sun King died in France in 1715. After five years of Tory government, the Whigs came to power in England in 1715, beginning a period of sustained political and economic stability. The Whig landowners were eager to consolidate power by acquiring yet more estates, and for both Whigs and Tories building and improving properties was an irresistible passion, although the Whig estates were by far the more prolific and significant. Houses and gardens were a visible symbol of power and prestige, of refinement and taste. They were one of the means by which a 'person of quality' could demonstrate his social superiority, his artistic discernment. As usual, the latest taste carried the greatest kudos, and new ideas were in the air.

Baroque architecture had triumphed for long enough; *how affected and licentious are the Works of Bernini and Fontana*, wrote Colen Campbell in his introduction to *Vitruvius Britannicus* of 1715. For Campbell, the architecture of ancient Rome, and Palladio's sixteenth-century interpretations of it, were the only acceptable sources of inspiration. The ideals of classicism, of all parts of a building interlocking together to form a harmonious whole, appealed to the rational eighteenth-century English mind in this Age of Reason. Classical decoration – columns, pediments, porticoes and arches – reminded scholars and travellers of the culture of Greece and Rome.

As well as architecture, the second decade of the eighteenth century gave birth to the most dramatic change in garden design that Europe has ever seen. The subject of garden design became an important intellectual talking-point, and its practice a means of expressing abstract ideas. Change was stimulated by paintings of wild, ruined or romantic landscapes, but the desire for change may even have been brought about partly by awareness of the great similarity of garden plans. Artists had produced imagined aerial views of gardens before, but bird's-eye views of country seats were produced in abundance by two Dutchmen, Knyff the draughtsman and Kip the engraver. These two travelled round England, recording houses, gardens and the surrounding landscape of avenues of trees and plantations, and publishing the results in 1707 and 1717. The collected views are like patterns stamped on the countryside by a giant woodblock, with a few alternative arrangements, but almost always conforming to regular shapes within a rectangle. The impression of sameness is more striking than the reality, but it was the impression that mattered. The fact that these gardens complemented their houses, being a logical extension of elaborate Tudor, Jacobean or baroque architecture, was sadly not enough to save them in the end.

Gradually, Renaissance parterres and terraces were modified. At

Domestick Pomegranate.

the start, long walks were replaced with serpentine paths, then undulations wormed their way into flat lawns, and straight lines were tempered with the beauty of natural growth. Garden buildings became the focus of a picture which the artist-designer was consciously creating. By the middle of the century, symmetry was tossed to the wind, and eventually the picturesque, romantic landscape garden became the only acceptable form. More or less the only gardens to escape the pickaxe and the shovel and the armies of earth-movers were those of impoverished gentry.

This change had a significant impact on the greenhouse for two reasons. First, since garden buildings were fashionable, and could not all be temples to Greek gods, some were conveniently designed for protecting plants in winter. A greenhouse was built for the sake of architecture; it was an ornament for the landscape gardener, a toy house for the architect. In the past, architects such as Wren, Vanbrugh and Talman had produced handsome designs, but more had been put up by local builders, perhaps with reference to John Evelyn's book or a neighbour's experience. Now, the serious glass house for sub-tropical and tropical fruit and flowers, known as a stove, was consigned to the kitchen garden, while the greenhouse became a building that had to be beautified, the decorative addition to a composed picture. Removable wooden sheds as used at Beddington were quite out of the question. Secondly, the change from the formal to the landscaped approach eventually liberated the design, allowing experimentation with different schools of architecture within the confines of a single garden. Adherence to classical rules became less strict as the century progressed. Since garden buildings were essentially frivolous, small and comparatively cheap, they became playthings for amateur gentleman architects as well as for established professionals, and they could look like classical temples, Palladian villas or, later, like tiny Gothic castles or Chinese houses.

The pioneers of change in garden design were, on the Whig side, the Earl of Burlington, with William Kent and Charles Bridgman, and, on the Tory side, Alexander Pope. For Pope, garden design was a challenge for the intellect and an appropriate subject for his teasing pen. In spite of political differences, Pope influenced Lord Burlington's garden at Chiswick, and developed his own garden at Twickenham from 1719 onwards, based on the new principles. At the far end of his garden he built a greenhouse beside a circular orangery, which was approached by no less than six paths. The form of this building is unknown, but it was doubtless designed to please the eye from each direction.

All these lofty ideals did not, however, preclude the practical side of gardening. Pope adored trees and loved growing – and moving – shrubs and plants. Fruit and vegetables were another passion, and he had a range of stove houses in the garden, hidden by a screen of hedges. These were for forcing early vegetables, and for more delicate fruit like grapes and melons, as well as the much prized pineapple. The great poet enjoyed all aspects of horticulture, and said that of all his works, he was most proud of his garden.[1]

Proof of this devotion to productive gardening is evident in an engraving of his house by Rysbrack of 1735. The house, designed by Pope with a little help from his friend James Gibbs, is a fairly orthodox Palladian villa, but with the surprising addition of glass frames for plants on the south side. Only the keenest gardener would have sited cold frames on the important river front of his house.

Pope's genius in literature and in the world of gardening allowed him to mix with anyone he pleased, but his main circle of friends were High Tories. One in particular, Allen Bathurst, 1st Earl of Bathurst, was also a garden lover. Bathurst was an enthusiastic creator of gardens, first at Riskins in Buckinghamshire and then at Cirencester Park in Gloucestershire. Major work was undertaken at Riskins in the 1720s, and the greenhouse was built by July 1725. Several years later, in 1739, it was described by Lady Hertford as containing a good collection of orange trees, myrtles, geraniums and oleanders. The greenhouse was not just for plants, however. She described it as one might describe a conservatory today: *This is a very agreeable room; either to drink tea, play at cards, or sit in with a book, in a summer's evening.*[2]

A good example of a classical Whig greenhouse was Wanstead House at Epping Forest in Essex, close to London. The house itself, amongst the first and finest Palladian houses in England, was designed by Colen Campbell in 1715 for Sir Richard Child, and the plans were published by Campbell in *Vitruvius Britannicus*. The newly built greenhouse was also illustrated at the same time, and Campbell said obscurely that it was *design'd by another Hand*, but he obviously thought it a worthy example of the new classical idiom, since he only published plans that he thought good enough to influence public taste.

Inspiration for building the Wanstead greenhouse must have come from family connections. The Child family was despised by some for being *nouveau riche*; Richard's father Sir Josiah, whom John Evelyn described in his diary as *sordidly avaricious*, had made a vast fortune from the East India Company; money helped the Childs climb the social ladder rapidly, and Josiah married his daughter to the elder son of the 1st Duke and Duchess of Beaufort. It was, therefore, not surprising that the Childs took on some of the activities of Whig nobility, such as growing 'Exoticks'. Seedlings, cuttings and expertise could be obtained from the Duchess of Beaufort at Badminton. That the greenhouse at Wanstead was impressive, both inside and out, was recorded by Daniel Defoe when he visited the house in 1722: *The greenhouse is an excellent building fit to entertain a prince; 'tis furnish'd with stoves and artificial places for heat from an appartment in which is a bagnio, and other conveniences, which render it both useful and pleasant.* The delights of Wanstead gardens were certainly well known, as Defoe went on to say that they were thronged with sightseers: *These gardens have been so the just admiration of the world, that it has been the general diversion of the citizens to go out to see them, till the crowds grew too great, and his lordship* [Richard Child was created Lord Castlemain in 1718

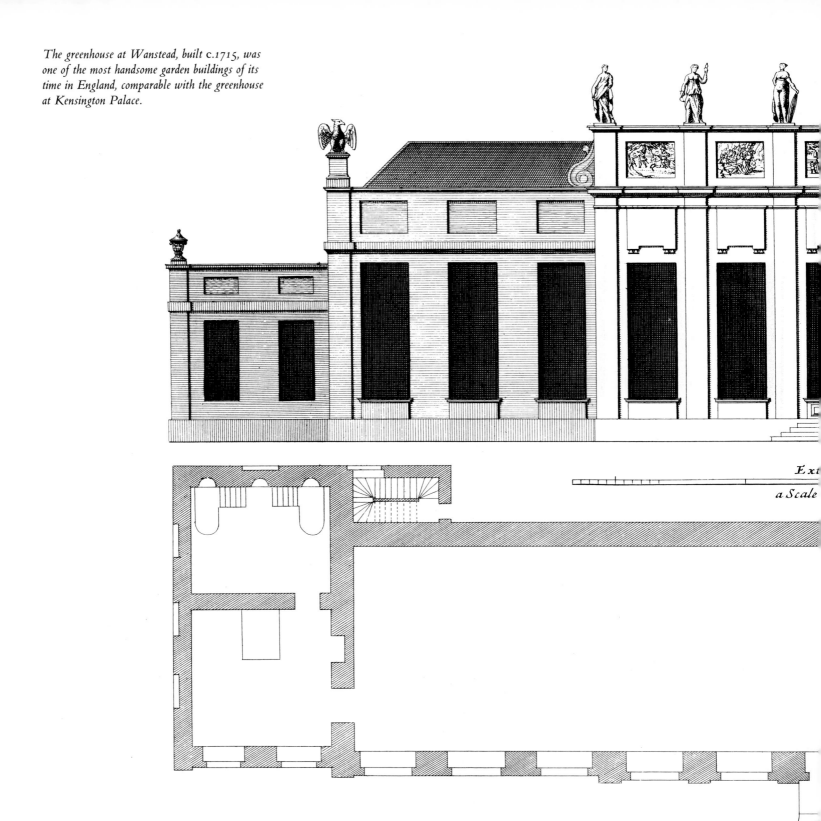

The greenhouse at Wanstead, built c.1715, was one of the most handsome garden buildings of its time in England, comparable with the greenhouse at Kensington Palace.

Ext

a Scale

The GreenHouse *at* WANSTED *in* ESSEX *the Seat of*

Waltham Forest *&c. to whom this Plate is*

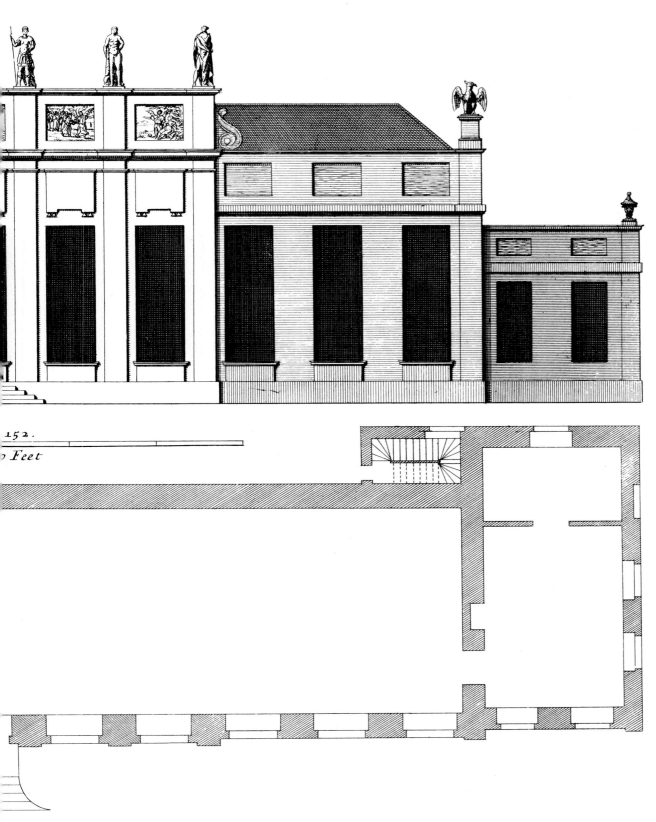

152.

Feet

RICHARD CHILD Baronet Hereditary Warden *of*

Humbly Infcribed

The Earl of Burlington's greenhouse at
Chiswick House, illustrated by Badeslade and
Roque in Vitruvius Britannicus, 1739, was
designed by the architect earl himself.

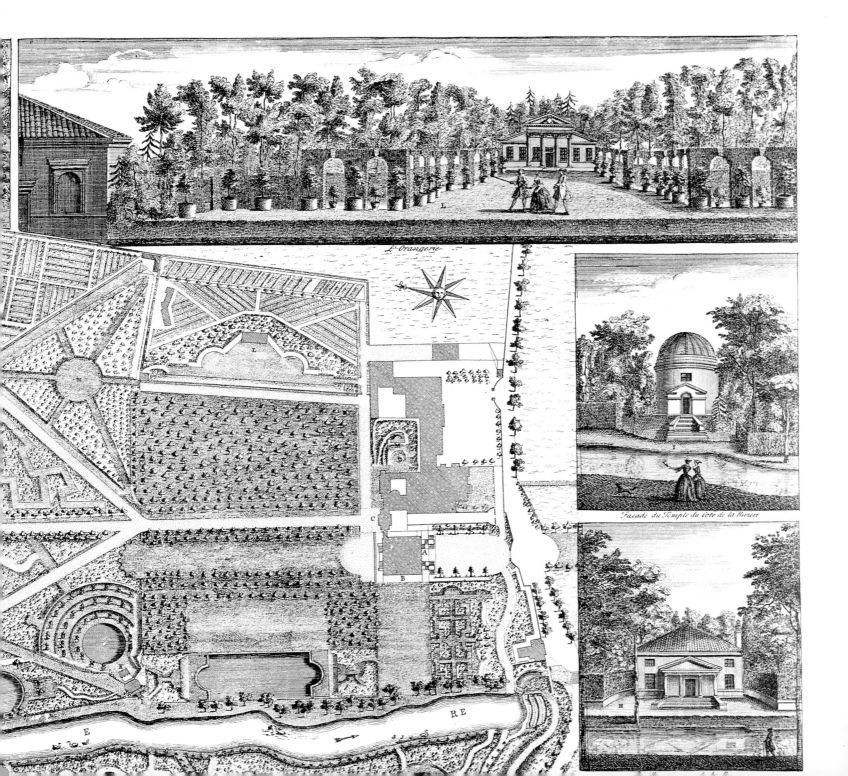

and Earl Tylney in 1724] *was oblige'd to restrain his servants from shewing them, except on one or two days in a week only.*[3]

Another famous early classical greenhouse was at Chiswick House in Middlesex. This had been designed and built by Richard Boyle, 3rd Earl of Burlington, great Whig patron of art and literature, and friend of Pope. His own interest in architecture was stimulated by not one but two Grand Tours of Italy, and he became a considerable amateur architect. For him, botany and horticulture were unimportant compared with the architectural embellishment of his garden. However, being one of the leaders of change in the sphere of gardens as well as architecture, Burlington started with the garden, like Louis XIV at Versailles. With the help of the landscape painter William Kent, from 1719 onwards the old straight parterres and canals were removed or altered, and turned into a series of pictures. This continuously evolving garden, as well as the revolutionary Palladian villa conceived in 1725, became a fashionable place to visit. Dilettantes, courtiers, gardeners and journalists made their way westwards to Chiswick to see this remarkable creation, of which garden buildings were such a prominent feature.

In spite of the emphasis on architecture, Burlington's greenhouse did house a large collection of citrus trees, which spent the summer in the garden. In his book *A Tour Through the Whole Island of Great Britain*, published in 1742, Daniel Defoe described it thus: *On the Right-hand, as you go from the House, you look thro' an open Grove of Forest-trees, to the Orangery; which is separated from the Lawn by a Faussee, to secure the Orange-trees from being injured by Persons who are permitted to walk in the Garden; so that they are seen as perfectly, and when the Orange-trees are in Flower, the Scent is diffused over the whole Lawn to the House, as if the Trees were placed on the Lawn.* What a delicious fragrance after the evil smells of London! Other orange trees were placed round the curved tiers of the amphitheatre, echoing the Renaissance gardens of Italy.

The house and gardens at Stowe in Buckinghamshire were being developed at the same time, and with the same emphasis as at Chiswick. Sir Richard Temple, Viscount Cobham, was assisted initially by Charles Bridgman, then William Kent and later Lancelot 'Capability' Brown, as well as by many noble friends who dabbled in garden design. Sir John Vanbrugh designed the house, built in the 1720s, and included two greenhouses, both attached to the house to the west; one was in line with the south-facing façade, and the other parallel to it to the rear. The most southerly of the two was demolished about sixty years later and the remaining greenhouse has been turned into language laboratories, for Lord Cobham's Stowe is now a major public school.

With the exception of Stowe, all these greenhouses have gone, but another from the same era still exists, at Hanbury Hall in Worcestershire. It was probably built between 1732 and 1735 by Bowater Vernon; he was recorded as being a vain, extravagant man for whom a greenhouse would have been a prestigious folly. The windows are larger and the brick piers between them are narrower than earlier examples at Hampton Court and Wanstead. The most interesting feature is the carving in the pediment, a latticed basket freely overflowing with flowers, foliage and exotic fruit.

Kent and Bridgman were the professionals in the new style of gardening, but gifted amateurs, such as Pope, were consulted by their friends too. Pope's advice was sought at Sherborne Castle in Dorset and Marble Hill in Middlesex, and it must be said that decorative greenhouses were not included in either plans. Greenhouses, while fashionable, were far from commonplace, and important new gardens did not automatically have a fine house for 'Exoticks'. Contemporary examples at Apethorpe Hall in Northamptonshire, Goldney Hall in Somerset, Carshalton House and Leoni's unexecuted plan for Carshalton Park, both in Surrey, were the exception. It is significant that when James Gibbs published a book of his architectural drawings in 1728, *A Book of Architecture,* while he was working at Stowe, he included summerhouses, pavilions and sundials, but not a hint of a plant house. Equally, Batty Langley's *New Principles of Gardening,* published in the same year, has no reference to any glass houses at all. Greenhouses or conservatories were still the prerogative of eccentric noblemen, of those who sought novelties or reminders of the warm south, of the real enthusiast or of the very rich.

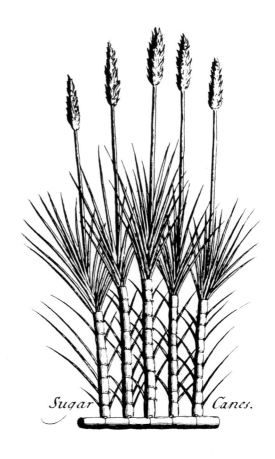

Sugar Canes.

The Practical Dr Bradley, FRS

How did the architects of greenhouses know what to do? The answer is that, generally, they didn't. Since they treated these buildings as architecture and not as places for plants, they paid scant regard to the needs of the plants. Windows sized for human use were sufficient for citrus trees and other old favourites, but the new varieties from the south that were arriving in Europe needed more light and heat, and therefore generally had to be grown in the stoves.

Dr Richard Bradley was the first person to publish a design for a decorative greenhouse with a partially glazed roof. He was a distinguished botanist, and had become a Fellow of the Royal Society in 1712. In 1718 he published a book called *The Gentleman and Gardener's Kalendar*, which included two chapters on the *greenhouse or Conservatory*, the first being mainly about design. Barely did Bradley disguise his scorn of current practices: *Green-Houses serve more for Ornament than Use; their Situation to receive the South Sun, is the only thing that seems to be regarded towards the Health of the Plants they are to shelter ... and sometimes where it happens that a Green-House has been well-consider'd in these Points, all is confounded by the Flues under it, which convey the Heat from the Stoves.*

The best aspect for the greenhouse was, of course, facing south, or possibly south-west. Bradley proposed the interesting alternative, *for the colder Parts of England,* of building the greenhouse in an outward-facing semicircle, which could catch every ray of sunshine from sunrise to sunset, a concept developed by Sir George Mackenzie a century later. In Bradley's view light was so important that not only were the windows to be from floor to ceiling, with no brick piers between them to cast shadows within, but the windows should be removable, so as to allow the whole glazed area to be open in summer. Shutters an inch thick should insulate the windows, and the attic above should either be a store for fruit or seeds, or filled with straw for insulation. The floor should be of stone tiles, and the walls lined with Dutch glazed tiles, *which are soon warm'd with the Sun, and reflect a great Heat into the House.*

Bradley was in favour of the greenhouse adjoining the house: *Can there be anything more agreable in the Winter, than to have a View from a Parlour or Study thorow Ranges of Orange-Trees, and curious Plants of foreign Countries, blossoming and bearing Fruit, when our Gardens without Doors are, as it were, in a State of Death?*

Bursting with all these sound ideas and a pioneering spirit, Bradley longed to influence the fashionable world, but knew that if he

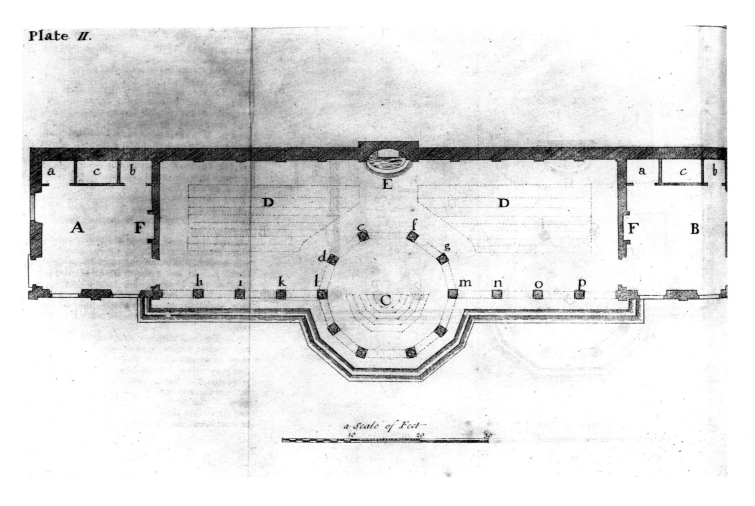

Plate II.

a Scale of Feet

produced a pedantic design he would be ignored. Luck was on his side. From 1717, he was employed by the Duke of Chandos at Cannons, in Hertfordshire, at the same time as an Italian architect called Alessandro Galilei. The Italian, who was much favoured by the aristocracy, produced an elegant, sophisticated design which was just what Bradley wanted, and proudly he incorporated it into *The Gentleman and Gardener's Kalendar*.

Galilei's greenhouse[4] sparkles with lightness and gaiety, and is far in advance of contemporary equivalents. The central feature is the classically inspired decagonal rotunda, under a cupola that was glazed on the south-facing half; aesthetically pleasing, it also satisfied Bradley's desire to catch winter sunlight from morn to night, and provide overhead light in the summer; the rest of the roof is opaque. The thirteen bays are separated only by Corinthian columns and topped by a row of attic windows for extra light, while the five windows around the rotunda can be moved from the external façade to the inner side, allowing the rotunda to be open to the elements in summer. A lantern, weather-vane, urns and potted aloes complete the exterior picture. The interior is graced with a small grotto, a pool and a statue, and the walls are decorated with pilasters and swags of flowers, while staging supports the rows of potted

The groundplan for Galilei's greenhouse, showing staging for plants at C and D, illustrated in Bradley's The Gentleman and Gardener's Kalendar, *1718.*

Galilei's superlative elevation of a greenhouse, as published by Bradley. Besides being a noble building, it was well advanced in horticultural terms.

Plate III.

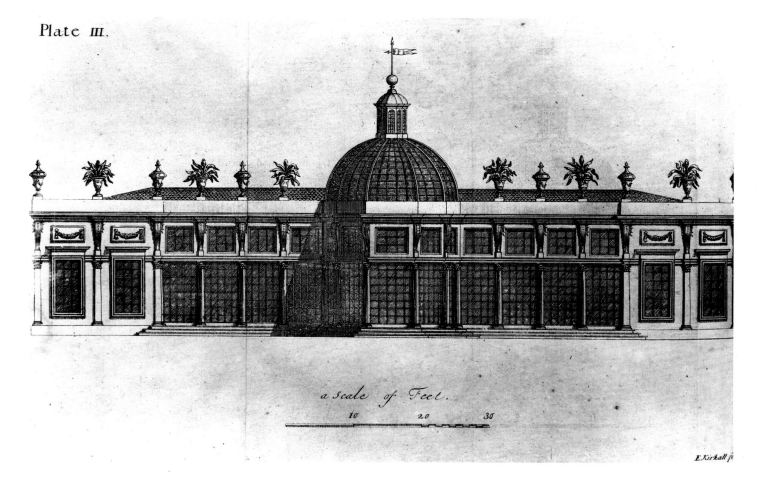

a scale of Feet.

10   20   30

E. Kirkall f.

plants and trees. In summer, when the plants were moved outside, this would have been a delightful *Room of Entertainment*, as Bradley proposed.

Old-fashioned charcoal was Bradley's choice of heating for most greenhouses; he considered it satisfactory provided it had stopped smoking before being taken into the greenhouse. He had obviously experienced problems with underfloor flues – in use at the Chelsea Physic Garden and Hampton Court and many other places – and he advised against them because the mortar between the bricks often cracked in the heat, allowing deadly smoke to fill the conservatory. This was a continuing problem until the introduction of steam and hot-water heating a century later; only when there was an alternative did most gardening writers groan about how difficult flues had been.

For Galilei's greenhouse, Bradley introduced a new design and position for a fireplace which might, he hoped, provide a better alternative to charcoal.[5] The idea was that at either end of the greenhouse should be a small room with a fireplace in the wall adjacent to the greenhouse. There is also the suggestion that the chimney flue might have one or two bends in it rather than going straight up, thereby heating more of the wall. Whatever the position of the flues, however, the wall could not have given off enough warmth to heat the entire greenhouse. Even if the flues warmed the wall all over, the area of heated wall would have been inadequate, so pans of charcoal were probably used too in frosty weather. However, the seed of the heated wall idea had been sown.

Specimens from other corners of the world were objects of curiosity, experiment and some misapprehensions. Bradley asserted that plants from south of the equator always grew best from August to November, even in the northern hemisphere. The growth pattern of

a plant grown from seed, however, is determined by the conditions surrounding it at the time, not by the seasons in its distant land of origin. Before being patronizing about this assertion — and perhaps some of today's beliefs will yet be exploded tomorrow — Bradley's mistake has to be seen in the context of the wisdom of the day, where pockets of proven truth subsisted with gulfs of ignorance and error. Pierre Pomet's *Compleat History of Drugs*, published in 1712 and reprinted in 1737, contains endless fallacies about flora and fauna; there are drawings of unicorns, and a whale with legs like a crocodile, beside which the minor botanical mistakes are insignificant.

Some of Bradley's expertise must have been acquired on trips to Holland. Social, economic and academic links with Holland were still strong, as were those in the gardening world, and English gardeners greatly admired the achievements of their Dutch counterparts. The Dutch led Europe in the seventeenth and early eighteenth century, both in plant collections and horticultural technology. England was a close second, with France and Germany following further behind. Bradley visited the botanical garden at Leiden, and was amazed particularly by the huge collection of aloes. These

plants had been grown in Europe since the beginning of the seventeenth century, but had recently become fashionable because of their shape; they have thick spiky leaves and a spectacular flower. The biggest was known as the American aloe (although actually it is native to southern Africa and is now called an agave), and it had a reputation for extremely rare but brilliant flowers. Another gardening writer, John Cowell,[6] tells how one absurd error gave rise to a generally accepted fact. In France, an ancient American aloe eventually produced such a superb flower that word of it spread far and wide. Its achievement was recorded in print, and expressed as *La Plante faisoit une si grande bruit . . .* This was translated into English, and commonly believed, as *the aloe, at the time of opening its Blossom, made a report as loud as a Cannon*!

Cowell wrote about growing *bonanas*, which need a high roof and might be planted in the rotunda of Galilei's greenhouse. He also mentioned other foreign fruit such as pawpaws, guavas and mangoes, but like all his contemporaries he enthused most about the queen of fruit, the greatest delicacy of all — the pineapple.

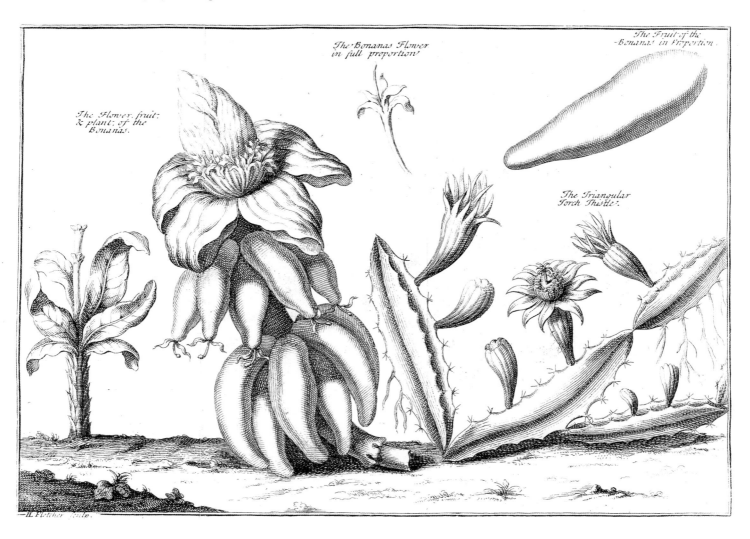

A Profusion of Pineapples

The pineapple, *Ananas comosus* or *A. sativus,* whose English name derives from the similarity of the fruit to the pine cone, is a native of Brazil and Columbia. By the seventeenth century it was also growing in the West Indies, and is first known to have been brought to England in 1657. John Evelyn tasted it at Charles II's banquet in honour of the French Ambassador in 1668, when the King kindly gave him a piece. *His Majesty having cut it up, was pleas'd to give me a piece off his owne plate to tast of.* Evelyn wrote that he did not think much of it, the flavour being *much impaired in coming so farr.*

There is a tradition that the pineapple was grown and fruited in England after the Restoration. A painting by Danckerts, who died in 1677, of a kneeling figure presenting a pineapple to Charles II[7] is said to be George Rose, the royal Gardener, offering the first home-grown fruit to the King. Were it possible to identify the large house in the background, this would lend credence to the event, but it remains a mystery.

Garden historians now also doubt if Rose had good enough heating techniques to bring the fruit to ripeness, since pineapples need prolonged, even heat around their roots. Furthermore, a respected later writer[8] stated that no stoves were built in England before John Watts's prototype at the Chelsea Physic Garden in 1684. Philip Miller, keeper of the Chelsea Physic Garden, asserted that the pineapple plant was introduced into England *so far back as the year 1690 by Mr Bentick,* presumably the Dutchman William Bentinck, later created Earl of Portland. It had fruited first in Holland for Agnes Block in 1687. The fruit certainly ripened at George London's Brompton Nursery in Kensington in October 1693: *Here is at this time a very fine Ananas near Ripe in the stove which is to be presented to ye Queen in a few days.*[9]

Another Dutchman, Sir Matthew Decker, is credited, erroneously, by many writers as the first to bring pineapples to maturity in England; he was certainly the first to get widespread publicity for the achievement. Sir Matthew was rich, thanks to his directorship of the East India Company and other interests in the City, and he also had *a truly Dutch passion for gardening.* He lived at Pembroke House on Richmond Green, and had a splendid garden, in which were *stove-houses, which are always kept in an equal heat for his Citrons, and other Indian plants, with Gardeners brought from foreign Countries to manage them,* according to John Macky in 1722. One of the foreign gardeners was Henry Telende, who had probably learned the secrets of pineapple culture from Pieter de la Cour at Leiden; gardening writers of that time mention *Monsieur La Cour of Leyden* and his stoves with positive reverence. La Cour sent plants to Richmond, and there were eventually no less than forty pineapple plants in Decker's stoves, producing fruit regularly. Decker was so proud of the achievement that he commissioned Theodore Netscher to commemorate the exotic fruit on canvas.

The Ananas or King of Fruits.

Telende's methods of cultivation were carefully described by Dr Bradley in his *General Treatise of Husbandry and Gardening* of 1724. A hot-bed, brick-lined and five feet deep, was filled with a twelve-inch layer of fresh horse dung, then covered with a much thicker layer of a new product, known as tanners bark. Tanners bark was *the bark of the Oak-tree, chopp'd and ground into coarse Powder, to be used in Tanning or dressing of skins; after which it is of great Use in Gardening. First in hot-beds, and then, when cooled, as manure in the Garden.*[10] It generated heat, just as manure did, but was more pleasant to handle. New plants were propagated by suckers or the crown of leaves, and then moved on to another hot-bed in what was called a succession house once the plant was established. From February to October, pots containing the pineapple plants (or pine plants, as they were usually called), were set into this warm mixture, and covered with a glass frame; in the coldest months the plants were moved to another hot-bed in a stove house with glass walls and roof, all within the kitchen garden. Telende made sure that the water he gave the pine plants was the same temperature as the soil; sensitivity to the needs of plants was doubtless the secret of his success.

Decker may have led the way in growing pineapples, but others followed quickly, despite the cost, as pineapples overtook the orange tree in novelty and chic. Philip Miller had a new frame built for them at Chelsea in 1723, and others who took up the challenge included the poet Alexander Pope. Being easy to propagate, plants were soon available from nurseries such as Mr Fairchild's at Hoxton in London. The pineapple train gathered pace as the years rolled on and the plants were more readily obtainable. Frequently, old garden records show that plants were also purchased from neighbours, or neighbouring estates in the country, as well as from nurseries. In Yorkshire, William Constable of Burton Constable built a greenhouse with two stoves on either side in 1758.[11] The total length was 206 feet and it was heated *with fire walls*, i.e. with the horizontal chimney flues gradually progressing up the wall. The stoves were for pineapples, and plants were bought from Lord Downe near Goole in that year, but they were also acquired from other estates at Cowick, Londesborough and Sledmere, and in 1761 the gardener was sent off to Castle Howard, seat of the Earl of Carlisle, to buy yet more plants.

Pineapple culture was popular in Europe too, particularly in France, where delicacies for the dining table were grown in all the aristocratic gardens. At the end of the eighteenth century in Poland, Prince Casimir Poniatowski, the King's brother, had a range of hot-houses 600 feet long containing no less than 5,000 pine plants.

English demand for pine plants was so great that it could not be satisfied locally, so plants were imported from Holland and also direct from the West Indies. The latter brought the scourge of gardeners: pests. Philip Miller moaned that those who selected plants in the islands of the Caribbean paid no attention to their condition, and sent infected specimens. Miller's time-consuming solution was to wash the leaves weekly with water infused with

tobacco stalks, but a badly infected plant should, he said, be removed from the pot, the soil shaken off, the plant immersed in tobacco water for twenty-four hours and then repotted. This treatment had to be repeated weekly. Since the leaves are edged with vicious little spikes, the job was hardly enviable. A further cure involving soot was recommended, as was quick-silver mixed with boiling water and cooled before application, with the possible addition of soft green soap.

Three more books about pineapples were published later in the century, full of contradictory advice. These were John Giles' *Ananas, or a Treatise on the Pine-Apple,* published in 1767; Adam Taylor's *A Treatise on the Ananas,* of 1769; and *A Treatise on the Culture of the Pine Apple and the Management of the Hot-House* published in 1779 by William Speechly, gardener to the Duke of Portland at Welbeck Abbey in Nottinghamshire. *Hot-houses are found by experience to be of so much importance, that no garden is esteemed complete without one,* he said. Together with John Abercrombie's *The Hot-House Gardener* of 1789, these books provide useful information about current practices.

Glazing was a matter that interested the writers; Giles proposed overlapping panes to give more light inside, welcoming the inherent draughts as a means of escape for the *rancid vapours* given off by fermenting manure. Speechly said that *the method of glazing in lead is now exploded; and what glaziers term flate-glazing in putty is most generally adopted.* Each pane of glass should measure about eight inches by six inches; larger panes cost too much and smaller ones meant that there was more wood to support them. The overlap should only be three-eighths of an inch, since the overlap cavity gets dirty, obscuring the light, and *contributes to give the house a gloomy appearance.*

Hot-house ranges or stove houses were widespread by the 1760s and 1770s; they were always hidden from the house and the landscaped park because of their functional appearance. They were replaced when old and rotten, or when new theories and new technology overtook their more primitive designs. Some were free-standing, and others were against a wall, and sometimes quite narrow. Some were for tropical fruit and exotic flowers, and some for forcing fruit and vegetables, or for peaches, cherries and grapes. Vines were almost as popular as pineapples, and some with knotted trunks and darkened, twisted stems still exist in old gardens.

The vinery at Hampton Court Palace houses the best known, indeed world famous, ancient vine. It was planted in 1768 under the direction of Capability Brown, and still yields the most delicious fruit. It is a dessert variety, called 'Black Hamburg'.

Most of the old stove houses have disappeared, but there is one pineapple stove that has partly survived destruction. It is in Stirlingshire in Scotland, and is known as the Dunmore Pineapple since it was built by John Murray, 4th Earl of Dunmore, in 1761.[12]

The identity of the architect of the Dunmore Pineapple remains a mystery, but the quality of design and of execution can still be admired. The giant freestone fruit is as crisp as new, and there is most delicate carving round the ogee-arched windows and above the portico. The circular chamber below the pineapple and the open loggia must have been built for pleasure visits from the Earl and his family. On either side of the portico were stoves for pineapples and other exotic fruit, each 45 feet long and with glass slightly angled from vertical; flued walls maintained essential heat, with chimney pots disguised, stylishly, as Grecian urns. Beyond these pine stoves stretched further glass houses, probably for peaches, cherries, melons and strawberries; rectangular holes high in the brick walls are the remains of a ventilation system. All the glass houses have now gone. Huge, high walls and Scots pine trees on three sides protected the stoves and garden from biting winds, and the gentle grassy slope where fruit and vegetables once grew is planted again with fruit trees. It remains an amazing piece of eighteenth-century eccentricity, the ultimate in pineapple mania.

The Dunmore Pineapple, built for the Earl of Dunmore in 1761, is a gigantic, flamboyant folly. Set in the heart of lowland Scotland, its absurdity is increased by contrast with the twentieth-century structures of the Forth valley – oil refineries and strings of pylons that lace the distant landscape.

The vinery at Hampton Court Palace houses an ancient vine of world-wide repute. An abundant annual crop – 840 lb in 1985, for example – is the result of good husbandry, since the vine receives the full-time attentions of one gardener. Nothing else is grown in the vinery, nor immediately outside where the roots have spread: the natural goodness of the soil plus a generous dose of fertilizer are for the vine alone. The vinery has been replaced five times in over two hundred years; the latest one in aluminium dates from 1970.

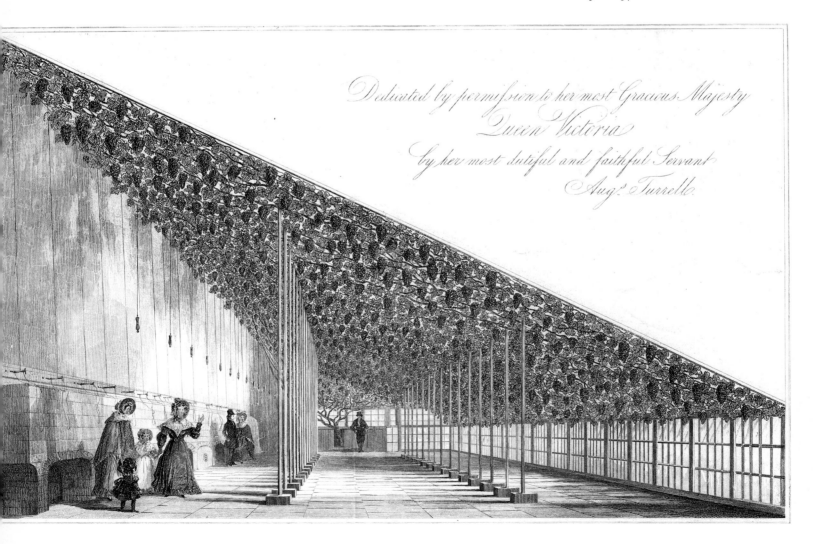

Dedicated by permission to her most Gracious Majesty Queen Victoria by her most dutiful and faithful Servant Augs. Turrell.

The Gardener's Challenge

Philip Miller, gardener to the Worshipful Company of Apothecaries and keeper of the Chelsea Physic Garden, was the single greatest influence on gardening in Britain in the eighteenth century. His best known publication is the famous *Gardener's and Botanist's Dictionary,* first published in 1731 with a further seven editions in the author's lifetime, and two more after his death in 1771. The dictionary covers houses for tender plants, which Miller described usually as a 'greenhouse', but occasionally as a 'conservatory'. He did not mention an 'orangery', but if he had, he would have meant the area in the garden where the orange trees were displayed in summer. Stoves were described in detail. Two editions are relevant to the greenhouse, the first and the sixth, both of which have diagrams and instructions which were widely followed. While details of design and heating may be somewhat turgid, they are very relevant in dating construction of a greenhouse: garden buildings are often poorly documented, and clues have to be sought anywhere, even under the floor.

Miller's first greenhouse was stone built, with huge windows, above which was a first floor for accommodation and storage. A central pediment was added to make the building look more important. On either side were stove houses, again with large glass windows but solid roofs. The idea was that the greenhouse had minimal heating, while the two stoves could be kept at a higher temperature; one was a 'Dry Stove' for aloes and cacti, and the other was for plants requiring both heat and humidity.

Miller recommended an amazing range of species for the greenhouse and the stoves: some little flowering plants, some succulent fruit, and some potential giants from tropical rain forests. It was an era when curiosity overcame practical difficulties, when compulsive collectors were daunted by nothing. The list makes truly impressive reading, given such far from perfect conditions. The quaint names that Miller used are given here, followed by their current common name, if different, and by the Latin name. Amongst the more spectacular are:

Acajou or cashew: *Anacaidium occidentale*
Allegator pear: avocado pear *Persea amencon 'Fuerte'*
Bastard locust of Barbadoes: rose acacia *Robinia hispida*
Cabbage tree: *Cussonia pomiculata*
Cocao tree: cocoa tree *Theobroma cacao*
Coconut
Dumb cane: *Dieffenbachia*
Fustick tree: iroco fustic tree *Chlorophora excelsa*
Ginger
Mahogany *Swietenia mahoganii*
Mimosa: *Acacia dealbata*
Sowre apple: prickly custard apple *Annona muricata*
Sugar apple: custard apple *Annona squamosa*
Tamarind tree: Indian date tree *Tamarindus Indica*

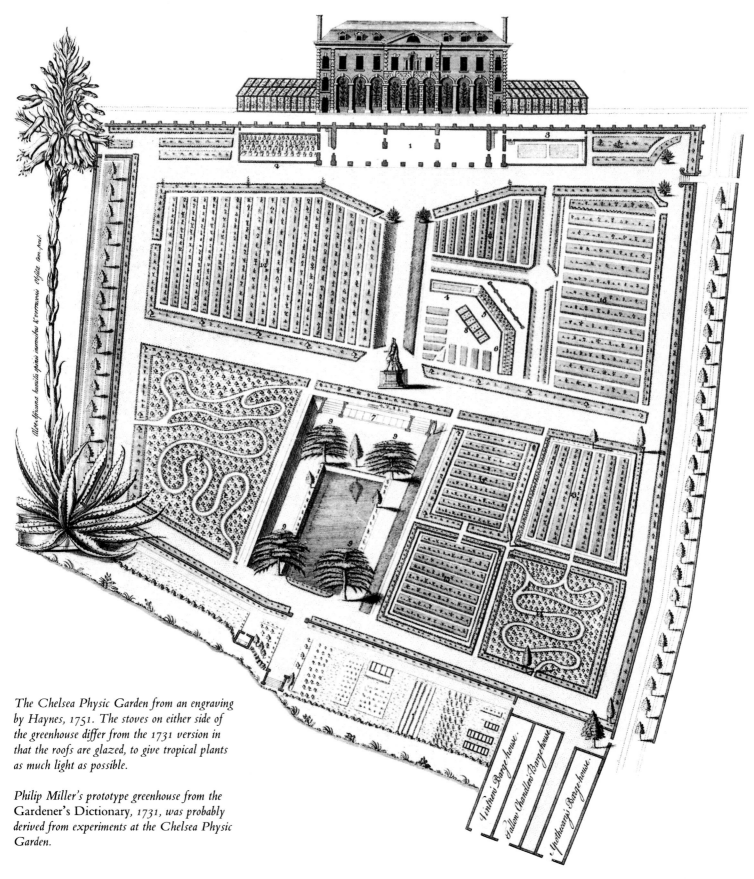

The Chelsea Physic Garden from an engraving by Haynes, 1751. The stoves on either side of the greenhouse differ from the 1731 version in that the roofs are glazed, to give tropical plants as much light as possible.

Philip Miller's prototype greenhouse from the Gardener's Dictionary, 1731, was probably derived from experiments at the Chelsea Physic Garden.

The eighth Lord Petre, who lived at Thorndon in Essex, was just the sort of expert amateur botanist for whom the plants in Miller's list would have been a fascinating challenge. At the age of nineteen he started collecting anything rare and tender that he could find, and by 1733 he had several stove houses for tropical fruit, and also a collection of exotic flowering plants, including a camellia.[13]

Colonial America was one of the richest sources of new species, and, following in Henry Compton's tradition, Lord Petre corresponded with the plant-collecting botanist, John Bartram of Philadelphia. This led to Bartram sending seeds and plants across the Atlantic to Thorndon, but this particular friendship came to an untimely end in 1742 when Lord Petre contracted smallpox, aged twenty-nine, and died.

At Chelsea in 1732, Miller built a new greenhouse with two stoves for £1,550 and then insisted on extra flues, presumably in the rear wall, at a further cost of £125. This prototype may well have had glass-roofed lean-to stoves, or been continuously modified by Miller as he sought improvements, and by 1751 at Chelsea there were stoves of familiar lean-to shape on either side of a very solid greenhouse.

The sixth edition of Miller's dictionary, which appeared in 1752, marks a watershed in published design. The main departures were that the stoves on either side of the greenhouse had glass roofs, and that not one but two furnaces were proposed per stove. One furnace had a traditional underfloor flue round the front of the house, and the other was beside the rear wall, with the flue going up within it. This heated wall, also described as a 'fire wall', was probably the product of experiments at various gardens, including Belvoir, where the effects of a warm wall had been observed by Dr Bradley in 1719 when a grape vine was planted next to a kitchen chimney.

Miller's dictionary was a mine of practical information about gardening and was widely read. Serious enthusiasts, however, probably visited the Physic Garden personally to study both plants and techniques. The designer, or owner, of the greenhouse at Gopsall Park in Leicestershire must have been influenced by developments

at Chelsea, for it bears a powerful resemblance to Miller's plan. It is thought to have been designed by William and David Hiorne for Charles Jennens[14] during the 1740s, and was completed by 1749. The greenhouse is an elegant building with classical decoration, while the stoves are plain but well proportioned. Both stoves have deep bark-pits; the stove for young plants has one furnace and the stove for fruit – guavas, mangoes, pineapples – has two furnaces because of the extra heat required. This basic design was followed widely throughout the country for the rest of the century.

There is an inherent flaw in creating an edifice that will deteriorate at different speeds, which may have been one reason why many rejected the greenhouse and stove, stone and wood combination. Another reason was that the combination had a touch of schizophrenia, lean-to stoves of that date being totally practical and very plain, in sharp contrast to the decorated greenhouse. Many people, therefore, opted for stoves hidden behind the walls of the kitchen garden, and the greenhouse next to the house, or within the pleasure garden.

The Oxford Physic Garden in 1766. The garden's noted collection of tender plants had been kept in a conservatory since 1675, but space and light there were inadequate, so these new greenhouses were built on either side of the Danby Gate to allow expansion of the collection.

The greenhouse at Norton Conyers, built by 1774, has one remaining hot-house stove.

Transatlantic Exchanges

A Country so delightful, and desirable; so pleasant and plentiful; the Climate and air, so temperate, sweet, and wholesome; the Woods, and Soil, so charming, and fruitful; and all others things so agreeable, that Paradice it self seemed to be there, in its first Native Lustre . . .[15] The new world began as a curiosity, a 'paradice' filled with exotic birds, beasts and plants and inhabited by strange and colourful Indians. It was a wilderness to be tolerated by some and to be tamed by others, a place for fortune or service.

By the second decade of the eighteenth century, a code for survival had been achieved and the quest for economic and social presence was established. Whether the colonist was a Virginia planter, Philadelphia Quaker, New York patroon or Boston merchant, the model of behaviour was that of the English gentry. Sons were being educated at Eton, Oxford and Cambridge, or in the newly founded colleges between Williamsburg and Boston. Fine libraries were being assembled and great mansions built. With an eye to the practical, the American garden for *meate and medicine* of the seventeenth century was extended to become the garden for pleasure and display. No longer was the traffic for exotic flora a one-way course eastwards.

As in England, enthusiastic gardeners shared eagerness for new plants with others of like mind. Many of these exchanges were organized through the Quaker plant collector from London, Peter Collinson. Collinson had an insatiable urge to collect plants from every quarter of the colonies, and he set up a sophisticated network of professional and amateur botanical contacts; seeds and plants were sent both up and down the Atlantic coast and back and forth across the Atlantic Ocean.

Amongst his many correspondents was William Byrd of Virginia. William Byrd II inherited Westover and The Falls from his father in 1704 at the age of thirty. He had been educated in England and had developed a keen interest in bulbs and plants which led to his election to the Royal Society, aged only twenty-two. It was not until 1726 that he left England to settle permanently at Westover and manage his estates. Perhaps encouraged by other beautiful estates on the James River or by the older expansive complexes at Green Spring or Bacon's Castle, he set out to change his father's frame house into a sizable brick mansion. Stimulated with fresh memories of Pope's garden at Twickenham, by other gardens belonging to his Royal Society friends, and inspired by Mark Catesby and Peter Collinson, he renewed his work on the Westover garden.

From Collinson's correspondence with John Bartram comes the description, albeit brief, of one of the earliest greenhouses in the colonies: *I am told that Colonel Byrd has the best garden in Virginia and a pretty greenhouse, well furnished with Orange trees. I knew him well when in England; and he was reckoned a very polite, ingenious man,* wrote Collinson in 1738.[16] In July 1740, Bartram recorded that

Colonel Byrd is very prodigalle . . . [with] new Gates, gravel walks, hedges, and cedars finely twined and a little green house with two or three orange trees . . . in short he hath the finest seat in Virginia.[17] The greenhouse was to be found on the same east–west axis as the house, on a site later occupied by the ice house.

Another of Collinson's correspondents was William Byrd's brother-in-law, John Custis of Williamsburg. Apart from discussing plants, Collinson wrote to Custis in 1737 advising him of the impending visit to Virginia of the foremost figure of eighteenth-century American horticulture, John Bartram of Philadelphia. Bartram was a *down right plain Country Man . . . His conversation I dare say you'l find compensate for his appearance. He is well Versed in Nature and Can give a Account of Her Works . . . He does not Value riding 50 to 100 Miles to see a New plant . . . His name is John Bartram. Your Friendship to him will be a singular favour.*[18]

Although they never met, Bartram and Collinson corresponded for thirty-nine years. Their letters often reveal great personal concern on the one hand, and a most abrupt and demanding attitude on the other: *I hope my old friend will not expose himself to Indian cruelties; and yet I want a dozen boxes of seed,* wrote Collinson in July of 1756, and in June of 1763, *O Botany! delightfulest of all sciences! There is no end of thy gratification. All botanists will join with me in thanking my dear John for his unwearied pains to gratify every inquisitive genius . . .*[19] It was only in 1760 that Bartram built his own greenhouse, telling Collinson that it was for *some pretty flowering winter shrubs and plants for winter diversion; not to be crowded with orange trees or those natural to the Torrid Zone, but such as will do, being protected by frost.*[20] Collinson's response was that he would send the seeds of the geranium to furnish it. He urged him to have a stove in the greenhouse, advice that reaffirmed what Bartram would have gleaned from his own copy of Miller's dictionary. The fact that Bartram did not build a greenhouse until he was sixty-one is evidence of the great variety of hardy plants that were available then in the colonies.

Just as Bartram introduced Collinson to a number of enthusiastic botanists in America, Collinson found scores of English subscribers for Bartram: in addition to his other great patron, Lord Petre of Thorndon, Bartram collected seeds and plant materials for the Dukes of Richmond, Norfolk and Bedford, Sir Hans Sloane, Philip Miller and Dr John Fothergill. The greatest honour was bestowed upon Bartram in 1765 by George III who made him his first – and last – Royal Botanist in North America. This title carried with it the sum of £50 per annum.

Mimosa grandiflora, *now called* Calliandra grandiflora, *is a native of Central America and was introduced into Britain in 1769. Another late eighteenth-century arrival was the climbing* Cobea scandens, *recorded in Britain in 1792. This painting is dated 1790, and was probably by Margaret Meen.*

The Architect's Influence

Here, far beyond
That humble wish, her lover's genius form'd
A glittering fane, where rare and alien plants
Might safely flourish; where the citron sweet,
And fragrant orange, rich in fruit and flowers,
Might hang their silver stars, their golden globes,
On the same odorous stem: yet scorning there
The glassy penthouse of ignoble form,
High on Ionic shafts he bad it tower
A proud rotunda; to its sides conjoin'd
Two broad piazzas in theatric curve,
Ending in equal porticos sublime.
Glass roof'd the whole, and sidelong to the south
'Twixt ev'ry fluted column, lightly rear'd
Its wall pellucid. All within was day,
Was genial Summer's day, for secret stoves
Thro' all the pile solstitial warmth convey'd.

William Mason, 'The English Garden', 1777

The decade of the 1730s brought new greenhouses, such as at Wrest Park, Bedfordshire, which Batty Langley built for the Duke of Kent in 1735, and at Windsor Park for the Duke of Marlborough. Charles Spencer, 3rd Duke of Marlborough, must have been rather fond of citruses, since he built a second greenhouse in 1750 at Langley Park in Buckinghamshire. This was designed by Stiff Leadbetter, a thorough but uninspired architect of the Palladian school. There is nothing original about the seven arched bays complete with pediment and hipped roof at Langley; however, the sash windows have one interesting feature: the semicircular top section is hinged along the diameter, so that it can be opened for ventilation, a very sound idea.

In Austria, the Emperor Francis I decided to start a collection of exotic plants.[21] There was already a 600-foot-long *Grosse Orangerie*, at the Palace of Schönbrunn, built in 1744 by Pacassi. In 1753 the emperor engaged two Dutch gardeners, one to supervise the gardens and hot-houses and the other to search for plants. An expedition was sent to the Caribbean in 1754, and for the next few years, plants, shrubs and trees were shipped back across the Atlantic to the Mediterranean port of Leghorn, and from there the precious plants were strapped to mules, who plodded all the way to Vienna. The collection flourished until 1780, when the ultimate gardener's nightmare was realized: one of the Dutch gardeners was sick, and the replacement gardener forgot to light the stoves. It was a bitterly cold night. In the morning, the unfortunate man tried to make amends

by making such a fierce blaze that the plants that had not already died of cold succumbed through the rapid rise in temperature. The collection was decimated, so the emperor, Joseph II, sent another expedition to Philadelphia and Florida for more plants.

Scotland's earliest remaining greenhouse was by William Adam, father of Robert Adam, built in 1750 to an earlier plan. Adam was commissioned by Robert Dundas of Arniston, Midlothian, to draw up plans for a house, which consisted of a central block with quadrant galleries and wings. The westerly wing was a greenhouse, with a central arched door, slightly recessed, three sash windows on either side, and at the westerly end a Venetian window. While Dundas's neighbours had gardeners skilled in producing fruit and vegetables, a greenhouse was quite a novelty for the area; perhaps Dundas brought the idea from Holland, where he had spent a year. The eastern portion of the main block of the house was built by 1732, as were offices in the east wing, and then work ground to a halt for financial reasons. In 1750, two years after the architect's death, the house and its wings were completed; the greenhouse at Arniston must have been quite a talking point in Edinburgh society.

If Adam's Arniston epitomizes Palladian simplicity, its opposite is the rococo frolic at Frampton Court in Gloucestershire, also built about 1750. At first sight it appears a most frivolous building designed entirely for appearance, a pastiche of Gothic architecture complete with defensive battlements. The design is

The orangerie at Huis Broekhuizen, Leersum, in Holland, was built in the eighteenth century and restored at the beginning of the twentieth century.

William Adam's greenhouse at Arniston, built for Robert Dundas in 1750, is probably the oldest extant greenhouse in Scotland.

The Frampton Court greenhouse, a many-faceted sparkling gem, was built during the 1740s for Richard Clutterbuck. The rococo Gothic detail of the doorcase and window is remarkably similar to plans in Batty Langley's Gothic Architecture Improv'd, *1742, for a Gothic window.*

based on three touching octagons, the rear one, a tower, housing a delicate stone staircase which ascends through two floors to the roof. Its very height might seem to disprove a horticultural function, but in fact two-storeyed greenhouses were quite the order of the day. At Frampton Court there were Gothic-inspired fireplaces, showing that these upstairs rooms were designed for social entertainment rather than as fruit stores. The two rooms on the ground floor, with their enchanting ogee-shaped windows, are exceptionally light and very suitable for over-wintering citrus trees. The arrangement of the panes of glass, and the exterior stonework around the windows and door, is a near replica of a design for a Gothic window published by Batty Langley in *Gothic Architecture Improv'd* in 1742. The overall shape of the building is a miniature of Stout's Hill, a nearby house designed by William Halfpenny.

One important change in design took place after the middle of the century: greenhouses lost their upper storey. The shift in perception of the ideal greenhouse came about during the 1750s, and was recorded by Sir John Hill in *The Gardener's New Kalendar*, published in 1758. He wrote, categorically: *It is common to load the greenhouse with upper rooms, but that is wrong. The back wall may serve for the erecting of sheds for the coals but nothing more should be done. No superstructure should ever be allowed, because it implies a solidity below which is out of the character of the building ... The sight is offended at a tall heavy building in a garden; and its shadow is hurtful. A greenhouse properly built is in character, and is an ornament: but such an edifice is a piece of lumber.* The greenhouses at Wanstead and Frampton Court could scarcely be described as 'lumber'. A late exception to the single-storey greenhouse was that built by George Steuart at Attingham Park in Shropshire in 1785, and others continued to be built across the Atlantic.

All the fashionable architects were asked to draw up plans for greenhouses, and Capability Brown, the landscape-gardener-turned-architect, had a positive field-day in combining two interests

The greenhouse at Woodside was painted by Thomas Robins the elder, c.1750. Through the windows a display of Chinese porcelain plaques can be seen on the walls.

at once. He seems to have designed more greenhouses than any other architect of his time. Most of Brown's greenhouses were free-standing, and he favoured a classical style. His first example in 1757 was quite different, however. This was for the Earl of Exeter at Burghley in Northamptonshire, where he designed a Gothic green-house adjoining Lord Burghley's Elizabethan mansion, set in a sheltered courtyard, with battlements and four little turrets which echo those on the house.

Brown drew up plans for alterations to the garden and for a greenhouse at Kimberley, Norfolk, in 1762, and in 1767 built three greenhouses: at Ashburnham Place, Sussex; at Charlton, Wilt-shire; and at Broadlands in Hampshire. The greenhouse at Broad-lands succeeded an earlier version, which was inadequate to cope with the volume of plants, and perhaps too plain to meet aesthetic demands. Here, Brown produced a classical façade for the west end of the greenhouse, while the south-facing front has plain, square-headed windows, later extended to the east. Both the view from the greenhouse over the gently flowing River Test, and towards it across acres of lawn, must have been carefully considered by the landscape gardener with 'the seeing eye'.

Brown's later commissions for greenhouses, all executed, in-cluded Redgrave in Suffolk, Stanstead Park in Sussex and Fisher-wick in Staffordshire, the latter demolished within fifty years of construction. He also built the now ruined greenhouse at Gibside in County Durham. Perhaps some of his buildings are a little ponder-ous and pompous when compared with equivalent buildings by Robert Adam; the derelict greenhouse at Redgrave, for instance, is a format devoid of inspiration. Brown's genius lay more in 'place-making', in siting the greenhouse on the ideal spot, rather than in creating the most desirable architectural design.

Most of the main architects of the day produced an example or two of a greenhouse. William Chambers, for all his many, varied and delightful garden buildings, designed remarkably few; one was Castle Hill in Dorset, later renamed Duntish Court, for Mr Fitz Foy. The best known, now called the orangery, is at the Royal Botanic Gardens at Kew, Surrey, and was built between 1757 and 1761 for Augusta, Dowager Princess of Wales. Its dimensions are impressive, and could have been overpowering had not rustications, painted stucco and the pattern of glazing bars lightened the effect.

James Paine's contribution was at Weston Park in Staffordshire, a greenhouse built in the late 1760s and known as the Temple of Diana. Another interpretation, and on the same scale as Kew, was James 'Athenian' Stuart's building at Shugborough. This was commissioned by Thomas Anson and started in 1764. It was posit-ioned to be admired from the house, free-standing and massive, in the classical mode that was James Stuart's hallmark. Along the south-facing front was a colonnade of columns, and in the west end there was a large alcove under a half-dome. The visitor who entered was transported to Greece by Anson's collection of classical sculpture amongst the orange trees, and by architectural frescoes.

'The Plan and Elevation of a Green House in ye Chinese Taste', one of three Chinese designs by William Halfpenny published in 1752 in Rural Architecture in the Chinese Taste. *Chinese-inspired greenhouses were also fashionable in France.*

The frescoes were accurate representations of Stuart's Greek drawings, and the work was painted in oil by the Danish artist Nicholas Dall. The temple of Minerva Polias was the main subject, with the ruins of the Odeum of Pericles in the background, but there was a surprise addition. In September 1770, Stuart wrote to Thomas Anson, communicating his pleasure in the finished fresco: *The water fall, with the scenery accompanying it, he has contrived with great ingenuity. I think it will have a wonderfull effect, it must astonish and delight every spectator.*[22] Enthusiasm and expense were lavished on this greenhouse, creating a place of great splendour; its destruction in 1800 seems all the more unfortunate.

In its brief heyday, a certain Miss Seward was so taken with the Shugborough greenhouse that she wrote the following lines:

See
Where the stately colonnade extends
Its pillar'd length, to shade the sculpted forms
Of Demigods or Heroes, and protect
From the cold northern blast each tender plant,
The fragrant progeny of milder climes.
Orange and lime, and cedars from the banks
Of Arno or Parthenope's soft shore,
There in fair order rang'd, stage above stage,
Rear to the lofty roof their green heads, crowned
At once with flowers profuse and golden fruit,
A sylvan theatre ...
Here while we breathe perfume, the ravish'd eye
Surveys the miracles of Grecian art.[23]

Composing poetry, landscaping the garden and designing suitable oranamental buildings were all agreeable activities for the upper classes in the later eighteenth century. Visiting the properties of others out of plain curiosity, to examine their art collections and their external 'improvements', was an accepted pastime.

Following in the tradition of the gifted amateur architect came Thomas Pitt, later Lord Camelford. He was invited to build garden buildings for friends, including a conservatory for General Conway in 1763 at Park Place, near Henley-on-Thames, and, most probably, the greenhouse at Mount Edgcumbe, Cornwall, built by 1780. Amateur opinion was also sought about the design of the greenhouse at Saltram, Devon. The building of this greenhouse is well documented, and family correspondence[24] shows the degree of pleasure involved in planning and using a greenhouse.

Saltram was owned by John Parker, later 1st Lord Boringdon; he and his wife Theresa divided their time between their house in town and their country estate near Plymouth. It was one of the largest and most important houses in Devon, and by 1773 the Parkers had decided to add a collection of citrus trees and a greenhouse. The plan was originally by a Mr Richmond, and had been further improved by the estate carpenter, Stockman. It was then sent by Theresa Parker to her brother, Lord Grantham, Ambassador in Madrid, who was the family arbiter of taste. From Spain, he wrote in September 1773: *I really like your Green house very much and think it a very handsome and proper building. I regret it's being in Wood, because it cannot last forever, and because Moor Stone is so beautiful, not perhaps so easily worked for a Doric Order if it is not upon a very great Scale.*

The following summer, Theresa sent him a progress report on the building: *Our green house is putting up and I think will look very handsome. I will send you the size of the inside Walls for your opinion how to ornament them. I want to have Niches and Statues for the Summer – exposed as it is, to the Sea air, and the Dampness there must be in the Walls sets aside all thoughts of Paintings. I have not had time to consider it, but I have a notion we may get good Medallions and Bas Reliefs in Artificial Stone, which properly arranged over Niches may make it clever.* Orange trees had already been purchased from Genoa in 1771; more arrived in 1775, costing £5. 9s. in freight charges, and further deliveries came in 1779 and 1780. Early in June in 1775, Theresa wrote again to her brother about how she was looking forward to returning to Saltram from London, and intended *sitting much in the Green House and drawing a good deal and I think the place must be in the highest Beauty.* The next month she was sitting inside it as she wrote:

Saltram Green House
July 10th 1775

Dear Brother
    You will see by the date that I inhabit this beautiful Room comfortably, I long much to shew it to you, and think it would meet with your approbation.

The niches and statuary were never acquired as Theresa died in November of that year, and the interior walls remain undecorated. The greenhouse was badly damaged by fire in 1932, justifying Lord Grantham's fears about a building in wood, but it has been carefully rebuilt.

The wooden greenhouse at Saltram was built for Theresa Parker in 1775. Inside, a small statue is framed by sweet-scented Trachelospermum jasminoides *and twin dracaenas. In winter the greenhouse is filled with a forest of healthy citrus trees.*

Robert Adam's unexecuted design for a greenhouse at Kedleston. The wealth of detail, from decorated panels to cornucopias to delicate moulding within the pediment, would have made this one of the most pleasing of Adam's garden buildings.

Following Theresa's death, her sister Anne took charge of household affairs and looked after John and Theresa's two small children. Anne continued the regular letters to her brother Grantham, and in January 1782 reported the following: *We have such mild weather that we are now planting and finishing the place for the orange trees, which is behind the Chappel, it is so warm a situation that we mean to plant all sorts of curious shrubs, myrtles we are sure will grow and Geraniums we mean to try.* This is the Orange Grove where the citrus trees are displayed in summertime to this day: their present positions are dictated by a diagram dated 1888. By tradition, the trees are moved out to the Orange Grove on Oak Apple Day, 29 May, and returned to the greenhouse on the day of the Tavistock Goose Fair, the second Wednesday in October.

Of all the greenhouses of the third quarter of the eighteenth century, Robert Adam's have perhaps the greatest appeal. Adam's

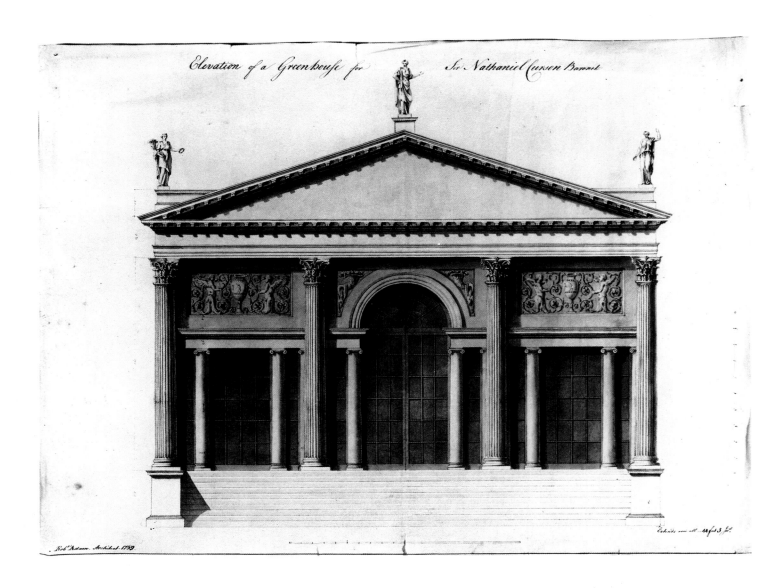

distinctive style, the lightness of his touch and the delicacy of his ornamentation were ideally suited for the subject. The Diocletian Wing at Bowood, Wiltshire, which was half menagerie and half greenhouse, is a prime example of his skill. It was built for the Marquess of Lansdowne in 1768, and was attached to the main portion of the house. The windows are large, allowing plenty of light inside, with fine glazing bars in a semicircular fan shape within the round head. The same fan pattern on a much larger scale is found in the fanlight above the central door. At Croome Court, Worcestershire, Adam again designed another quite different yet pleasing building, a large hexastyle classical greenhouse with huge windows separated by simple Doric columns. Lightness and delicacy are provided by the fineness of the entablature and the elegant stonework of fruit and flowers trailing from a basket in the pediment.

Robert Adam built this greenhouse, known as the Temple Greenhouse, for the Earl of Coventry at Croome Court in 1760, while Capability Brown was completing the house and landscaping the park. It is an intrinsic feature of the landscape, visible from the house but some half mile distant from it, and approached by a serpentine path through a shrubbery. Crossed cornucopias are carved above the side doors, and in the pediment a basket overflows with fruit and flowers, reminiscent of the not-so-distant carving at Hanbury Hall. While the stonework is well preserved, the absence of the original sash windows, a victim of spiralling costs, intensifies the air of an abandoned temple.

Robert Adam's elevation for Kenwood, 1764.
The greenhouse, already in existence, was
incorporated into Adam's new plan in the west
pavilion, and a music room was added as the east
pavilion.

The immense length of Anthony Keck's plan
for Margam is most apparent in this elevation.

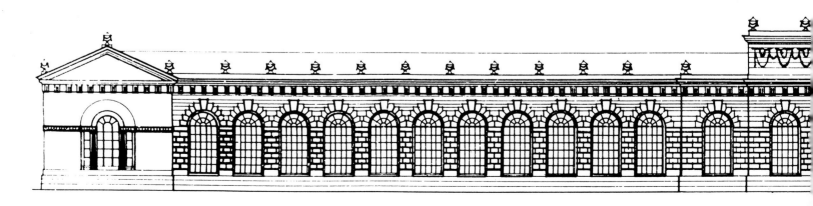

Robert Adam designed a greenhouse in one of the two south front wings at Kedleston in Derbyshire, which were never built, and at Compton Verney in Warwickshire. At Kenwood, Hampstead, he remodelled the house for the 1st Earl of Mansfield in 1764, and extended it as far as an existing greenhouse. This was refaced, in keeping with the new façade, and to maintain symmetry a similar wing on the east side was built as a music room. Perhaps the most appealing of them all were the greenhouse and the garden room built for the Earl of Jersey at Osterley in Middlesex in 1780. The greenhouse has been demolished, but the garden room, which could equally well have been used for plants, is semicircular, stuccoed and painted in pale blue and white. It is like a wedding cake, or a trinket, another frivolous jewel in the spirit of the greenhouse at Frampton Court.

Classical decoration was used for Britain's largest greenhouse, the immensely impressive Margam in West Glamorgan, South Wales. In many ways, this is the climax of the classical era in the eighteenth century, the grandest of a long, prestigious line. Designed by a relatively minor West Midlands architect, Anthony Keck, it was started in 1787 and completed three years later. The external façade is 327 feet long, and has no less than twenty-seven round-headed windows, plus two more Venetian windows in the end pavilions. It is richly decorated with vermiculated, deeply incised stone dressings round the windows, and above the three central windows is a panel carved with bulls' heads and garlands, whilst a row of urns ornaments the roof line. An explanation for the enormous size of the greenhouse, and the purpose of the two large end pavilions, is revealed by a quick glance at the owners of Margam and its history.

Margam was owned by Thomas Mansel Talbot, who set off on a Grand Tour of Europe in 1768 – and a very Grand Tour it turned out to be, for it took four years. Like his contemporaries he bought furniture and jewellery, paintings and statues, and these he had shipped back to Swansea. He also acquired ideas of architecture on the grand scale, and garden designs to match. Doubtless he had visions of Versailles, Kassel and Schönbrunn when he returned to Margam.

Margam already had one of the largest collections of citrus trees in the country. Various fanciful traditions declare that orange trees were grown at Margam in previous centuries, having been part of a cargo either shipwrecked or seized by pirates. The orange trees were said to have been destined for several alternative monarchs – Elizabeth I, the King of Denmark, Charles I, Catherine of Braganza (Charles II's bride), or Mary, wife of William of Orange – but they ended up on the shores of South Wales. Whatever their age or their origins, there were plenty of citrus trees at Margam, including some giants 20 feet high and 18 feet wide, by 1753.[25] Keck's masterpiece was therefore built to accommodate a large number of trees, and tall ones at that; the main entrance for plants was in the centre of the rear wall, where there were doors almost up to the eaves. Margam estate accounts show that the greenhouse cost £1,600 to build, but that figure does not include the value of many of the materials, which came from the estate.

The pavilions at either end were fitted up to display Talbot's treasures. The east pavilion was a gallery for statues, and the one at the west was a library, with a marble fireplace, an elaborate plasterwork frieze, vases of alabaster and porphyry and pumice models of Roman buildings, as well as a collection of books.

Small wonder that people called at Margam to see this magnificent greenhouse and its contents. In 1802, Sir William and Lady Hamilton, travelling *à trois* with Lord Nelson from Milford Haven to London, stopped at Margam. They visited the greenhouse, and Lord Nelson gave the gardener a tip of three shillings for showing them around.

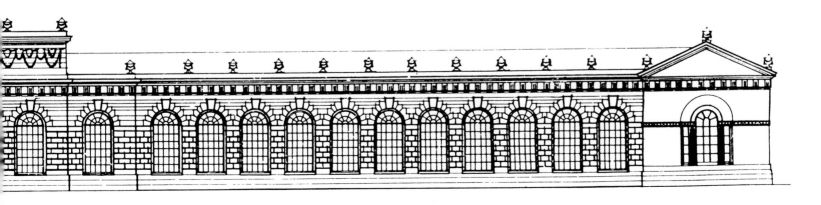

The Colonial Gentleman's Greenhouse

It is indisputable that the eighteenth-century colonial gentleman looked to England, both before and after the Revolutionary War of 1776. When the best kitchen and greenhouse gardener was sought, the London agent was put to work to find him. The gardening guides of Dr Bradley, Philip Miller and Thomas Whately, and the architectural builders' manuals of Langley, Price, Salmon and Gibbs found in the colonial gentleman's library, were becoming as commonplace as the English furniture, porcelain and textiles in his elegantly appointed Georgian house.

The designs of Batty Langley, James Gibbs and William Kent dominated the American architectural landscape. The Palladian design of a major centre block with side pavilions became the standard layout for the country houses, which were multiplying rapidly along main rivers and highways from Williamsburg to Boston. Punctuating the extremities or the boundary walks of the garden were summer-houses, and, if the owner was of substantial wealth or possessed a sophisticated knowledge of plants, a greenhouse was sometimes built. Smaller, less ornate and not as well stocked as its English counterpart, it was no less romantic or appealing.

Covered with Virginia creeper and buttressed by the entangled trunks of the iron-like trumpet vine stands the picturesque ruin of the once noble greenhouse and stove at Mount Airy, built by

Colonel John Tayloe II between 1748 and 1758. This very large estate on the Rappahannock River in the Northern Neck region of Virginia was inherited in 1744 by Tayloe from his father. A small manor house situated close to the river was soon abandoned for a site on a higher, cooler knoll on one of the estate's many farms, where he built a much larger villa.

Mount Airy is regarded as the most important, and perhaps the most handsome, eighteenth-century stone Palladian house in Virginia; it took ten years to complete. On the edge of the right lawn and in line with the central bay of the north-west façade stood the imposing greenhouse. Built of rich red brick and randomly placed glistening blue-grey headers and stretchers, the greenhouse complemented the colour scheme of the house. Approximately 48 feet long and 18 feet high, it had five large bays with fanlight, or arched, windows flanked by two smaller doors also capped with fanlights. The shorter doorways led into two *Hot-houses*, one described as *pt* [part] *top covered with glass* and the other as having one wall of glass and one of brick.[26] The greenhouse had *walls of brick covered with wood,* and underfloor heating.

Among the records of visitors to Mount Airy is one of May 1827 when an English diplomat by the name of Nicholas St John Baker spoke of the *very large conservatory with orange and lemon trees put out upon the grass.* The biography of Thomas Dabney of Gloucester recorded *a small dish of Antwerp raspberries sent by Mrs Tayloe of Mount Airy in February. They came from her hot house and were set before General Lafayette.* Other reports indicate that before the Civil War, tropical and out-of-season berries, pineapples and grapefruits were grown at the Mount Airy greenhouse. It was destroyed soon after the Civil War and many of its bricks used to build tenant houses on the farms.

John Tayloe II had been a member of the King's Council under Lord Dunmore – the builder of the Dunmore Pineapple in Scotland – and later served on the first Republican Council. The Tayloes were known for their love of the turf, and Mount Airy was the scene of great hospitality and frequent lavish entertainments. It is therefore not surprising that the Tayloes' many children married into the best families of Virginia and Maryland, and the influence of Mount Airy was felt throughout the eighteenth century.

The Tayloes' eldest daughter Elizabeth married Edward Lloyd IV of Maryland. After the beginning of the Revolutionary War, the Lloyds started to build a new house at Wye, between the Wye and Miles rivers. It consisted of a main central block flanked laterally with service wings, and, at the far north end of the bowling green, a greenhouse. The strong architectural vocabulary at Mount Airy without doubt influenced the Lloyds with the expansion and alteration of the greenhouse at Wye, making it the most aesthetically pleasing structure of its kind. Still standing, it is long, measuring over 85 feet, with windows almost 6 feet wide and an upper floor used as a billiard room. Curiously, the four wedge-shaped voussoirs and keystones over the square-headed windows are of wood, painted and sanded to appear as stone; the second storey and wings are constructed of brick but are stuccoed to look like stone.

Fruit from the citrus trees at Wye was enjoyed by the family, and shared with neighbours. In 1810 a local doctor prescribed a lemon supplied from the Wye greenhouse to help cure an illness. Some years later, C. Howard Lloyd, who was born in 1859, recalled that he was often sent to the greenhouse to fetch a lemon; and that the tubs at the *orangerie* at Versailles were the same as those he knew in the greenhouse at Wye.[27]

Another very prominent Maryland family, related to the Lloyds and the Tayloes, were the Carrolls, Charles and his wife Margaret Tilgman, of Mount Clare in Baltimore. After their marriage in 1763, they developed their colonial estate overlooking the Patapsco and its gardens, whose elaborate series of terraces falling down to the river would cause many pens to scratch. Charles Carroll frequently sent to London for goods and plants, including a thermometer for the greenhouse in 1760 and lemon trees and grape vines in 1768. Delays and casualties were endlessly frustrating. By 1770, a visitor from Jamestown, Virginia, was admiring the Carrolls' greenhouse, *with a good many Orange & Lemon Trees just ready to bear besides which he is now buildg a Pinery where the Gardr expects to raise about 100 Pine Apples a Year. He expects to ripen some next summer.*[28]

When Mount Clare and its successful greenhouse were fifteen years old, Charles Wilson Peale painted the garden front, showing its interconnecting dependent wings, the westernmost being the

Colonel John Tayloe II's greenhouse at Mount Airy, now a picturesque ruin, must have been one of the finest in the colonies in the middle of the eighteenth century. Its present romantic state would have been much admired in the eighteenth century, when overgrown ruins were built for effect.

Wye House greenhouse may have been constructed in 1755 and then enlarged c.1780.

four-bay, hipped-roof greenhouse. Carroll died in 1783, and left his widow a life interest in Mount Clare; she spent the rest of her life altering and improving the house and garden. She even had her portrait altered to record the changes. In 1788, Peale repainted his 1770–71 portrait of her standing proudly in her garden: the central block of the main garden façade behind bears a new lunar window in the pediment. In her left hand she holds a spray of orange leaves from which an orange once dangled.

General Washington was known to everyone and an acquaintance to many. During the Annapolis racing season he socialized with the local gentry and particularly with those who shared a keen interest in experimental agriculture, such as Charles Carroll. After the war the acquaintanceship was rekindled, and by August 1784 the well-known correspondence between Mrs Carroll and the General had begun.

Although there exists documentary evidence pertaining to its conception, design, construction and contents, the Mount Vernon greenhouse of today is not the original, but a reconstruction built on its former site and completed in 1951. Its historical and archaeological accuracy is a testament to the professionalism of the Mount Vernon Ladies Association which saved Mount Vernon in 1858, and to the early historic preservationists and archaeologists who painstakingly sifted through both soil and manuscripts to design the present structure.

An undated memorandum in Washington's own hand, perhaps to Lund Washington, indicates the initial plan for a square greenhouse with long, narrow slave quarters attached to either side. Two more undated sketches by Washington show a more rectangular greenhouse, to which he alluded in a letter of 11 August 1784 to Tench Tilgman, Mrs Carroll's brother-in-law. Washington sought precise details about the dimensions of the Mount Clare greenhouse, and also about the heating system. Tilgman replied with an informative account and a sketch of the flue system. One particular piece of advice concerned the position of the orange trees: *It is the Custom in many Green Houses to set the Boxes upon Benches – But Mrs Carrol says they do better upon the Floor, because they then received the Heat from the Flues below to more advantage.*[29]

Construction, however, did not begin until the winter of 1787, and it was still not finished in September 1789 when Washington wrote to Mrs Carroll, asking for *such aids* [from her greenhouse] *as you can well spare and as will not impair your collection.* What ensued could be dubbed 'The Orange Affair'.

What Washington thought was a simple request for a few small trees, which he could then transport without too much cost, became an embarrassingly expensive gift. Mrs Carroll eventually despatched *five boxes and twenty small pots of trees, and young plants among which were two Shaddocks – One Lemon and One Orange; of from three to five feet in length, Nine small orange trees; Nine Lemons, One fine balm-scented Shrub; two potts of Alloes and some tufts of knotted Marjoram.*[30] The collection had to be specially packaged, and

a vessel chartered to transport it from the Patapsco to the Potomac River. The President wrote that he was overcome with her generosity.

The greenhouse was valued for insurance purposes in 1803 at $800, compared with $15,000 for the dwelling, and again in 1805 at $1200. It burned down on a bitterly cold morning in December 1835.

Massachusetts has always laid claim to the first greenhouse built in the colonies. The harder winters of Boston meant that fewer plants could survive the winter outside, and therefore there was more reason to enhance the garden with orange trees in summer. Andrew Faneuil, a French Huguenot merchant who was first listed on the Boston tax list of 1691, had moved to a large stone house on Treamont (Tremont) Street by 1710. There in his garden a greenhouse was built sometime between 1710 and his death in 1738. A neighbour, Gardiner Greene, also built one soon after 1738, undoubtedly inspired by Faneuil's building and its contents.

North-east of Boston on the road to Portsmouth was the wealthy port of Salem, a mercantile centre for New England populated with prosperous shipowners, captains and merchants. Elias Hasket Derby was a resident of Salem, a merchant, a man of taste and intellect. Perhaps reminiscent of Nicholas Fouquet at Vaux-le-Vicomte in the seventeenth century, Derby combined the talents of Samuel McIntire, the architect, and George Heussler, his Alsatian gardener, to create a superb house, more like a palace than a dwelling for a merchant. House and garden are long since gone; we are left with McIntire's drawings, which date from the last few years of the eighteenth century.

As at Wye and Mount Vernon, the McIntire plan shows a two-storey greenhouse, by then out of fashion in England. There are five large recessed bays under a simple cornice which balances four delicately carved urns silhouetting the skyline. No doubt constructed of wood which would have been painted or stuccoed white, this attractive greenhouse, if built, must have added a princely pose to Mr Derby's garden.

New York City was, of course, the other hub of new arrivals, new ideas and new commodities. A series of advertisements placed in the weekly *New York Mercury* for September and October 1758 by a surveyor, Theophilus Hardenbrook, suggests that greenhouses were not uncommon by this time. *Designs all Sorts of Building, well fitted to both Town and Country, Pavillions, Summer-Rooms, Seats for Gardens, all sorts of Rooms after the Taste of the Arabian, Chinese, Persian, Gothic, Muscovite, Paladian, Roman Vitruvian and Egyptian; ... Studies in Parks and Gardens, Green Houses for the Preservation of Herbs, with winding Funnels through the Wall, So as to keep them warm ...* Ten years later, a similar series of advertisements appears in the *New York Journal or the General Advertiser*, inserted by a Thomas Vallentine, recently of Ireland.

Could it have been Hardenbrook or Vallentine who built the first recorded greenhouse in New York City for James Beekman at

Samuel McIntire's drawing for the E. H.
Derby greenhouse at Salem, before 1799, has
three unusual features. The first is that the
greenhouse faces east, an orientation doubtless
dictated by space in the garden; secondly, the
central section, or Stove, for tropical or sub-
tropical plants, has windows too small for good
growth year round, and would probably have had
to be used as a green house. The third, and most
attractive, feature is the dovecote above the
Green House at the south end.

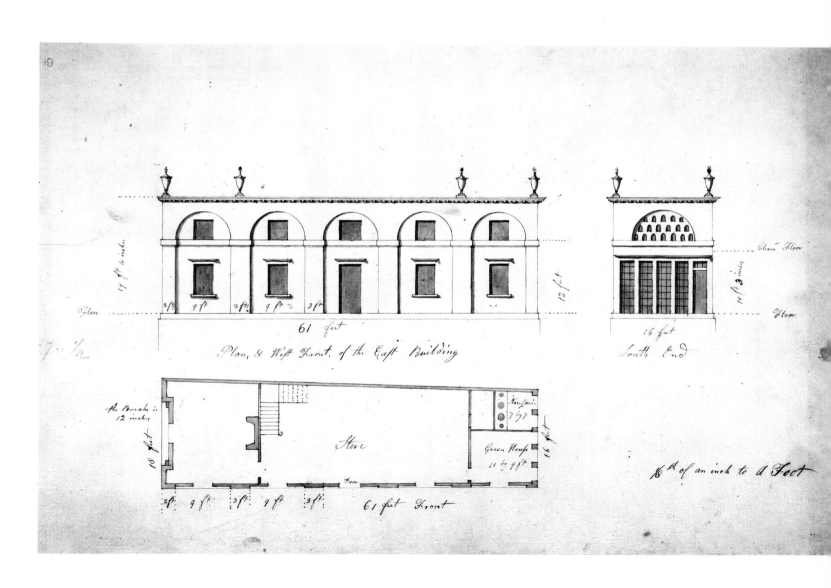

John Woodside's painting of Lemon Hill, 1807, on the northern bank of the Schuylkill River, Philadelphia. The enthusiasm of its owner, Henry Pratt, for exotic plants is apparent from the size and the close proximity of the earlier greenhouse to his 1799 mansion.

A nineteenth-century sketch of James Beekman's greenhouse of c.1764, from The American Florist.

Mount Pleasant on the East River at Turtle Bay? The greenhouse may have been built in 1764, and was doubtless used much like any other until 1776, when it became a prison for one night. During the Revolutionary War, Mount Pleasant was the headquarters for the British Generals Howe, Clinton and Riedesel. On Saturday night, 21 September 1776, the British had captured the American spy-patriot, Captain Nathan Hale, and had taken him to General Howe, who ordered Hale to be hanged the next day. That night, a disastrous fire raged in lower New York, so Hale's last hours were spent confined under a strong guard in a place not often thought of as a gaol: the Beekman greenhouse, *filled with exotic shrubbery and plants.*[31]

After the war, the Beekmans returned to New York and re-established their active social life, but by 1852 Mount Pleasant's period of magnificence had passed and the estate was demolished. The prolific American historian Benson Lossing made a sketch of the greenhouse and the mansion a few days before demolition, and in 1887 it appeared in *The American Florist* with the caption *First American Greenhouse ... an illustration of considerable historical interest to the trade.* A small, neat building, it holds no surprises in its design, but offers a glimpse of the accepted standard city greenhouse of pre-revolutionary New York.

Further south was Philadelphia, a prosperous cultural and intellectual centre, a city with significant institutions and a tradition of beautifully manicured town gardens and elegant country estates. As the city grew, houses with gardens and orchards were built in nearby Germantown and along the Schuylkill and Delaware rivers. By the middle of the eighteenth century over two hundred country houses were found within a ten-mile radius of the city, many of which were equipped with all the essential features of a well-appointed garden. Greenhouses and hot-houses were part of the picture, as they were in England. They were to be found in the gardens of John Penn at Lansdowne, James MacPherson at Mount Pleasant in Fairmount Park, John Cruikshank at the Grange and Isaac Norris at Fairhill. There was also a greenhouse at Gray's Ferry, one of the first public gardens in Philadelphia; it was large, *having three stories in front, and two in the rear.*[32] The most significant and largest estate belonged to William Penn, at Springettsbury, just west of the city, now the Fairmount Park area. Orange, lemon, lime and citron trees graced the gardens, and hot-houses provided out-of-season delicacies.

William Logan, a keen botanist, had a greenhouse in town and another at his Germantown estate, Stenton. He had a good stock of citrus trees, some of which found their way to The Hills, a property on the banks of the Schuylkill River. It had been owned by Robert Morris, a signer of the Declaration of Independence, who sold it to Henry Pratt in 1799; it was Pratt who changed the name to Lemon Hill, built a new mansion which stands today, and expanded Morris's villa into a greenhouse, as seen in the painting of 1807 by John Woodside.

FIRST AMERICAN GREENHOUSE.

A few years before Pratt's death in 1838, *The American Gardener's Magazine* bore an article on Philadelphia gardens, which observed that at Lemon Hill *the range of hothouses and greenhouses, is about two hundred and twelve feet in length, and is divided into six compartments; or rather they are additional houses, built on since the erection of the first … the largest one is built in the old style, with upright sashes or large windows in front, and with a dark roof … filled principally with the different species and varieties of oranges and lemons — among which are some of the very largest species.* Although the appearance was thought to be somewhat neglected in 1835, the contents were found to be *unrivalled in the Union.*

Another fine estate on the Schuylkill was Woodlands, built by William Hamilton and described by Thomas Jefferson as *the only rival which I have known in America to what may be seen in England.*[33] The Reverend Manesseh Cutler was enchanted by the greenhouses: *Every part was crowded with trees and plants, from the hot climates, and such as I have never seen … there was not a rare plant in Europe, Asia, Africa, from China and the islands of the South Sea, of which he had any account, which he had not procured.*[34] Hamilton and Pratt represented the new generation of greenhouse gardeners. Although lemons and oranges continued to find their advocates, the new species from South America and China were collected with great enthusiasm.

Unfortunately, very few of these eighteenth-century buildings exist outside of diary description, the artist's eye or the archaeologist's probe. They were very much a symbol of wealth and status, a luxury for any prosperous man who loved his garden and wished to adorn it with exotic fruit trees in summer and enjoy their fruits in winter. Yet it was an ephemeral structure, often the object of attention for one generation only. *The greenhouse lover is like an actor,* wrote a reviewer in the middle of the nineteenth century, *remembered by his contemporaries, and by them only.*[35]

The cast-iron greenhouse at Chiselhampton,
c.1800. The identity of its architect remains a
mystery but, as the finest and oldest glass-roofed
cast-iron greenhouse in Britain, its importance is
not in doubt.

The First Glass Roofs

A steady change in perception of the greenhouse emerged towards the end of the eighteenth century, with the realization that overhead light benefited the increasing variety of plants within. Why should only hot-house plants have this great advantage? Light, its quantity and quality, depended on glass. Glass was made by the same process as in the past, either as a round disc – crown glass – or on a cylinder that was slit down one side to make a rectangle – plate glass. It was still an expensive commodity to produce, and was taxed according to size, so smaller panes were used for greenhouses and hot-houses. Greenhouse glass was thick, and therefore relatively cheap, and it often had a slightly greenish tinge. Faint though it was, this tinge helped protect plants from the fiercest heat of the sun, so shading was not as necessary as it became after the introduction of colourless sheet glass in the 1830s.

The advantage of glazing plant houses with panes that overlap, instead of being set into timber mullions, was that more light reached the plants. This had been established in the 1760s, but overlapping panes have their own problems. The overlap eventually becomes discoloured, thus reducing the light inside. Furthermore, water collects in the overlap when the temperature drops below freezing, so the panes may be cracked by expanding ice. A partial solution to the problem was to curve the pane top and bottom, so that the water could collect naturally at the lowest part of the curve and drain away easily. Putty was often used to seal the overlap, and the recommended width of the overlap was reduced from three-eighths of an inch in the 1780s,[1] down to as little as one-eighth of an inch by the 1830s.[2] Where putty was not used, certain draughtiness was inevitable with scalloped glazing, but this never seemed to concern the gardeners. Indeed, had airtight glazing been thought imperative, sash windows would not have been used either, since they are invariably draughty. Neither did cold air coming through cracks seem to be related in gardeners' minds to temperature control. There appears to have been a surprising degree of tolerance to draughts in greenhouses – and in private houses too – in Britain, in contrast to concerns with *courants d'air* on the Continent, where the better fitting French windows were always used, in both house and *orangerie*.

Scalloped or fish-scale glazing was used for a very early cast-iron greenhouse at Chiselhampton in Oxfordshire. Here each pane of glass had straight sides with an identically curved upper and lower edge. Curved glass was doubtless used for practical reasons, but the aesthetic effect is delightful, lending a delicate touch that complements the fine pentagonal structure.

Chiselhampton is a milestone from the point of view of design and materials, but unfortunately the identities of designer and manufacturer remain a mystery. Nor is there documentary proof of its date of construction, although this is most likely to have been about 1800. It bears a close resemblance to Humphry Repton's

The iron roof at Chiselhampton has a simple yet effective cap for ventilation.

trellised greenhouse, published in 1803 in *Observations on the Theory and Practice of Landscape Gardening,* and is also similar to a design by Sir John Soane for Henry Peters of Betchworth Castle in Surrey, dated 1800, except that Soane's version was to have been built in wood.[3] This would have made the roof both heavy and solid at the apex, which may have been why iron was chosen in preference.

Good quality cast iron was readily available from the 1760s onwards, when coke replaced charcoal in the smelting process, producing a runnier molten metal that could be moulded into more complex patterns. It was a stimulating material for imaginative architects. At Chiselhampton the sturdy cast-iron uprights were moulded with a pattern of trailing vines, and the umbrella-shaped roof was made up of many slender bars of iron. There is a first-class ventilation system. At the apex of the roof, a little cap of cast iron

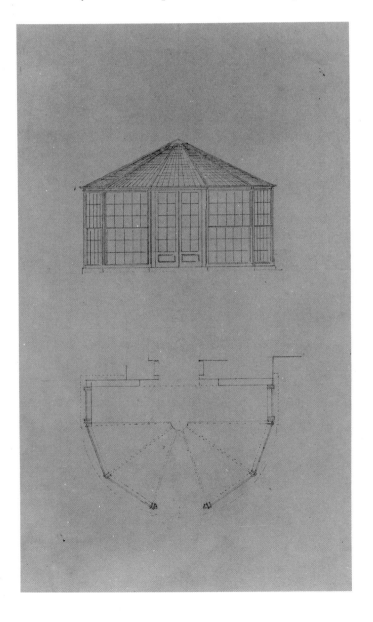

and glass can be raised several inches to let hot air escape; its weight is counterbalanced by an iron ball, so that it can be opened easily by pulling on a rope. It is a simple principle that could well be used nowadays, instead of temperamental so-called 'automatic' ventilators. Unfortunately, a gale in 1986 brought a large bough from a swamp cypress crashing down through the roof; many of the roof ribs were smashed, and the whole building was badly twisted. This tale, however, unlike so many others, does not end with demolition. The vinery, as it is now called, has been carefully restored by local craftsmen to mint condition. The task of reglazing with scalloped panes was simplified by making each pane twice the length of the originals, but in the same curved shape. Thus the vinery now has a mere 4,000 panes of glass, instead of the 8,000 it had when built.

Other buildings of this type in England, the glass and iron semi-domes of W. and D. Bailey, are later than Chiselhampton, whereas in Germany a hot-house made of iron was built in 1789, and another was built in 1807 in the Royal Castle Gardens, Nymphenburg, in Munich.

If iron-framed buildings were rare at the turn of the century, so were glass roofs. Greenhouses with glass roofs may possibly have been built before the 1790s, although they are hard to find. There is a puzzling reference in Mason's poem, 'The English Garden' written in 1777, to a greenhouse which was *glass roof'd the whole.* Mason stressed that the building in his vision was a *glittering fane* or temple of noble form, certainly not a common stove.

Maybe he was dreaming of a brighter form of Galilei's greenhouse. However, it is most unlikely that any greenhouses were built with completely glass roofs before the 1770s. J.C. Loudon's well-known claim that Wollaton Hall in Nottinghamshire had a glass-roofed greenhouse at the end of the seventeenth century is dubious, for his opinion was based merely on Jan Siberecht's painting of Wollaton in a London saleroom.[4] Painted in 1695, it shows the greenhouse from the rear, having a flat roof of a grey colour which could be mistaken for glass.[5] Both the idea and the construction technology were lacking at the end of the seventeenth century; had such a building been contrived, it would have made a huge stir in the horticultural world.

By the 1790s transparent roofs were beginning to replace opaque versions, prompted by horticultural necessity. Tropical plants had to be kept inside all the year round, but they were beautiful and sweet-smelling and therefore highly desirable in the greenhouse near the house, rather than in the distant kitchen garden. Since they could not be moved out even in summer, they were often planted in the ground inside, and sub-tropical flowers and trees could also be planted in beds. All these plants needed top light to flourish, as well as light from windows, hence the arrival of the glass roof. Writing in 1803, Humphry Repton, Capability Brown's successor as the foremost landscape gardener of the day, noted that *the numerous tribe of geraniums, ericas and other exotic plants, requiring more light, have caused a very material alteration in the construction of the greenhouse; and,* perhaps, the more it resembles the shape of a nurseryman's stove, the better it will be adapted to the purposes of a modern green-house.[6]

Repton, however, thought the shape of a slanting glass roof was ugly, and therefore often advised siting the greenhouse in the flower garden rather than adjoining the house. He also considered that *the smell and damp from a large body of earth in the beds, or pots, is often more powerful than the fragrance of the plants; therefore the conservatory should always be separated from the house, by a lobby, or small anti-room. But the greatest objection arises from its want of conformity to the neighbouring mansion, since it is difficult to make the glass roof of a conservatory architectural, whether Grecian or Gothic.* In spite of his own misgivings, Repton was induced by clients to design attached conservatories. One of his specialities was the 'flower passage', which connected the conservatory with the house, and also had a glass roof, with one heated wall and one glass wall.

Sir John Soane's plan for a greenhouse at Betchworth Castle, remarkably similar to Chiselhampton and dated 1800.

This sketch by Repton for a flower passage with a curvilinear roof appeared in Fragments on the Theory and Practice of Landscape Gardening, *1816. An earlier version with a flat roof was published in* Designs for the Royal Pavillon, *1803.*

Repton followed previous writers in using the term 'greenhouse' and 'conservatory' without differentiation. However, the question of what the Englishman called the glass buildings in his garden – or the rooms in his house – is more thorny than an acacia. Repton may have interchanged the terms, but for another contemporary expert, Dr Thomas Martyn, who edited the final tenth edition of Miller's dictionary, published in 1807, they were not identical. Martyn thought a greenhouse was for over-wintering potted plants and trees, while a conservatory had beds in which plants grew permanently, and a roof that was removed in summer. Another glass house expert, George Tod, writing in the same year, gave similar definitions, although his conservatories always had fixed glass roofs.[7]

From these descriptions, it can be seen how and why the later definitions arose: conservatories had planted beds, and were therefore landscaped and made to look attractive all year round. Greenhouses, whose main purpose was to shelter plants in winter, became a practical place also for raising plants; they were filled with staging, and ideal for seed trays as well as potted plants. The difference between the two at that time lay in the internal arrangements, not necessarily in design. As the century progressed, the glass house in the flower garden was more likely to be called a greenhouse, and the landscaped glass house near the house was more often known as a conservatory.

When was the word 'orangery' adopted? In France, *orangerie* referred both to a building and to the collection of orange trees, but in Britain throughout the eighteenth century, 'orangery' meant only 'a plantation for orange trees'; dictionaries in the middle of the nineteenth century continued to give this as the sole meaning. Humphry Repton was amongst the first to adopt the Continental practice and use the word to describe a building, but neither of the two examples he gave were orangeries in today's sense, although both were built for orange trees. An orangery he designed for the Prince Regent, at the Royal Pavilion in Brighton, he described as a *chiosk*; it had a glass roof and removable side walls, and looked rather like a bandstand *à la chinoise*. The other had solid walls and a fixed glass roof, and was between a music library and a flower passage. George Tod's version of an orangery was all glass against a stone wall, with trees planted in the ground.

H. Repton Esq.r del.t   J. C. Stadler sculp.

DESIGN for an ORANGERIE.

The frame & Glass removed in Summer, it forms a Chiosk

It is impossible to be definitive about the form of an orangery in the early nineteenth century other than to conclude that some masonry was involved in the construction, with varying quantities of glass in the walls and the roof. The word itself was doubtless brought back by travellers to Europe, where *orangeries* and *Orangerien* were to be found in all the best gardens. By the 1840s, however, it was the term used in Britain for the stone or brick, solid-roofed greenhouse of the eighteenth century, and for any subsequent, similar buildings; and so it has remained. The new term also had the advantage of distinguishing variety of form, material and contents. The establishment of any self-respecting nineteenth-century gentleman included a glass house adjoining or near the house: a conservatory; plus a glass house in the flower garden: a greenhouse; plus ranges of glass houses in the kitchen garden: hot-houses, forcing houses, stoves, peach houses and melon beds, pineries and vineries; plus a masonry opaque-roofed glass-windowed house: an orangery.

This is a glimpse of the future; let us return to the conservatory, *whether Grecian or Gothic*, in the words of Mr Repton.

Humphry Repton's Design for an Orangerie *was for the Prince Regent at the Royal Pavilion, Brighton. Not only was the orangery to be transformed from winter to summer by removal of the glass roof and fixed and swivelling windows, but glazing in the arcades on either side would also have been dismantled. Sadly, this plan was never executed.*

Who loves a garden loves a greenhouse too.
Unconscious of a less propitious clime
Where blooms exotic beauty, warm and snug
While the winds whistle and the snows descend.
The spiry myrtle with unwithering leaf
Shines there and flourishes. The golden boast
Of Portugal and western India there,
The ruddier orange and the paler lime,
Peep through their polished foliage at the storm,
And seem to smile at what they need not fear.
The amomum there with intermingling flowers
And cherries hangs her twigs. Geranium boasts
Her crimson honours, and the spangled beau
Ficoides, glitters bright the winter long.

    The sight is pleased,
The scent regaled, each odoriferous leaf,
Each opening blossom, freely breathes abroad
Its gratitude, and thanks him with its sweets.

William Cowper, 'The Garden', 1784

William Cowper's fragrant, smiling picture of greenhouse flowers was familiar to increasing numbers. By the 1780s, the smaller gardens of the gentry were usually equipped with a range of hot-houses in the kitchen garden, and a modest greenhouse too. A good example of a small domestic one was built by Mr and Mrs Philip Lybbe Powys. Mr Lybbe Powys and his diary-writing wife lived agreeably but not extravagantly at Hardwick, in Oxfordshire. Tender greenhouse plants were kept in the summer-house, and were killed off during a cold spell in 1776, which vexed the diarist considerably. In 1782, the summer-house was pulled down and a greenhouse erected in its place. It was 27 feet long, 12 feet wide and 10 feet high, and built of stone. An economy drive prevented its completion: *Put no windows till the next year, as we waited for the old sashes from the breakfast parlour*, noted Mrs Lybbe Powys.[8]

Another example of a greenhouse built with existing materials is at Williamscote, also in Oxfordshire, dating from 1787. Converted from the lower part of the old dovecote, it was turned into an intimate little building by the addition of four Gothic windows. Most building façades have an uneven number of windows, a practice considered architecturally correct, but this one proves that rules can be broken with great success. The owners of Williamscote were minor Oxfordshire gentry; it was a sign of the times that they

felt it appropriate to their status to have a house for exotic flowers, albeit one converted from a dovecote.

An interesting fact emerges from studying greenhouses of this period: whilst the great gardens of dukes boasted greenhouses as a matter of course, whatever their location, a pattern was developing of concentrations of greenhouses, belonging to major and minor landowners, in particular counties. Oxfordshire is a good example: perhaps stimulated by the Duke of Marlborough's greenhouse at Blenheim Palace, and the botanical rarities at the Oxford Physic Garden, greenhouses were built in the 1780s at Hardwick, Chisel-hampton, Tackley and Williamscote, and, just over the border in Northamptonshire, at Eydon Hall. There was a cluster of them put up in the 1780s in Norfolk and Suffolk, at Beeston, Blickling, Gunton and Heveningham, inspired by Holkham Hall and Redgrave. Hampshire, on the other hand, with the exception of Broadlands, is singularly devoid of greenhouses of this period.

As far as architectural tastes were concerned, classical and Gothic styles were jostling for supremacy; Robert Adam's finely decorated buildings were out of fashion — he built no greenhouses after 1780 — and the classical movement, with 'Athenian' Stuart's Greek revival ideas, was developed instead by various other archi-tects, including Anthony Keck at Margam, and John Nash. The form of an Ionic temple was one that appealed to Nash, and he used it most successfully at Barnsley Park in Gloucestershire for Sir

The greenhouse at Williamscote, modest yet appealing, was converted from a dovecote in 1787.

The orangery at Barnsley Park was designed by John Nash and built in 1807.

James Musgrave in 1807. Here he also mixed stone with cast iron, so that there are large circles of iron inside the pediment, where before there would have been a solid wall. The roof is glass too, in accordance with the latest ideas. Witley Court, Worcestershire, built for Lord Foley in 1810, is another example of Nash's neo-classical temple style. The versatile Nash turned his hand to any school of architecture, be it classical, Gothic or exotic, while keep-ing abreast of new ideas of the ideal environment for plants, and using new materials as they became available.

Greenhouses like Greek temples reflected the current Greek revival movement in architecture, which continued in garden buildings until the middle of the nineteenth century. Glass-roofed examples were built at Deepdene in Surrey by William Atkinson in the early 1820s, at Glevering in Suffolk by Decimus Burton in 1835, and at Camerton Court in Somerset by G.S. Repton in 1840. The Aroid House in Kew Gardens is another, better known example. It was originally designed by John Nash for the gardens of Buckingham Palace, and was transferred to Kew in 1836 to serve as a palm house. Sir Jeffry Wyatville was partly responsible for various alterations, including the addition of twelve columns that had come from the colonnade at Carlton House, Pall Mall.

Not everyone considered a classical temple appropriate for a plant house, however. Walter Nicol, Secretary to the Caledonian Horticultural Society in Edinburgh, and a sound, experienced builder of glass houses, was adamant that temple-type greenhouses, particularly those with opaque roofs, were unsuitable because they did not admit enough light. Writing in 1810, he also dismissed them because they looked *more like tombs, or places of worship, than compartments for the reception and cultivation of plants, which ought always to be light, airy and cheerful.*[9]

A domed octagonal glass house, c.1830, by J. A. Repton, is as fanciful a folly as Halfpenny's Chinese buildings of the eighteenth century. This is a conservatory for the landscape garden, decorated with treillage and dripping with bells.

The hipped-roof conservatory with classical motifs was also designed by J. A. Repton. This form was popular in the 1830s since it blended well with neo-classical architecture and could be simplified for plainer Palladian houses. Such conservatories were often joined to the house by a glass passage, as at Halton in Hampshire.

Eastwell Park was designed by Joseph Bonomi in 1794, and published in Richardson's New Vitruvius Britannicus. *According to the architect, a curved conservatory passage led to a greenhouse in the east pavilion. The house was demolished in 1926.*

Exuberant exoticism was also in the air at the time, epitomized by Samuel Pepys Cockerell's masterpiece at Sezincote in Gloucestershire. Both house and conservatory were designed for his brother Sir Charles Cockerell in 1805 in the Indian manner, and the resulting glass house is a novel interpretation of English form with Hindu decoration. The house is on rising ground, and the conservatory curves back into the hillside, nestling comfortably near the trees, and terminating in an oriental octagon.

Sezincote was one of many houses with a curved conservatory. The idea came from the Palladian villa with dependent pavilions, often attached by means of a curved colonnade. Joseph Bonomi, an Italian architect who practised in England, turned this colonnade into a conservatory at Eastwell Park in Kent, a house he designed in 1794 for G. F. Hatton.[10] The conservatory curved downwards as well as round, and terminated in a greenhouse with large windows and low-pitched opaque roof. Bonomi's designs for Eastwell were twice exhibited at the Royal Academy, so the curved conservatory idea would have been well known in the architectural world. Others were built at Dodington Park, Gloucestershire, by James Wyatt, and at Gaddesdon in Hertfordshire and Gatcombe in Gloucestershire.

One advantage of the curved conservatory was that it was an agreeable way of extending a house without adding a symmetrical block, and asymmetry was becoming popular, especially when combined with the romanticism of Gothic architecture. A reaction to the tightly balanced proportions of classicism, this yearning for the confused, irregular charm of medieval buildings accelerated during the late eighteenth century, reflecting the romantic movement in literature and music. Gothic greenhouses proliferated like crockets on a Gothic spire.

The pavilion and conservatory at Sezincote. S. P. Cockerell designed the house in the Indian manner in 1805, including a fashionable curved conservatory. Sezincote's exotic style compares with contemporary plans for oriental buildings by Repton and Nash for the Prince Regent at the Royal Pavilion, Brighton.

A Chinese garden, c.1814, has orange trees in porcelain pots. Greenhouses were not unknown in China by this time, according to J. C. Loudon in the Encyclopaedia of Gardening.

Brandard's 1840 lithograph of the Warwick Vase gives a rare contemporary interior view of a greenhouse: the curve in the rear wall, shaped to offset the vase, is just discernible. The bent figure with a cane was John Humphries, a local character who took visitors round the castle and gardens.

The most spectacular Gothic greenhouse of the late eighteenth and early nineteenth century was the building at Warwick Castle. It was designed by a local Warwick architect, William Eboral, and built in 1788 for the specific purpose of displaying the huge vase found at Hadrian's villa at Tivoli, now known as the Warwick Vase. George Greville, 2nd Earl of Warwick, had acquired the vase in 1778 after the British Museum had turned it down. For the first few years the vase was in the courtyard, until it was decided that it ought to have some protection from the climate. By a stroke of genius, it was decided to combine its shelter with shelter for tender plants, and Eboral created a perfect setting for both: a greenhouse with large pointed-arch windows and with a semicircular bow in the rear wall to accommodate the vase. *I built a noble green house, and … placed in it a vase considered as the finest remains of Grecian art extant for its size and beauty,* wrote the Earl.[11] (In fact, the vase turned out not to be Greek; much later, experts decided it was Roman, made in the fourth century AD.)

The 'noble greenhouse' was expensive. William Eboral was paid £1,260. 12s. 10d. over three years, the best quality crown glass ordered from Bristol cost £77, and the glazier charged £200. 7s. 6d. for his labour. A further £81. 5s. 8d. was paid to the slater for the roof, and the carpenters charged separately for making the windows. Other costs of materials were absorbed into the estate accounts, so the final bill is impossible to calculate. The windows are a particularly attractive feature, since the Gothic arch is accentuated by tracery of local Hornton stone, dark brown and full of iron, contrasting well with the thin white glazing bars. The original crown glass still gleams, even on grey days. In 1900, the slate roof was replaced by a glass ridge roof supplied by Richardsons of Darlington; the bill for refurbishment, including the roof, came to £1,397. 19s. 11d. The roof is currently slate.

The vase soon became an attraction for visitors. It remained at the castle for nearly two hundred years, until it was sold to the Burrell Museum in Glasgow, where it is now on display. In 1800, the Duke of Bedford, not wishing to be upstaged, bought another vase that came from Hadrian's villa, known as the Lanti vase, and placed it in the greenhouse at Woburn.

At the time of writing, there are no plants in the Warwick Castle greenhouse. In the last century it housed a collection of exotic flowers, and was much used by the family. It also served as a temporary prison for its owner; a rare claim to fame. The 2nd Earl was an important collector of works of art, with an extravagant lifestyle too; the combination led to bankruptcy. As a result, his family locked him out of the main part of the castle, and an indignant friend, Mrs Serres, wrote: *From their taking this step, Lord Warwick, the Rightful Owner, was compelled to eat his dinner in the Green-house of the castle gardens!!*[12]

In 1830 planting beds were added, and a little later the magnolias that still blossom on the walls outside, were presented to Lord Warwick by the Emperor of China.

Part of the appeal of the greenhouse lay in its situation. Acres of smooth green lawn rolled down to the river Avon which twists its way into the distance. Capability Brown had planted specimen trees and thickets of shrubs, creating *the grandest association of beautiful objects; the green-house, its shrubs, and velvet turf to the left; beyond it a mass of wood, its dark line broken by proud towers and spire.*[13] It was the epitome of 'the picturesque feeling', the romantic mood of the early nineteenth century. The contrast with the gardens surrounding the greenhouses of 1700, such as Hampton Court and Bretby, could hardly be more dramatic.

There were many other greenhouses in the Gothic taste built from this time onwards. Sir Richard Hill of Hawkestone Hall, Cheshire, had what sounds like a twin to the one at Warwick, apart from the antique vase. It was *built in the Gothic style, and placed so as to take in a grand view of the adjoining superlatively fine scenery.*[14]

Thomas Hopper designed a large conservatory for the Prince Regent in 1807 at Carlton House Terrace. It was a clever, original construction to suit the Prince's tastes, with Gothic arches based on those in Henry VII's Chapel at Westminster Abbey. The vaulted roof was made of a dramatic combination of cast iron and coloured glass. It was short-lived, however, for the entire house was demolished in 1827. John Nash included greenhouses or conservatories as an integral part of various houses, such as Hafod House in Cardiganshire, Longner Hall in Shropshire and also Luscombe in Devon, where he worked with Humphry Repton.

If a greenhouse or orangery was a fashionably irregular addition to a house, it could also have a practical purpose in concealing servants' offices and thwarting prying eyes, such as at Nash's Hafod House, while the orangery at Culzean Castle in Ayrshire was positioned to mask some water tanks.

Minor and amateur architects could copy the published designs of successful exponents, such as Humphry Repton and J. B.

Papworth. Many a delightful Gothic greenhouse must have been built according to Papworth's plans.[15] The camellia house at Culzean Castle, which was designed in about 1818 by James Johnson, typifies the best of these late Georgian Gothic garden buildings; the stone frame is light and delicate, with finely chiselled Gothic detail. Although now roofless and windowless and sans camellias, it retains a noble air in its peaceful woodland glade.

One of the last stone Gothic greenhouses was built in 1831 by John Nash's adopted son, Sir James Pennethorne, at Dillington House in Somerset. Gothic decoration continued to be used in the cast-iron conservatories that were becoming increasingly popular, largely because of the extra light they afforded. The revolution in heating by hot water, so much more effective than underfloor and wall flues, also meant that the heat-retaining qualities of stone were much less important. Stone was used for aesthetic reasons, to blend conservatory with house, but there was every reason to build entirely in glass for the benefit of plants.

The orangery at Culzean, c.1815, was crenellated to blend with Robert Adam's romantic Gothic castle. This photograph was taken in 1885.

J. B. Papworth's plan for a Gothic conservatory, published in Rural Residences, *1818. Papworth proposed that the conservatory be attached to the house by a passage and used as a breakfast room or morning room. It was to be heated by* ingenious stoves *or apparatus and a* steam tube which could produce *abundant vapour.*

PLAN

A GOTHIC CONSERVATORY.

The greenhouse at Ammerdown Park was built in 1793 when James Wyatt's design for the house had been completed. It is now one of the focal points of the Lutyens garden.

The interior of the Ammerdown greenhouse, empty in summer.

The Wyatts

James Wyatt was the most prolific country house architect in the reign of George III, and his houses had almost as many variations in style as there were styles to be copied. His greenhouses were just as diverse, sometimes totally integrated into the body of the house, as at Bowden House in Wiltshire, often free-standing and in any manner of shapes. There is a vast difference between the examples at Ammerdown Park in Somerset, a traditional stone greenhouse flanked by stoves, and the elegant Adam-like pavilion at Heveningham in Norfolk. Nor is there any telling link between the heavy flinted form of the greenhouse at Goodwood in Sussex, the curved glass-roofed wing at Dodington in Avon and the Gothic conservatory at Ashridge Park in Hertfordshire.

Ashridge Park was one of James Wyatt's most important Gothic houses, where his profound understanding of the principles and decoration of Gothicism were adapted to suit current tastes. Replacing an older mansion that had an attractive greenhouse added to the south front, Wyatt designed the major part of Ashridge for the Earl of Bridgewater in 1806, including the conservatory which joined the dining room to the chapel; it had a roof of plate glass and a long line of Gothic windows.

Wyatt must have had a good reputation as a designer of successful greenhouses,[16] which may have secured him commissions at the expense of his rivals. Sir John Soane, for example, built many a country house but fewer greenhouses. Wyatt could have had even more commissions had he not been hopelessly inefficient in carrying projects through to completion. Talent, enthusiasm and a polished social manner charmed his clients initially, but they were later driven to distraction by his lack of interest once work was under way.

James Wyatt's older brother, Samuel, was much more business-like, and a successful architect too; not versatile, not particularly imaginative, but sound and reliable, and with an interest in using cast iron where appropriate. Medium-sized country houses were his speciality, usually neo-classical and elegant, such as Coton House in Warwickshire and Tatton Park in Cheshire, both built in 1785, and Belmont Park in Kent, c. 1790; all three had attached greenhouses or conservatories designed at the same time as the house. Samuel Wyatt also extended Gunton Park in Norfolk in 1781 for Lord Suffield by adding an eight-bay colonnade of Tuscan columns with greenhouses at either end, and it is thought that he designed the greenhouse at Blickling, just a few miles away, for the Earl of Buckinghamshire at the same time.

The Blickling greenhouse incorporates one of Samuel Wyatt's trade-marks: the wide, flattened arched doors that are in the pavilions at either end. The proportions of the sash windows and pilasters, cornice and roof are almost identical to those at Belmont, which point to Samuel as the most likely architect. The glass in the fanlights is set in metal. The situation of this greenhouse is unusual,

The greenhouse at Blickling, attributed to Samuel Wyatt, was built in 1781. The Green house is spacious and elegant, containing Orange Trees and other Exotics, particularly thriving, wrote William Angus in The Seats of the Nobility and Gentry in Great Britain and Wales, 1787.

for it is visible neither from the house nor from the pleasure garden, being right on the perimeter of the park; other south-facing locations could have been found closer to the house. A possible explanation lies in the character of Lady Buckinghamshire, who was very interested in gardening and also extremely energetic. It was apparently her decision to build the greenhouse there, and she would doubtless have enjoyed walking through the park to inspect the orange trees. The greenhouse still contains a selection of citrus plants, camellias and fan palms, *Trachycarpus fortunei,* plus a statue of Hercules probably carved by Nicholas Stone in the 1640s.

Other members of the Wyatt family left their mark on the gardens of England. The conservatories at Tatton Park and Lyme Park in Cheshire and at Heaton Hall in Lancashire are by Lewis Wyatt, but the most numerous examples were by Sir Jeffry Wyatville, nephew of James Wyatt. More than a dozen were designed by him, ranging from the orangery wing at Chatsworth to the camellia houses at Wollaton in Nottinghamshire and Bretton Hall in Yorkshire. There was also a royal commission from George IV in 1829 for a huge octagonal conservatory at Royal Lodge, Windsor. This was an exotic affair, 120 feet long, with cast-iron trellised pilasters and a central trellised temple.

After James Wyatt's death in 1813, Wyatville was called in by Lord Bridgewater in 1815 to build the stables and add another wing at Ashridge Park, this time an orangery with a tower. Wyatt's conservatory faces south, while the new orangery was angled towards the south-east, showing that the overall irregular appearance of the house and wings was more important than orientation for maximum winter sunlight. Lord Bridgewater, being exceedingly rich, could afford to ignore some free heat from the sun.

Wyatville drew several versions[17] of the orangery, the early plans having a plate glass roof supported by a cast-iron framework rich in trefoils and quatrefoils. In the executed plan, however, the roof frame was made entirely in wood and embellished with a pattern of stags horns. A description written in 1836[18] records that the conservatories were abundant not with variety but with plants *of the most showy kinds* which were grown elsewhere and moved into the conservatories *when in flower or in their best state.*

Holkham Hall, Norfolk.
A view through the entrance to the sloping roof of the vinery, designed by Samuel Wyatt in the early 1780s.

Wyatville's sketch, one of many versions, for the orangery at Ashridge Park. Although Loudon and Paxton are commonly credited with formulating the ridge and furrow roof (see the photograph of Paxton's greenhouses at Somerleyton on page 123), Wyatville's plan here suggests that he was working on similar lines, but without running the ridges on a north–south axis.

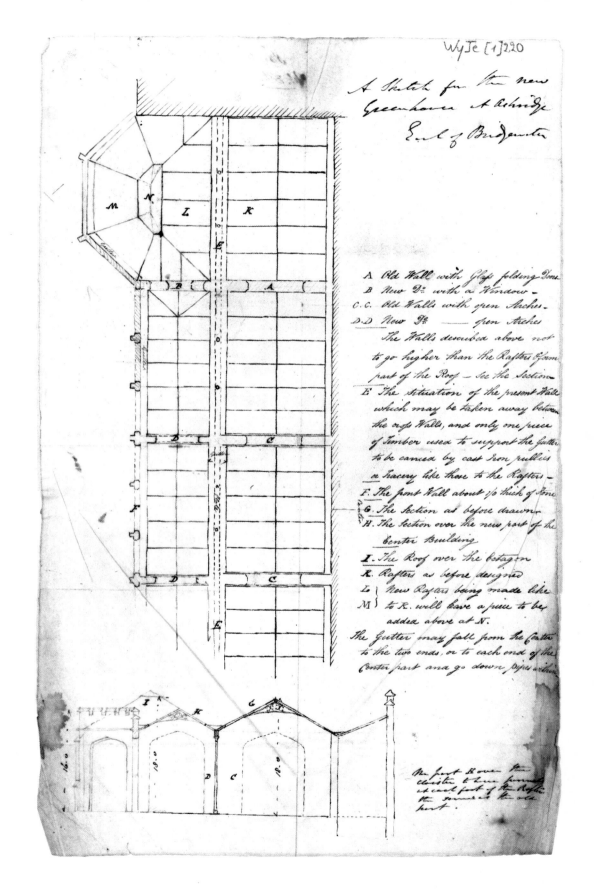

A Sketch for the new
Greenhouse at Ashridge
Earl of Bridgewater

A Old Wall with Glass folding Doors
B New D.º with a Window
C.C. Old Walls with open Arches
D.D New D.º ——— open Arches
The Walls described above not
to go higher than the Rafters & form
part of the Roof — See the Section
E The situation of the present Wall
which may be taken away between
the cross Walls, and only one piece
of Timber used to support the Gutter
to be carried by cast Iron pullies
a tracery like those to the Rafters —
F. The front Wall about 1/o thick of Stone
G. The Section as before drawn
H. The Section over the new part of the
Center Building
I. The Roof over the Octagon
K. Rafters as before designed
L } New Rafters being made like
M } to K. will have a piece to be
added above at N.
The Gutter may fall from the Center
to the two ends, or to each end of the
Center part and go down pipes within

The front D over the
cloister to have formed
at each part of the Rafter
the same as the old
part.

The orangery at Longleat, c.1812, designed by Sir Jeffry Wyatville, has windows large enough to allow a good collection of plants to flourish. It is similar to other orangeries by Wyatville, such as Belton, Badminton and the plan for Thoresby.

The typical Wyatville greenhouse or conservatory was free-standing, stone-built, and with seven or nine huge squared sash windows on the south front. The roof was generally opaque, and the façade kept simple with restrained classical decoration. The greenhouses at Belton in Lincolnshire and Longleat in Somerset are examples which stand today, and another very similar one was designed for Thoresby Hall in Nottinghamshire, which may never have been built. Wyatville's last conservatory was for the Duke of Bedford at Woburn Abbey, Bedfordshire, in 1837. It has very little stone compared to his earlier designs; the roof is glazed, and supported by cast-iron braces that stretch from wall to wall in a rippling, swirling pattern. Along with many others of this era, such as Alton Towers and C. R. Cockerell's conservatory at The Grange in Hampshire, this is a transitional building: one facet reflects the past history of brick and stone, while another catches the spirit of experimentation, the new era of flowers flooded with sunlight.

The conservatory at The Grange, designed by C. R. Cockerell in 1824, made the columns of the Gardeners Magazine *in 1826 and 1827, and was also praised by Charles M'Intosh in* The Greenhouse, Hot-House and Stove, *1838.*

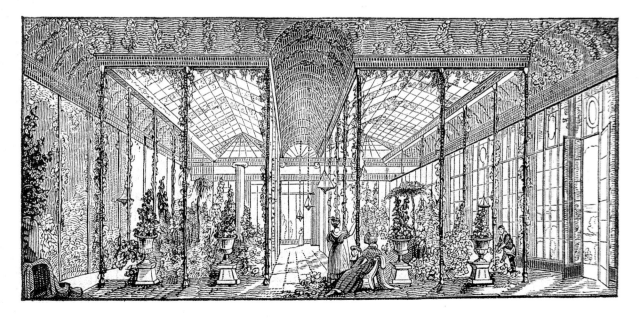

Cast Iron and Curves

A revolutionary plan for a glass house was aired in 1815. Instead of being basically a glass box with squared sides and an angled roof, the new shape was a half-dome, curved from side to side and top to bottom and set against a straight wall. It was the brainchild of Sir George Mackenzie of Edinburgh, designed for forcing fruit rather than growing tropical flowers. Sir George said that this was the best design for receiving *the greatest possible quantity of the sun's rays, at all times of the day and at all seasons of the year ... since the use of cast iron has become so familiar, I have lately turned my attention to the subject; and am happy to find that, in reality, there is no difficulty in the case, even if the work was to be constructed in wood.*[19] It was to be heated by an underfloor flue which led to a chimney disguised as an urn; good ventilation was provided by sliding shutters at the base of the dome and more shutters along the top of the back wall.

This was the first of many new shoots in the theory of design. The second came from J.C. Loudon, another Scot who had a formidable influence on gardening affairs until his death in 1843. Loudon was clearly fascinated by the horticultural possibilities of the shape, and also by the construction, and he wanted to improve the appearance of the traditional lean-to design. Cast iron had proved too brittle under tension, and in 1816 Loudon devised a wrought-iron sash bar that could be curved without losing strength, making Sir George's design a practical reality.

To substantiate his theories, he built a row of both curvilinear and traditional glass houses in the garden of his house in Bayswater. Loudon then gave the principles of his invention to a firm called W. and D. Bailey of Holborn and their business thrived as a result. Designed either as one half-dome rising to a pointed apex, or alternatively as three integrated half-domes, these bulging curved glass houses were sold all over the country. During the following twenty-five years from 1818, W. and D. Bailey built them at Loddiges Nursery in London, for Lord St Vincent, for Lady Rolle at Bicton in Devon, at Dallam Tower in Cumbria, and others. They even exported a pair of curvilinear hot-houses to Belgium, to a Mr Caters-de-Wolf of Berchen, near Antwerp.

One of Bailey's most renowned products was at Bretton in Yorkshire, built for Mrs Beaumont in 1827. It was a triumph in engineering, being circular and 60 feet high, the wrought-iron sash bars that supported the entire roof measuring only two inches by half an inch. While under construction, the frame swayed alarmingly in the wind, but once glazed, it was as firm as a rock. It cost £10,000.

Besides this conservatory, Mrs Beaumont had quite a collection of glass houses. There was a stone-built conservatory, Sir Jeffry Wyatville's camellia house, probably built in 1815, a curvilinear vinery also supplied by W. and D. Bailey, and *several culinary hot-houses*. So many, in fact, that Loudon thought the quantity of chimneys gave Bretton Hall *the air of an iron foundry*[20] — not quite the idyllic rural scene one might have imagined. The clouds of smoke

Sir George Mackenzie's revolutionary glass half-dome, 1815

Mrs Beaumont's dome, built by W. and D. Bailey in 1827

were partly caused by local coal, which gave off more soot than Newcastle coal. A solution for removing these sooty emissions from the immediate area was to take the chimney flue underground for some distance, and then make a feature of it. This practice was widely adopted, for example at Kew, where the Palm House chimney was turned into an Italian campanile. Bretton's famous dome stood for only five years; Mrs Beaumont died in 1832, and the conservatory was sold by auction and taken down.

Conservatories of wrought and cast iron were more expensive than their counterparts in timber, even after a new processing technique in the 1820s allowed a small reduction in price. It was the elegance and grace of their lines and the possibility of moulded fittings that endeared them to owners and architects. Amongst professional gardeners they were not so popular, due to condensation, heat loss and the need for endless maintenance. Like many others, Joseph Paxton, Charles M'Intosh, head gardener at Claremont, and the head gardener at Syon Park in Middlesex all preferred wooden structures.

The Palm House at Bicton, built by W. and D. Bailey, c.1820. Its bulbous curves are made from scalloped glass set in neat seams of iron. Ventilation is by metal flaps that open in the rear wall.

J. C. Loudon was the first to think of another important contribution, the ridge and furrow roof. He devised it as a means of taking maximum advantage of the sun's rays. Early in the eighteenth century a Dutchman called Boerhaave had theorized that maximum heat was gained by rays hitting the glass at a right angle and therefore being able to pass through it rather than bounce off it. Thoughtful gardeners had pondered long about how to achieve this, but it was a contentious subject.

Mackenzie's dome was one method, and Loudon's was another. The idea was that the roof was made up of several ridges on a north—south axis, so that the angles of the glass were facing east and west, thus catching more sun in the early morning and afternoon, rather than in the middle of the day. Loudon did not pursue the idea, but Joseph Paxton developed it at Chatsworth, and ultimately used it for the Crystal Palace in 1851. Commercial greenhouses and new botanic conservatories such as the Princess of Wales Conservatory at Kew continue to be built on a north—south axis.

An exuberant series of domes on the greenhouse at Alton Towers, built in 1827 by Robert Abraham. This, a pagoda and other follies were part of the eccentric Earl of Shrewsbury's pleasure garden.

The combination of cast iron and narrow panes of glass on the domes ensures a delicacy that would have been impossible if wood had been used in place of iron.

Besides his inventions, Loudon was a respected landscape gardener and the designer of hot-houses proposed for the Birmingham Horticultural Society, although these were never built. His numerous publications made yet another major contribution to gardening. Amongst these were *The Encyclopaedia of Gardening,* first published in 1822, and the *Gardener's Magazine,* which appeared monthly from 1826 until 1843; both are mines of information about what was happening in Britain and in Europe. If Loudon's judgements of gardens were sometimes too hasty, or sometimes biased, they were informative and lively. Never at a loss for an opinion, his explanation of current fashions was firmly based on reality. He was a middle-class enthusiast for middle-class greenhouses, at a time when greenhouses were no longer the sole preserve of the nobility and gentry.

The conservatories of the 1820s and 1830s that have survived are, however, largely to be found attached to houses where the owners have maintained their wealth for over a century and a half. Most are therefore on country estates, where repair costs were absorbed by estate revenues. Middle-class incomes could not always stretch to the conservatory in times of war and economic depression. Maintenance is always a burden, and the cost of restoration immense.

Of those that remain from this era, the Camellia House at Wollaton is an important milestone. It was designed in cast iron by Sir Jeffry Wyatville, and made by Jones and Clark of Birmingham in about 1823. The roof is a mixture of shallow glazed pyramids, with cast-iron barrel vaulting above the paths. The cast-iron columns were used to drain water away from the roof, a new idea that became current practice whenever such columns were required to support the roof of a conservatory. Jones and Clark made a similar roof for Charles Robert Cockerell's conservatory at The Grange in Hampshire, built in 1825. To reduce heat loss, the iron barrel vaulting was composed of two layers, two inches apart.

Swirling patterns in cast-iron braces at Wrest Park, Bedfordshire. The conservatory is attached to the house, which was designed by James Clephan and Earl de Gray between 1834 and 1839.

Sir Jeffry Wyatville designed this glass-roofed camellia house at Wollaton in about 1824. It is an irregular octagon, and is made of cast iron decorated with Elizabethan detail to echo the mansion seen behind it. The roof, a complicated pattern of ridges, pyramids and curved vaulting, is similar to the roof at The Grange.

The orangery at Ripley Castle, built in 1823 for Sir William Ingilby, is reminiscent of an eighteenth-century greenhouse. It is decorated with neo-classical pilasters and a balustrade, and has adjoining glass-roofed hot-houses just visible on the right.

Inside are raised beds, typical of their time, for the display of plants too delicate for an English summer.

The recently restored conservatory at Syon Park was designed and completed by Charles Fowler in 1827, one of the grandest built during the prolific decade of the 1820s. It is 382 feet from the end pavilions round its curved wings. The Palm House, the central pavilion, has a steep-sided dome made of wrought-iron ribs supported by cast-iron pillars and trusses and façades of Bath stone.

The Barton Seagrave orangery (below) has an originality and delicacy that makes its unknown origins even more tantalizing.

Charles Fowler's conservatory at Syon Park, Middlesex, built in 1827 for the Duke of Northumberland, was and is one of the finest examples of its day. Its central, giant-domed palm house has two curved wings, terminating in classical pavilions reminiscent of the late baroque German *Orangerien*. Another is at Alton Towers in Staffordshire, built by Robert Abraham in 1824 for the eccentric Earl of Shrewsbury. The seven domes still sparkle as new, the centre dome topped with the Earl's coronet, the others with pineapples. Nearby, another conservatory is awaiting restoration.

Perhaps the stone frame still typical of this era has saved many conservatories from destruction, such as the three at the Sheffield Botanical Garden and the mysterious domed buildings at Barton Seagrave in Northamptonshire. No clues about the latter's architect or date of construction have been found. The roof is opaque except for three glazed, flattened domes made of cast iron like the window glazing bars, possibly again the product of W. and D. Bailey.

Heating and Glass

The columns of the *Gardener's Magazine* became the airing ground for countless theories about how to design, how to glaze, and how to heat glass houses. Heat was as controversial as roof angles. No one disputed that flues were far from perfect, but not everyone thought that steam heat, invented in 1788 by a Mr Wakefield of Liverpool, was the answer. It was much used in the first thirty or more years of the nineteenth century, in the Bailey dome at Bretton, for example; but a steam boiler was expensive to buy, temperamental, liable to explode, and the furnace had to be stoked frequently day and night. There was another novel idea by a Scot in 1831, a Mr M'Diarmid, *the very intelligent editor of the Dumfries and Galloway Courier*, who was persuaded that the best way of heating hot-houses was by the breath of cattle, a method he assured was common in Russia.[21] This romantic notion made no headway in the age of engineers.

Heating by hot water eventually won the day, because it was so much more efficient and reliable than steam. It had first been thought of by a Frenchman in 1777, M. Bonnemain, who was raising chickens and wanted to keep their eggs warm. Prince Potemkin's greenhouse near St Petersburg was said to have been heated by a mixture of flues in walls and pillars, and *earth leaden-pipes ... incessantly filled with boiling water*.[22]

The idea was developed in 1816, as a means of heating his house, by another Frenchman, Count Chabannes, in exile in England; but it was William Atkinson, an architect, who was the first to evolve a successful system for heating greenhouses by hot water in 1826. Water was heated in a boiler, located either underground or in a rear shed, and circulated round the greenhouse or conservatory through cast-iron pipes. It provided a more even, controllable heat than steam or flues, and did not need to be stoked so regularly. Usually the pipes were routed above the floor along the sides and front of the building, but they could also be sunk into the floor where the flue had been, and covered by an iron grille. This was often done in the old greenhouses, such as at Powis Castle.

Hot-water heating was a most significant breakthrough for the horticultural world, but even more so for architecture. Had an efficient system for heating a vast volume of air in an all-glass house not been perfected, the soaring forms of the Great Conservatory at Chatsworth and the Palm House at Kew could not have protected tropical plants, and might therefore never have been built.

French glass manufacturers had also developed techniques for making much larger panes, by using compressed air to blow glass in cylinders. By 1832, Chance Brothers of Birmingham had imported the technique, and were making sheets of cylinder glass that were 36 inches long and 10 inches wide, a good 14 inches longer than the longest panes of crown glass. Output increased considerably after this milestone, especially after 1845, when the existing duty on glass was removed, and *a great impulse was given to the glass trade by the extraordinary quantities that were required for horticultural purposes*.[23] As a result of the increase in size there was no need to overlap, so there were no draughts and more light passed through. However, this new sheet glass was clear, with no greenish tinge to protect the plants. The glass revolution that had seemed like a blessing turned into a nightmare of scorched leaves. Anguished gardeners had to experiment with blinds, or re-glaze with tinted glass.

Paxton and Burton

Any discussion of glass house design and materials from 1830 onwards leads inevitably to Chatsworth, to Joseph Paxton and to his employer, the 6th Duke of Devonshire. A descendant of Bess of Hardwick, builder of the glass-fronted Hardwick Hall of Tudor days, the Duke developed the ancestral tradition of glass and green-houses to make Chatsworth world famous.

The Duke appointed Paxton as head gardener at Chatsworth in 1826, when Paxton was only twenty-three years old. This was another brilliant gardening partnership, in which invention, skill and enthusiasm were married with encouragement and resources. As with Louis XIV and Le Nôtre, it was based on mutual respect, esteem and affection.

Paxton arrived at Chatsworth to find a patchy collection of glass houses: Talman's greenhouse of 1697 had been moved, but contained nothing remarkable; Wyatville's orangery was as yet unbuilt, and there were two good peach houses plus some shambolic vineries and pineries. Paxton started to rebuild and make improvements to the design of the hot-houses. Having worked previously at the Horticultural Society's garden at Chiswick, he knew the large curved span greenhouse for stove plants, but his mind was working on other lines.

In 1832 he designed a ridge and furrow roof – whether as a result of his own deliberations or through studying Loudon's sketch, we do not know. The old greenhouse was reroofed accordingly, in order to make it a *plant stove*.[24] Another 97-foot-long greenhouse followed, with cast-iron columns for drainage and a wooden ridge and furrow roof, while ranges of forcing houses, hot-houses, vineries, pineries and orchid houses sprang up over the next decade. Paxton also designed the ridge and furrow roofed passages joining the three conservatories at the Sheffield Botanic Garden in 1836.

The atmosphere of bustling activity that pervaded Chatsworth is evident from the account books.[25] Expenditure on building and maintaining all the glass houses rose from £467 in 1830 to £1,769 in 1840, continuing around that level for several years. This did not include the cost of the Great Conservatory. Bills for coal fluctuated wildly from year to year, probably through stockpiling, but possibly

also due to surface coal being found on the estate. Expenditure on coal for 1830–34 came to £245; over the next five years it nearly trebled. It is not surprising that various shafts were dug on the Devonshire estates to see if a private supply of coal could be found. Paxton's salary was initially £70 per annum, but by 1838 it had risen to £276, the clearest possible proof of the Duke's confidence in his young gardener.

A part from building, the Duke and Paxton were also avidly collecting plants. A total of eighteen suppliers sent plants to Chatsworth in 1830. A few years later, when plant collecting had reached fever pitch, plants were sent direct to Chatsworth from Calais (orange trees), The Cape (bulbs), Malta (vine cuttings), and from Paris, Rouen, Dresden, Odessa, Vera Cruz, Madras, Calcutta and Seringapalam. Many specimens were sent as presents to the Duke, whose passion for rarities was renowned. A new dwarf banana, which Paxton named *Musa Cavendishii* after his employer, was one of the great successes of 1836. The Duke was also financing expeditions to the tropics and western Canada, and subscribed to Dr Lippold's expedition to Brazil in search of new plants.

Paxton's first major triumph, the Great Conservatory at Chatsworth, which he designed with Decimus Burton. Ridge and furrow glazing rippled over its billowing curves, protecting a tropical garden within. So well built was the Great Conservatory that when beyond repair it took no less than six attempts to blow it up.

One of a pair of ridge and furrow roofed greenhouses at Somerleyton, designed by Paxton c.1850. This photograph shows how the ridge and furrow system worked: it was a series of adjoining ridges, the furrow being the gulley in the middle, which ran north–south. In this case the entire roof is sloped, but it could equally well be flat, as in the Crystal Palace. The Somerleyton greenhouses are similar to but much larger than the 1832 prototype at Chatsworth, and are made mainly in metal. Each one is 90 feet long and 21 feet deep, and is ventilated by a complex system of shafts in the rear wall.

The conservatory at Capesthorne Hall in Cheshire was built to Paxton's design by 1845, complete with ridge and furrow roof.

With this burgeoning collection of very exotic 'Exoticks', extra space was clearly needed. Since domes and half-domes could not provide sufficient height, the shape that emerged was like a curved cathedral in cross-section, as Loudon observed, a central span buttressed by two side aisles. Paxton conceived the idea of the Great Conservatory in 1836 and discussed it with Decimus Burton, a trained architect whose initials are on the 1836 plans. To Paxton must go the credit as initiator and as designer of the ridge and furrow glazing system; the detail of the form itself should perhaps be credited to Burton, who later claimed that he was the architect. The Duke, however, clearly regarded it as Paxton's plan, describing it as *this extraordinary monument of Mr. Paxton's talent and skill, in the execution of which he was cordially met and assisted by Mr Decimus Burton.*[26]

The Great Conservatory, or Great Stove as it was sometimes called, cost £33,000 to build, and was more or less complete by 1841. It was 277 feet long, 123 feet wide and 67 feet high at the apex of the roof, by far the largest glass building in existence. Cast-iron columns and a cast-iron frame up to the top of the first curve supported wooden ribs which held ridge and furrow glazing. Paxton had always preferred wood to iron, since it was both cheaper and needed less maintenance, and he had evolved a means of bending timber to give it the necessary curve.

Seven miles of four-inch pipes, fired by eight boilers hidden underground, were needed to heat this massive edifice. Any hint of a man-made mechanism was out of the question: this tropical forest in Derbyshire had to appear uncontrived. Coal was brought to the boilers on an underground railway, and the chimney flues taken underground to a chimney stack some distance away in the trees.

The Duke was ecstatic about it. *Its success has been complete, both for the growth of plants and the enjoyment it affords.* With enormous pleasure, he described its ravishing contents: *the Walton date-palm, growing every day more like that of Posilippo; Hibiscus splendens; Erythrina arborea; ...the various creepers and passiflorae; Bougainvillea spectabilis; and Stephanotis floribunda, ascending even to the roof; ... Sabal Blackburniana, the very first stove plant I acquired, from Mrs. Beaumont of the North: then Cocos plumosa, easily surpassing all others, a present from the Sheffield Horticultural Society; the Rose Hibiscus, and more lofty Musa; ... Lord Fitzwilliam's present, Dracaena Draco, that promises to rival the Dragon tree of Java.* These plants are familiar now, but how amazing they must have been to the early Victorians. And so the Duke continued for pages, finishing with a poem composed by a French visitor:

> *A Chatsworth quel Dieu nous amène?*
> *C'est un Dieu cher à tous les coeurs,*
> *Qui sur la prison d'une Reine*
> *A bâti le Temple des Fleurs.*

The Queen referred to was Mary, Queen of Scots, who was a prisoner at Chatsworth briefly in 1570 while in the custody of the Earl of Shrewsbury.

Queen Victoria, Prince Albert and the Duke of Wellington came to Chatsworth in December 1843. They drove in an open carriage at night down the central aisle of the conservatory, which was lit by 12,000 lamps. The Duke of Wellington was said to have remarked thereafter: *I have travelled Europe through and through and witnessed many scenes of surpassing grandeur on many occasions, but never did I see so magnificent a* coup d'œil *as that extended before me.* Hoards of public visitors pressed through the gates; entry was free and they came by the train-load from neighbouring towns: *there has been a perfect tribe at Chatsworth today,* wrote Mrs Paxton in 1845.[27] The crowds were kept outside the conservatory for fear of damage to its precious contents. The Great Conservatory flourished through the Edwardian era, but the First World War and taxation were death-blows, for both maintenance and fuel costs. This tropical paradise was deliberately blown up in 1920.

The Great Conservatory at Chatsworth inspired other private pavilions, while its public successor was the Palm House for tropical plants at Kew. Decimus Burton is credited with the design of the Palm House, but just as he may have been the dominant influence at Chatsworth, so was he heavily influenced in turn at Kew by Richard Turner. Turner, of the Hammersmith Iron

The Palm House at Kew, completed in 1848

Works in Dublin, brought considerable expertise to the project, having already designed conservatories at Killilee near Dublin and for the Belfast Botanic Garden, and manufactured various others. One of his suggestions was to make the main ribs of wrought iron rather than cast iron, as Loudon had advocated earlier. Burton, too, had experience of building other conservatories besides Chatsworth; while still in his teens he designed Holme House in Regent's Park in 1818, which, significantly, had a small pentagonal greenhouse attached to the library. In 1824 he designed a half-dome for Grove House, now called Nuffield House, also in Regent's Park. This was built by W. and D. Bailey and still stands, and there were others at Park Hatch and Painshill in Surrey, and Ven House in Somerset. The building at Kew had echoes of Chatsworth in outline, but unlike Chatsworth the entire structure at Kew was made of metal, and glazed more simply with curved glass. Surveys of the Palm House have shown it to be a brilliant example of intuitive engineering, marking the emergence of the structural engineer.

The central section of the Palm House was considerably smaller than the Great Conservatory, being 137 feet 6 inches long by 100 feet wide by 63 feet high, but with the addition of wings at either end, the overall measurement was 360 feet. It was glazed with sheet glass slightly tinged with green, which, according to conventional wisdom, would prevent scorching. However, the quality of this glass must have differed from the old green crown glass that had always been used in greenhouses before, for *the plants refused to grow properly under it*.[28] There were also cold down-draughts just inside the glass skin, which meant that some tropical palms would not grow. Not that early visitors found the plants stunted or peevish, but the range of species was limited by both factors. In 1895 the green glass was largely replaced with clear glass, with beneficial results. In more recent years, improvements in the heating system have cured the problem of cold air near the glass.

In the words of the official guide book, the *Kew Guide* of 1850, *The Palm-House or Palm-Stove . . . may be said to be the glory of the Gardens*. It is as gracious as a crinolined lady, as smooth as a camellia. The Palm House remains one of Kew's greatest attractions, and probably the best known botanical building in the world.

The beauty of Turner and Burton's arches and decorative detail can only be fully appreciated when the house is empty. After 140 years, extensive restoration is taking the Palm House into the twenty-first century. The wrought-iron ribs are being repaired, but the glazing bars, impossibly corroded, will be replaced by ones of stainless steel.

Glass Houses in Society

The middle years of the nineteenth century saw the proliferation of a close relation of the botanical hot-house, the public winter garden. According to J. C. Loudon, the idea originated in Berlin after the peace of 1814, and they were soon to be found in Potsdam, Strasbourg and Vienna. The Berlin winter garden was stone-built with a solid roof, and filled in winter with scented bulbs such as hyacinths and narcissi, plus heaths, camellias and acacias. The proprietors also brought in *curious and showy stove plants* as novelty attractions, including, of course, pineapples in fruit. Entertainment included music, poetry recitals, readings and lectures. *If you enter these gardens in the early part of the morning, you will find gentlemen reading the newspapers, taking chocolate and talking politics ... When the audience leave the theatre in the evening, a great number of well-dressed people, of both sexes, are in the habit of visiting these gardens before they go home, to see the beauty of the vegetation when brilliantly illuminated by artificial light, and to talk of the plays and the players.*[29]

In England, Burton and Turner worked together again to build the winter garden at Regent's Park for the Royal Botanic Society in 1846, while another glass building, this time for animals, had already proved a great attraction at the Surrey Zoological Gardens. The iron and glass menagerie was built in 1831 by Henry Phillips. All these spectacular glass palaces were the delight of the English, and soon objects of admiration for foreign visitors. The expertise that British architects and iron-founders were developing was ahead of their European counterparts, and the latter crossed the Channel to observe and learn. One of these was a Frenchman, Rohault de Fleury, whose glass buildings included the vast range of glass houses in the Jardins des Plantes in Paris, started in 1833.

Another was Hector Horeau, the builder of the second Jardin d'Hiver in Paris of 1848. The first version of this had been put up in 1846, but it was a plain building, more like a commercial greenhouse than a place for elegant entertainment. Parisian society demanded something more stylish, so within six months it was torn down and replaced with a spacious, curved-roof pavilion that instantly won approval. This was 300 feet long, and 180 feet wide across the centre of the wings. Inside was a ballroom, a café, a *pâtisserie* and a reading room, and there were promenades, a *jardin anglais* complete with lawn, and several fountains. The air was filled

with the scent of orange blossom and the song of birds. Paxton admired the interior landscape when he attended a concert at the Jardin in 1848, adding that balls and *fêtes* were frequently held there.

What of the inside of the private conservatory? With the advent of the glass roof, the interior had changed dramatically from the plain halls of the old greenhouses or orangeries. Fountains played, grottoes dripped and goldfish swam around in water-lilied pools. Song birds were often to be seen flying through the trees, or warbling in gilded cages: *At the farther end of a most magnificent greenhouse is an aviary full of all kinds of birds, flying loose in a large octagon of gilt wire, in which is a fountain in the centre, and in the evening 'tis illuminated by wax-lights, while that water falls down some rockwork in form of a cascade,* wrote Mrs Lybbe Powys in 1796 of Temple House in Berkshire.[30] Exotic birds and wild animals from faraway lands were still part of the rich man's paraphernalia, a remnant of Stuart collections of rarities.

The taste for *chinoiserie* was fashionable throughout the end of the eighteenth century and well into the nineteenth. The Prince Regent had a Chinese greenhouse at the Royal Pavilion in Brighton,

Ladies 'botanizing'

In 1849 the Illustrated London News *printed this engraving of* Victoria amazonica *flowering for the first time at Chatsworth. The little girl standing on one of the leaves gives an idea of their size and strength.*

THE GIGANTIC WATER-LILY (VICTORIA REGIA), IN FLOWER AT CHATSWORTH.

although it succumbed to damp and drips within a few years. Chinese porcelain was a favourite decoration; porcelain plaques had been hung on the walls of the greenhouse at Woodside in Berkshire in the mid-eighteenth century, and there were vases and figures in the Chinese garden at Cassiobury in Hertfordshire beside the pagoda-like greenhouse. Plants from the East were considered appropriate for this Chinese greenhouse, including camellias and bushes of green and black tea.

Plants were being sent back from all the corners of the globe, and previously unseen specimens were as precious as gold-dust. Nathaniel Ward's invention of a protective case for transporting living specimens was a boon to botanists. The introduction in the late 1830s of the Wardian case, as it became known, meant that instead of one in twenty plants surviving the journey from the tropics, only one in twenty perished.

Competition between gardeners reached peaks of intensity that are normally not associated with this gentle art. Charles M'Intosh, gardener to the King of the Belgians at Claremont in Surrey, was extremely proud of his large tropical collection, which included perfumed caladiums and rare orchids. Paxton was desolate about the lack of blossom on the Chatsworth *Amherstia nobilis,* which Kew succeeded in flowering first. When the *Victoria regia*[31] water lily – for which Paxton designed a special house with a ridge and furrow roof – produced a flower in November 1849, it was headline news in the horticultural world and even merited an article in the *Illustrated London News* of 17 November 1849. Paxton took a flower bud and one of the giant leaves to present to the Queen.

Mature shrubs and trees changed hands as well. The Duke of Devonshire bought an enormous palm tree from Lady Tankerville's palm house at Walton in Surrey to help fill the Great Conservatory. The circumference of the trunk was 8 feet 4 inches and the tree and root ball weighed 12 tons. The palm house had to be taken

down, and turnpikes demolished on the long road from Surrey to Derbyshire. What an extraordinary sight it must have been on its journey northwards! The Duke was also very proud of four orange trees that had belonged to the Empress Josephine at Malmaison, and of a rare specimen of *Altingia excelsa,* which although bought in London from Lowe's Nursery, had come all the way from St Petersburg. It cost nearly £50.

In Russia, Prince Potemkin, Catherine II's favourite, built a semicircular greenhouse in the 1780s that was much used for evening entertainments. Decorative gardening, indoors or outdoors, was in its infancy in Russia; it was a dilettante fashion for the richest of the rich, and middle-class Russians did not even indulge in more mundane gardens. Potemkin's greenhouse was packed with exotic trees brought in from kitchen garden stoves and sunk into the earth. Paths meandered through flowery hedges and fruit-bearing shrubs, past Greek sculpture, curious fish in crystal vases and a grotto of

The conservatories at Fairlawne, 1834. The first conservatory of classical proportions appears to have had a later half-hipped extension, emphasizing the conservatory fever that was sweeping through country houses. Both were removed at the end of the nineteenth century and replaced with a stone and glass version by Mackenzie and Moncur of Edinburgh.

The Grosse Orangerie in the gardens of the Palace of Schönbrunn, Vienna. The Orangerie was built in 1744 by Pacassi, and was used not only for plants but also for court entertainments. The diners at this magnificent banquet in March 1839 are dwarfed by the table decorations, glittering chandeliers and banks of fruit-laden orange trees.

looking-glasses. A German traveller in 1802 was transfixed by its night-time beauty: *The genial warmth, the fragrance and brilliant colours of the nobler plants, the voluptuous stillness that prevails in this enchanted spot, lull the fancy into sweet romantic dreams; we imagine ourselves in the blooming groves of Italy.*[32] Catherine's own winter garden at the Hermitage was another marvel. These glassed gardens must have been even more astonishing in the winters of Russia than elsewhere in Europe.

Although lofty, glassy pleasure domes proliferated in the early part of the nineteenth century, more modest greenhouses and conservatories were fast becoming fashionable in Britain. *A Green-house, which fifty years ago was a luxury not often to be met with, is now become an appendage to every villa, and to many town residences and suburban villas,* wrote Loudon in 1824.[33] He was of the opinion that looking after the greenhouse was a matter for the ladies of the house, and that it should be stocked with a few choice plants rather than a plethora of curiosities that were difficult to grow. He had seen too many greenhouses *filled with sickly naked plants in peat soil, with hard names, which one half of people of taste and fashion, and nine-tenths of mankind in general, care nothing about.* In this Loudon was supported by

The winter garden of Prince Lichtenstein, which was, according to Loudon, justly considered one of the most luxurious promenades in Germany.

William Cobbett, the great egalitarian and rural historian. He suggested that various outdoor plants — snowdrops and crocuses, primroses and violets, cowslips and daisies — should be grown in the greenhouse to make them flower earlier.

Cobbett also saw a heavy moral value in greenhouse gardening that transcended the mere pleasure of watching plants grow. *How much better for daughters, or even sons, to assist, or attend, their mother, in a green-house, than to be seated with her at cards, or in the blubberings over a stupid novel, or at any other amusement that can possibly be conceived! How much more innocent, more pleasant, more free from temptation to evil, this amusement, than any other!*[34]

By the second quarter of the nineteenth century most middle-class families had a gardener or two to look after a hot-house and perhaps a peach house and a melon bed, and to lend a hand in the conservatory. Country gentlemen were expected to have several gardeners and a range of hot-houses for flowers, fruit and plants. Noble lords were deprived if they did not have a complete set of every kind of hot-house: *One wonders how a Duke could live without peaches and grapes, not to say pine-apples, forced strawberries, and kidneybeans.*[35]

This orangerie *at the Bagatelle, in the Bois de Boulogne in Paris, was built in 1844 for the 4th Marquess of Hertford. It follows the conventional form of many French orangeries, such as that at Breteuil which was built in the late seventeenth century.*

The Republican Greenhouse

During the eighteenth century every plantation or country estate library of any quality in America possessed a well-worn, much annotated edition of Philip Miller's *Gardener's Calendar* — highly instructive, but not for an American climate. It was not until 1806 that the *American Gardener's Calendar* was written by Bernard M'Mahon, nurseryman, seedsman and florist of Philadelphia. M'Mahon's *Calendar* gave month-by-month instructions on caring for plants in the greenhouse, hot-house and cold frame, and also explained the construction techniques for the buildings themselves.

M'Mahon recommended that the greenhouse *generally stand in the pleasure ground, and if possible, upon a somewhat elevated and dry spot fronting south.* He made no innovations but kept to the traditional design, although dismissing two-storey greenhouses as being heavy and expensive to build. The purpose of the greenhouse was to provide shelter for plants in winter. M'Mahon refrained from discussing style, later stating that most greenhouses were commonly built *more for ornament than use,* and that style was a matter for architects. His definition of a conservatory was similar to the English concept, for it had a removable glass roof and *beds and borders — made up of the best composition of soils.* However, as in England, the two words, greenhouse and conservatory, were sometimes interchanged, without reference to M'Mahon's distinctions. The *American Gardener's Calendar* was widely distributed and went through several editions in the nineteenth century. From its emphasis on greenhouse culture it is clear that greenhouses were popular, and that many important examples of such buildings have since been lost completely.

The Elgin Botanic Garden in New York City was one such greenhouse, demolished just two decades after construction; nonetheless, it was in its own time a symbol of the coming age of American horticulture. The founder was David Hosack, a young doctor trained in New York, Edinburgh, London and Philadelphia, and Professor of Botany at Columbia University. In September 1801 he purchased a twenty-acre site, with his own money, in an uninhabited suburb over three miles from the city. It was an appropriate site for the Elgin Botanic Garden, named after his family's home town in Scotland, in that it sloped south and east, and its soil was very varied.

L. Simond del.   Leney sc.

View of the BOTANIC GARDEN *at* ELGIN *in the vicinity of the* CITY of NEW YORK.

The Elgin greenhouse was completed by 1803; it was a pleasing structure, not unlike the one at William Hamilton's estate, Woodlands, 62 feet long and 23 feet wide and 20 feet high in the clear.[36] A certain resemblance to the Mount Airy greenhouse was evident in the small doors on either side of the arcaded front. Here, the four central bays projected slightly forwards, and a string course encircled the building at the level of the lunar windows.

I shall heat it by flues, they will run under the stays so they will not be seen — my walks will be spacious ... My collection of plants is yet small, I have written to my friends in Europe and in the east and West Indies for their plants. I will also collect the native productions of North and South America. What medical plants can Mr. Bartram supply — request him to send me a catalogue ... I hope Mr. Hamilton will have duplicates of rare and valuable plants — I will supply him anything I possess, wrote Hosack to Dr Thomas Parke in 1803. Hosack also received plants from Mr Prince's nursery in Brooklyn, from Bernard M'Mahon, from Monsieur Thouin at the Jardin des Plantes in Paris, and from William Curtis's own botanical garden at Brompton in London. The ever-increasing collection was housed in the conservatory or in two spacious hot-houses. Hosack published a twenty-nine page catalogue of the Elgin collection in 1806, expanded into a more comprehensive *Hortus Elginensis* of 1811, covering some two thousand plants and exotics.

What could have been its saviour in fact was the garden's death knell. Since 1806 Hosack had been trying to find a major financial backer for the garden; on 3 January 1811, the State of New York became its owner, but its management was given to the College of Physicians and Surgeons. By 1812 the hot-house plants were gone, the greenhouse plants had not been removed in the summer, and the shrubbery was overgrown; only the greenhouses remained in 1817, and by 1825 Columbia University took over the property for its new campus. Today the only evidence of the Elgin Botanic Garden is a plaque in the centre walk of its latest tenant, Rockefeller Center.

The Elgin Botanic Garden may have failed in 1811, but Dr Hosack's dream was eventually realized in the New York Botanical Garden at the end of the nineteenth century, and in many other botanical organizations throughout the United States.

Among M'Mahon and Hosack's most avid patrons was Thomas Jefferson. A man of unlimited accomplishments, Jefferson used his estate at Monticello as a base for his interests as naturalist, farmer, architect and landscape gardener. Monticello was the great magnet in his life, from the first planting recorded in his *Garden Book* in 1767 until his death in 1826. It was designed, redesigned, altered and rebuilt on paper and in practice for over forty years during two major periods: 1769–82 and 1793–1809. Despite early plans, a detached greenhouse was never built. Instead, when Jefferson expanded Monticello, the single-bay extension on the southern wing became his greenhouse.

The greenhouse extension was begun in 1806, and a network of

The excellent, yet short-lived, conservatory and hot-houses at the Elgin Botanic Garden, c.1806. A plaque dedicated to David Hosack at Rockefeller Center is now the only tangible evidence of its existence on this site.

Thomas Jefferson's greenhouse at Monticello is a very small, simply designed glazed loggia, one bay deep and three bays long, balancing in design the open piazza on the north end of the house.

amateur and professional gardeners was tapped for specimen plants. To William Hamilton of Woodlands in 1806, Jefferson reported a flourishing *Mimosa Julibrisia,* but a failure with *Mimosa Farnesiana or Nilotica* which he had sent; it had perished during Jefferson's absence from home. He continued with a request: *I remember seeing in your greenhouse a plant of a couple of feet height in a pot the fragrance of which (from its gummy bud if I recollect rightly) was peculiarly agreeable to me and you were so kind as to remark that it required only a greenhouse, and that you would furnish me one when I should be in a situation to preserve it, but it's name has entirely escaped me . . .*[37]

Although the greenhouse was not quite finished, Jefferson wrote to Hamilton in March 1808, thanking him for a specimen from his collection and pointing out that *my green house is only a piazza adjoining my study, because I mean it for nothing more than some oranges, Mimosa Farnesiana & very few things of that kind.* He enquired again about the odiferous plant in Hamilton's greenhouse, repeating his desire to have it and more mimosa seeds. In addition, he hoped Hamilton would visit him some day at Monticello *where I shall be very happy to receive you & be instructed by you how to overcome some of its difficulties.*

The first mention of a greenhouse in correspondence with M'Mahon was in a letter of March 1811, when M'Mahon asked Jefferson, by now retired from the presidency, if he had both a greenhouse and a hot-house. Jefferson reported sadly a month later: *I have only a green house, and have used that only for a few articles. My frequent & long absences at a distant possession render my efforts even for the few greenhouse plant I aim at, abortive. during my last absence in the winter, every plant I had in it perished . . .* Undaunted by these remarks, M'Mahon sent a snowberry bush, *Symphoricarpos leucocarpa,* which would *retain its beauty all the winter; especially if kept in a Green House,* and three lily roots, *Amaryillis belladonna.* The greenhouse received little attention after this date. In November of 1816, Jefferson indicated that it was used for storage *where a bushel of Orchard grass-seed out of the large box* can be found. Mr A. B. Woodward, from Tallahasse, Florida, sent a dozen orange seeds in April 1926, but their fate is unknown as Jefferson died that year.

Classical greenhouses continued to be built in the United States in the nineteenth century, such as the one at Hampton in Maryland, c.1828, and the attached twin orangery pavilions of 1849 at Westend in Louisa County, Virginia. A Philadelphia architect, John Haviland, was responsible for designing the early Greek Revival Moody house in Haverhill, near Boston, Massachusetts, whose plan incorporated a small conservatory wing off the dining room, balanced by a corresponding study wing off the library. *The Builder's Assistant,* published by Haviland in three volumes between 1818 and 1821 which included the Moody design in Volume I, is important as the first instance in an American work where the plates of the Greek orders were shown. An Ionian villa was built for J.W. Perry in Brooklyn, possibly by James Dakin, an early partner of

Alexander Jackson Davis. Forming the left wing of this delicate building was *one of the most beautiful conservatories attached to a dwelling,*[38] and there was another spacious conservatory adjoining William P. Van Rensselaer's mansion at Beaverwyck.

The most palatial of Grecian buildings with an attached conservatory was the house A. J. Davis designed for John C. Stevens in 1844–45. One writer in *Putnam's Monthly* reported that *the conservatory to the right and the dome upon the roof extend and raise the composition to a good proportion.* Reproduced in a line engraving, the conservatory appears as a two-storey structure rising to the level of the engaged capitals.

An idea of the atmosphere of these early classical conservatories is found in Isabella Lucy Bird Bishop's description of the Richard K. Haight mansion in her book, *The Englishwoman in America,* published in London in 1856. An Italian Renaissance palazzo designed by Trench and Snook between 1848 and 1849, this *fairy palace of taste & art possessed a large wintergarden.* It sounds remarkably like Morton Peto's winter garden at Somerleyton in England, with which it is a close contemporary. *It was a glass building with a high dome; a fine fountain was playing in the centre, and round its marble basin were orange, palm, and myrtle trees, with others from the tropics. . . . Every part of the floor that was not of polished white marble was thickly carpeted with small green ferns. The gleam of white marble statues, from among the clumps of orange trees and other shrubs, was particularly pretty; indeed the whole had a fairy-like appearance about it.*

Such mansions as these, however, contradicted Isabella Bishop's preconceptions of American republican simplicity: a naïve attitude at the time, for this complex artificial scene was by no means unique. The ornate and well-supplied greenhouse or conservatory was an accepted appurtenance, in part because of fashion, economics and improved construction techniques, but more importantly because of an avalanche of interest in horticulture and exotics first fostered on the estates along the Hudson River.

John Cox Stevens's New York house, complete with attached conservatory, was designed by A. J. Davis in 1845. In 1854 Davis executed a set of plans for Stevens's country estate, Mount Sterling in New Jersey, which included designs for Landscape Gardening, Garden Temple and Tank, Grapery, Greenhouse *and* Conservatory.

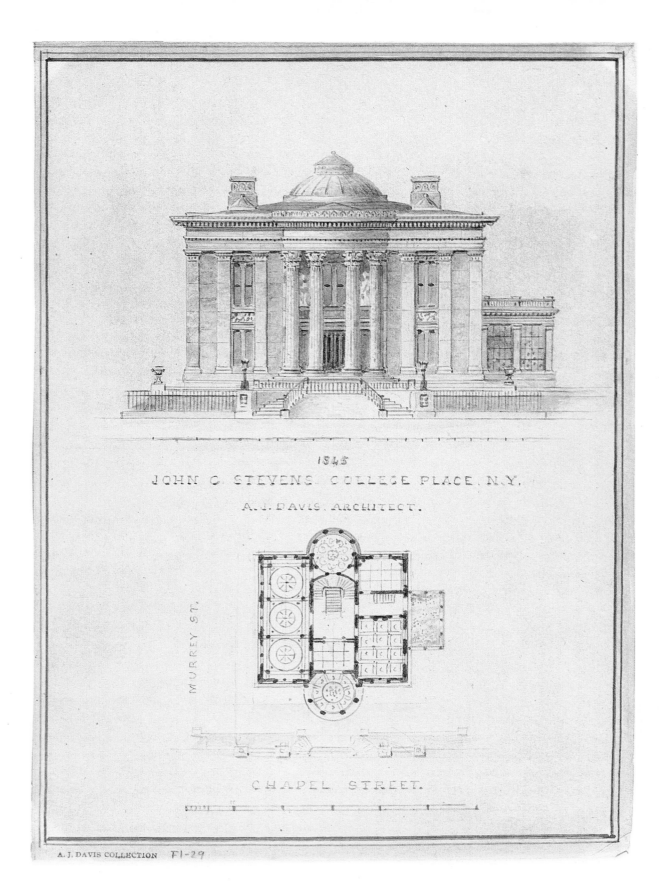

1845

JOHN C. STEVENS, COLLEGE PLACE, N.Y.

A. J. DAVIS, ARCHITECT.

MURREY ST.

CHAPEL STREET.

The Hudson River Style

There is no place in the Union where the taste in landscape gardening is so far advanced as on the middle portion of the Hudson, wrote A.J. Downing in his second edition of *A Treatise on the Theory and Practice of Landscape Gardening* in 1844. Downing was clearly the most enthusiastic and eloquent writer on landscape gardening of his day. The *oracle of the Hudson,* he was to America what Loudon had been to England less than a generation before. Essays, editorials and critiques poured from his pen to educate Americans in landscape gardening, rural architecture and horticulture. His congenial, persistent and ebullient personality convinced many architects of the day to collaborate with him, until his untimely death by shipwreck on the Hudson River in 1852 at the age of thirty-seven.

A movement for improving the tasteful quality of rural architecture and landscape design had been brewing since the 1830s, but it was Downing's contemporary, Alexander Jackson Davis, who first articulated a rural style in *Rural Residences,* written in 1837. Davis and Downing were kindred spirits. Together the versatility of Davis the architect and the practicality of Downing the designer would create the Gothic vocabulary for the picturesque American cottage and villa.

Important to Downing's overall schemes were the architectural, rustic and floral embellishments by which the *union between the house and grounds* was to be achieved. The greenhouse or conservatory was one such embellishment: if designed properly, it could be *an elegant and delightful appendage to the villa.*

Judging from the many entries in his daybooks and journals, one can conclude that Davis designed a number of greenhouses and graperies, even though only a few drawings exist today. Designs for conservatories attached to houses, on the other hand, are many and often ingeniously placed. Davis had designed country villas in the Gothic style, but had never adapted these designs for a suburban villa until 1844, when he was commissioned by William Coventry H. Waddell to plan the first Gothic villa in New York City.[39] It was enclosed in its own garden on Murray Hill, which sloped northwards along Fifth Avenue to the area once occupied by the Croton Reservoir on 42nd Street. The large, glazed conservatory extending west from the double crenellated towers was a simple complement to the picturesque exterior of the house, saving a more flamboyant statement for its interior. This was described in Ann S. Stephens' contemporary novel, *Fashion and Famine:*
The conservatory was filled with blossoming plants, and lighted entirely by lamps, placed in alabaster vases, or swinging-like moons, from the waves of crystal that formed the roof. Masses of South American plants sheeted the sides with blossoms. Passion flowers crept up the crystal roof, and dropped their starry blossoms among the lamps. Trees, rich with the light feathery foliage peculiar to the tropics, bent over and sheltered the blossoming plants. An aquatic lily floated in the marble basin of a tiny fountain, spreading its broad green leaves on the water, and sheltering a
host of arrowy, little gold-fish, that flashed in and out from their shadows. The air was redolent with heliotrope, daphnes, and cape-jessamines. Soft mosses crept around the marble basin, and dropped downward to the tesselated floor. It was like entering fairy land, as you came into this star-lit wilderness of flowers, from a noble picture gallery, which divided it from the reception room ... No artist ever arranged a more noble picture – no peri ever found a lovelier paradise.

A few years later, in 1854, Davis was asked by Robert Donaldson to draw up plans for a greenhouse at his estate, Edgewater, overlooking the Hudson River. *The Green House is to be placed on a terrace – to be octagonal with Iron Rafters 28 feet Diameter & glazed with large glass on the sides with bold mullions.*[40] Could he have been inspired by John Notman's smaller Gothic conservatory which he added to the Nathan Dunn house in 1838 and which Downing illustrated in his *Treatise* of 1841?

In addition to commissions for Stevens and Donaldson, Davis designed greenhouses for various other clients, including a Mr Strange and a Mr Litchfield, and a most individual greenhouse for J. Smith Ely on Staten Island in 1849–50. The Ely house was in the Pointed Gothic style, and the greenhouse an ambitious interpretation of a favoured idea, a glazed verandah. Unique to the rural villa was the verandah, an open porch or ombra; Davis would wrap the verandah around a corner, separate it by a projecting entrance tower or *porte cochère,* or add it as a one-storey wing off the dining room or drawing room. Its slightly slanting roof would rest on a frieze of Tudor or Gothic arches, supported by slender single or engaged columns. For the winter months, Davis advised some of his clients to transform the verandah into a *plant cabinet* by placing movable sashes in between the columns. Downing noted that this clever device offered *an air of summer, even in the depths of a northern winter.* Equally, it introduced colour to the exterior in the bleak grey months.

Often Davis would be asked by Downing to make drawings of his or other architects' buildings which would then be illustrated in *The Horticulturist.* For Downing's article of October 1847 about Montgomery Place, not far from Edgewater, Davis made two drawings of the conservatory, one of which has survived. Designed by Frederick Catherwood, an English architect and artist, in 1839, it was somewhat altered by 1847. The conservatory was a large, free-standing building in the ornamental pleasure ground, and could be seen from the main drive approaching the house which had been altered by Davis. Construed out of many conventional sources, its delicate façade was distinguished by small panes of glass set into prominent Gothic arches.

If the Hudson Valley led in the initial development of a characteristic American horticulture, the environs of Boston soon vied at the beginning of the nineteenth century for the lead. As early as 1800, Theodore Lyman was growing pineapples in his modest hillside greenhouse at his estate, The Vale; this and more expansive lean-to glass houses, which still stand, were to be inspirations for Lyman's neighbour John Perkins Cushing at Belmont.

Known for its exotic plants from China, Trinidad and London, Belmont's range of greenhouses formed one side of an enclosed 300 foot square. On the north end was the conservatory and graperies built into a wall, behind which were potting sheds and plant houses, a design reminiscent of W. and D. Bailey's 1820 plan for a half-dome and lean-to houses at Hackney in London. Cushing, however, embellished his half-dome with Moorish arches and built a baroque gabled brick wall to silhouette the semicircular lantern. Although the date of this house is not known, one can surmise from the literature that it predates the Crystal Palace.

A. J. Davis suggested a more ambitious interpretation of the glazed verandah for the former mayor of New York, J. Smith Ely, on Staten Island in 1849–50: a glazed passage connected the main house with its service wing.

The conservatory at Montgomery Place was designed by the English architect and artist, Frederick Catherwood, c.1839, for Mrs Edward Livingston. This isolated ornament in the pleasure ground is a larger, more elaborate version of J. A. Repton's glass houses.

Curvilinear greenhouses, more simple than the Gothic and more graceful than the half-dome, were to be found along the Hudson as well as in Boston before 1850. The Vinery at Clinton Point, inspired by the Boston type, and Wodenethe on the estate of Henry W. Sargent represent two important styles. For his collections of vines, Stephen Van Rensselaer designed a building of wood and glass at Clinton Point.[41] Although the central columnar supports, as well as the poles controlling the ventilators, may have been of cast iron, the rafters and mullions were all wood, unlike their English counterparts in iron. John Notman, on the other hand, had suggested using cast iron throughout the Gothic building he had proposed for the new Smithsonian Institution in 1846, which included an octagonal conservatory and greenhouse. *By using cast iron for beams, they can be made ornamental to the ceilings,* stated Notman. His building was not chosen.[42]

In September 1849, William Resorr of Cincinnati wrote to *The Horticulturist* with his plan for an iron-roofed vinery, the first documented cast-iron greenhouse in America. The critique which followed in November 1849 in the same periodical was admiring but hesitant: *I should like to hear from Mr. Resorr five years hence, when the frosts, and the damps, and the shrinks, and the swells, and the lightnings and the electricities of all sorts, have played their pranks around it* ... The critic, who may have been Mr Downing himself, concluded his remarks with a challenge which the second half of the nineteenth century would accept with alacrity and success: *Iron is yet to be — when it can be made cheap enough — introduced into a great many structures that we hardly yet dream of; and if the same advantages can be had in the construction of conservatories, vineries and hot-houses, with iron, as with wood, its durability will prove its greater merit.*

The graceful, cold vinery at Clinton Point on the Hudson, illustrated in The Horticulturist, *October 1849. Then considered* the best model for a curvilinear house, *it was placed on a north–south axis so that the vines might receive maximum sunlight.*

A blazing arch of lucid glass
Leaps like a fountain from the grass
To meet the sun!

Tennyson, 'May-Day Ode', 1851

Public Palaces

The Crystal Palace stunned the world when the Great Exhibition was opened on 1 May 1851. Not for its elegance – Kew and Chatsworth and many others far surpassed it in beauty of form – but because this enormous, glittering masterpiece rose from the grass of Hyde Park in a matter of months, leaving Londoners gasping in amazement. And that was before they had gone inside to see the prize exhibits of British industry.

The complicated story of why and how it was built is well told elsewhere; its details make today's reader, too, gasp in amazement. Entries for an international competition, announced in January 1850 by a Royal Commission headed by Prince Albert, had been disappointing; the best, a massive brick pile by Brunel, could probably not have been built in time for the scheduled opening in May 1851. Joseph Paxton was told of the commissioners' dilemma on 11 June 1850. A few days later he doodled the first embryonic plan on some blotting paper during a meeting, and by 22 June he had presented his plans to the Commission. After some discussion, they were accepted on 26 July. For the commissioners, this glass design was a gamble – new technology only partly tested, and the designer not a professional architect or an engineer but a gardener – but it was a gamble they had to take, otherwise there would be no Great Exhibition.

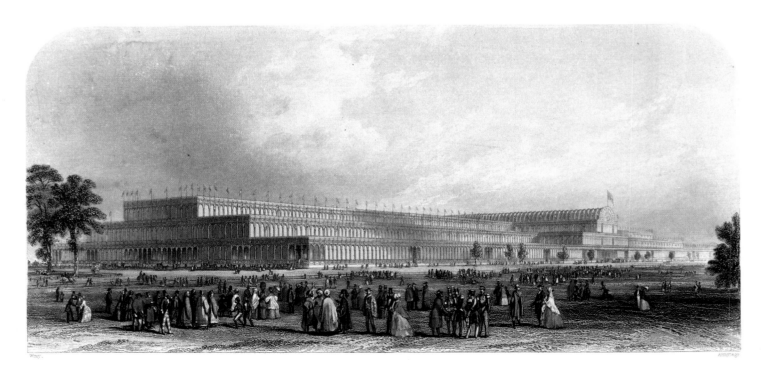

A VIEW OF THE GREAT INDUSTRIAL EXHIBITION IN HYDE PARK.

Paxton and the contractors had precisely five days in which to produce an estimate for a building that used 3,800 tons of cast iron, 700 tons of wrought iron, 600,000 cubic feet of timber, 24 miles of guttering and 205 miles of glazing bars — and a staggering 900,000 square feet of sheet glass, about a third of the country's annual glass output. The glass manufacturers had to be persuaded to produce panes twelve inches longer than ever made before, in order to meet Paxton's specification for the ridge and furrow roof, and they had to take on thirty-two extra skilled glass-blowers from France. Standardization was the key to assembling the materials, so that identical units could quickly be locked together on site, time and time again. The overall length of the main building was 1,848 feet, more than six times longer than the Great Conservatory at Chatsworth, and the width was 408 feet, three times wider than Chatsworth. It was four times the size of St Peter's in Rome. Within twenty-two weeks the structure, complete with barrel roof and rose window, was finished and ready for painting and for the army of exhibitors to move in.

One of the building's greatest assets was its name, coined by a journalist writing for *Punch*. It is so familiar now that it is hard to imagine the impact of these words; they conjured up something out of fairyland, as did Tennyson's lines in 'May-Day Ode'.

The magic image appealed to the public. In only twenty-five weeks, between 1 May and 15 October when it was closed, the Palace attracted over six million visitors, an amazing figure when one considers that there was no underground railway and only horse-drawn buses for public transport within the capital. People walked for miles to see it, buying cheap season tickets for repeated visits, for it was not only the affluent in carriages who flocked to Hyde Park. Queen Victoria, who opened the building and was a regular visitor, saw it as the greatest triumph of her beloved Albert. The exhibition inside was crammed with a mixture of the latest inventions, the products of British industry at its best, with the cream of foreign competition too, while at the other end of the scale there was much tawdry machine-made rubbish. The building, its aspirations and its displays were an accurate mirror of colonizing, trading, industrializing, Victorian Great Britain.

Paxton's great achievement was to produce a design with enough decoration to please, but simple enough to construct, for in that lay the speed of execution. From his gardening experience he readily acknowledged the lessons learned at Chatsworth, and the constant support of the Duke of Devonshire. Being a shrewd businessman as well, Paxton also patented the ridge and furrow roof design.

What the Crystal Palace showed was that huge spaces could be enclosed by glass, with the aid of iron and wood. The formula could be adapted to cover any area and various heights; iron could be moulded and wrought into curves and patterns to give variety of form; and the structure could be mass-produced and assembled more quickly and cheaply than conventional buildings in bricks and mortar. The technology could be used for all manner of public buildings, from exhibition halls to shopping arcades to railway stations, and to glass houses for plants.

Another advantage of this new type of construction was that it could be taken down and reassembled elsewhere, which is precisely what happened to the Crystal Palace. It had been intended as a temporary edifice in Hyde Park, and the year after its closure it was dismantled and moved to Sydenham Hill in south London. The flexibility of its design allowed alterations to be made, and it was reopened in June 1854, again by Queen Victoria. Part of it was a winter garden stocked with orange trees and pomegranates that had belonged to King Louis-Philippe of France. There were other tropical plants for visitors to admire, as well as many educational exhibits, a concert hall and several restaurants. The Palace was always beset by financial crises, but it was a popular centre of entertainment for Londoners until, on 30 November 1936, it was burned to the ground in a raging fire.

Immediately following the success of the Hyde Park Great Exhibition Building, Paxton entered a competition to design a similar building for the United States' first World Fair in New York in 1853. His entry was not successful, but the winning plans of the New York architects George Carstensen and Charles Gildemeister had echoes of Paxton's Crystal Palace. The glass was framed in cast-iron wall panels, arched like Paxton's but more elaborate, the detail generally was much more ornate. The roof was opaque, but crowned with a huge semicircular glazed dome, whose cast-iron construction acted as a support for its wide span as well as being highly ornamental. In spite of a claim that it was fireproof, this building too was destroyed by fire, only five years after it opened.

Other architects challenged Paxton's early supremacy, such as Owen Jones who built the Crystal Palace Bazaar in Oxford Street in London, and the People's Palace in Muswell Hill, north London's answer to the south's Sydenham Hill. In Munich, a glass house based on much the same principles as Paxton's was designed for the old botanical garden by August von Voit.

There were other influences, however, particularly as far as style was concerned. More and more travellers were going beyond the shores of Greece to look for architectural inspiration in the Middle East. A whiff of the mysterious excitement of Constantinople could enliven a plain glass wall, and make the building exotic. Saracenic motifs in cast iron were applied to the structure of the conservatory at Wilhelma, Stuttgart, built by Ludwig von Zanth between 1842 and 1853. In other places, such as Enville Hall in Staffordshire, the Saracenic touch was visible in onion domes on the roof-line, as well as in the decorated panels. The Far East also had its influence, again in Germany, in the Great Palm House in the Royal Botanical Garden at Berlin-Schoneberg. Built by Bouche, Herter and Nietz in 1859, it was an oblong building in three sections, with the central part much raised to accommodate lofty palms; the roof was ridged and furrowed. The structure was essentially dominated by right

angles, which the architects counteracted by setting the glass in diagonal sash bars, giving a mildly Oriental effect. It was demolished in 1910.

In the midst of these rectangular panelled buildings, the curves of Loudon, Turner and Paxton were not forgotten. In 1865 a Scottish engineer-architect called John Kibble built a curvilinear conservatory at Coulport on Loch Long, one of the sea lochs in the Clyde estuary. It was designed by James Boucher and James Cousland and made of cast iron by James Boyd of Paisley, a conservatory manufacturer. It had two domes, one small and one large, glazed with greenish glass. Inside were many rare specialist plants, including a dozen different varieties of araucaria from South America, a dracaena twenty feet high that flowered — quite an achievement — and a collection of fruit-laden citrus trees. In the centre beneath the large dome was a big pool of water with a rocky island and a fountain, like many another conservatory. But to this rocky pile Kibble added models of the ruins of ancient Rome and Greece, and then — joy of joys for small boys — two or three model ships at anchor in the island harbours, and a tugboat, fifteen inches long and equipped with a steam engine so that it could pull the other vessels round the island.

A few years later, Kibble realized that his family had no interest in his conservatory and its tender plants, and would let them fall into ruin on his death. So he approached the Glasgow Botanic Garden and offered to transfer the building there at his own expense, provided he could manage it commercially for twenty-one years. Agreement was reached, and the dismantled frame was towed up the Clyde on a raft. At the new site in the affluent West End of Glasgow, the conservatory was much enlarged; the wings and corridors were planted; and the main dome became a popular concert hall, the orchestra playing from the island in the wide round pool. For public meetings the pool was covered; two Rectors of Glasgow University, Disraeli and Gladstone, delivered their rectorial addresses under the giant dome. In 1881 the agreement between Kibble and the Botanic Garden was terminated, and the conservatory was planted with species from temperate zones, requiring little winter heat. Many of the tree ferns from New Zealand originally planted there flourish still, surrounded by camellias of every hue from purest white to deepest red. The delicate fronds of ferns and deep green leaves of camellias are a perfect foil for statues, of which there is a fine collection: an icy Eve waits silently; an elf gazes over a billowing, ferny sea.

The Kibble Palace is an immensely impressive building. The diameter of the main area is a vast 146 feet, with the dome constructed in two parts. The upper dome rests on a frame supported by a dozen columns, spiralled like barley sugar and attached by filigree brackets. Another circle of twenty-four columns supports the roof of the lower dome. Where the two domes meet there is a clerestory circle of swivelling ventilators, and more ventilators are positioned under the cupola and low in the glass walls. The temperature is

The lush, cool interior of the Kibble Palace, where statues are enhanced by tree ferns. Like the Crystal Palace, this circular glass house was moved from its original site, in this case up the river Clyde to a prime position in the Glasgow Botanic Gardens.

further controlled by daily spraying with water in summer, since tree ferns need high humidity.

Glasgow Botanic Garden has a range of hot-houses nearby, built on traditional lines with straight walls and ridge roofs. During winter gales these may lose maybe fifty panes of glass in one night, whereas the glass in the Kibble Palace is unbroken. The wind flows over its gentle curves, leaving it intact.

Another surge of interest in public glass houses swept across Europe in the 1870s. It was a matter of prestige, botanical and probably social too, that stimulated their construction. German cities blossomed with *Flora*, glass halls for displaying exotic flowers. At the botanical gardens of Copenhagen and Florence stately palm houses were built, both finished in 1874, and in 1880 at the Parc de la Tête d'Or in Lyons five vast conservatories were built in a row, each with a different climate. What is interesting about these three

buildings, started and finished within an eight-year period, is the diversity of shape. The Copenhagen building, designed by Rothe and Jacobsen, was reminiscent of the Kibble Palace without the curves, with a wide two-tiered flattened dome and wings. The other two were based on the Gothic arch. In Lyons, the arch faced the front in the central conservatory, and in the two smaller adjacent buildings, while in the Florence version the arch faced the ends of the building. All were covered with cast-iron decoration, appropriately restrained in Copenhagen and riotous in Florence.

The beauty of the internal structure of these nineteenth-century pavilions could not be appreciated once the plants were moved in. Their full glory can only be seen when total restoration is in progress, such as in the Palm House at Kew and Stanford White's conservatory at the Brooklyn Botanic Garden in New York, or in the empty, decaying ribs of the Orto Botanico in Florence.

The large glass house business continued to boom in countless cities. In 1887 Velasquez Bosco designed the Palacio de Cristal, in the Parque del Retiro in Madrid. This is an extremely elegant building. Rounded arches dominate the structure, inside and out, and the only non-structural decoration is to be found in the capitals of the cast-iron columns. It is used now not for plants but as an exhibition hall. In 1896, Liverpool erected its botanical glass house in Sefton Park, and in the same year Glasgow built a People's Palace on Glasgow Green. This was a cultural centre for the working classes of Glasgow, for whom the Kibble Palace was too distant and too expensive to visit. The Great Palm House in the Berlin-Dahlem Botanical Garden was one of the few to be built after the turn of the century; it was designed by Alfred Koerner and finished in 1907.

The tale of these sunlit, ever warm flower gardens returns always, like a homing pigeon, to Kew. The Temperate House was designed by Decimus Burton in 1860 for the garden's collection of Australian, Chilean and Mexican plants. The centre pavilion with its hipped roof and the twin octagon glass rooms were completed by 1862 for £29,000, but the additional conservatory wings were not built at the time because of rising costs. The roof was glazed with green glass, in accordance with contemporary practice. The idea that a conservatory should have a removable glass roof was still popular, and an ingenious device to enable the glass panels in the upper part of the roof to slide down was evolved by the builder, W. Cubitt and Co. The contract for completing the original plan was awarded to the conservatory manufacturers Mackenzie and Moncur of Edinburgh, in 1894 and the extensions finished in 1898.

The Temperate House has recently undergone thorough restoration. The heating and ventilation systems have been reorganized to work efficiently, since in the building's early days many plants failed to grow well there. It was reopened by Queen Elizabeth II in June 1982. The Temperate House provides a pleasing contrast to the curves of the Palm House; for some years it was considered the latter's plain sister, but since its refurbishment it looks magnificent.

The stuccoed porches, iron structure and urns have all been painted brilliant white.

The Temperate House is 553 feet long overall, and now houses the garden's collection of species from China and Japan, Tasmania and New Zealand, southern Africa and the Mediterranean. With a minimum winter temperature of 45° F, the house contains some enormous trees, like the feathery blue-grey Kashmir cypress which touches the roof. Other giants are the fan-leafed *Brahea edulis* and *Washingtonia robusta,* and the Japanese banana. Shrubs and smaller plants also abound. This, like other temperate houses, is a good place to visit for inspiration for the private conservatory. There are fine daturas, varieties of brunsfelsia, climbing cestrums, and another climbing favourite, the sweet-scented, June flowering *Trachelospermum jasminoides,* all of which the amateur can enjoy growing.

The conservatory at the Orto Botanico in Florence is now a magnificent ruin, a reminder of the need for constant maintenance of these fragile buildings.

The Temperate House at Kew by Decimus Burton, which dates from 1862 and 1898.

Flower Conservatory; Plan of Second Story, *signed by Calvert Vaux and Jacob Wrey Mould, c.1860. With an overall length of 370 feet, Vaux's conservatory has a central hall with two double-storeyed circular pavilions, a unique feature. The Central Park Commissioners were much more interested in having a conservatory and flower garden as part of Central Park than was Olmsted, who stated that they were* scarcely a necessary part of a park . . . [only the] *accessories of a composition.*

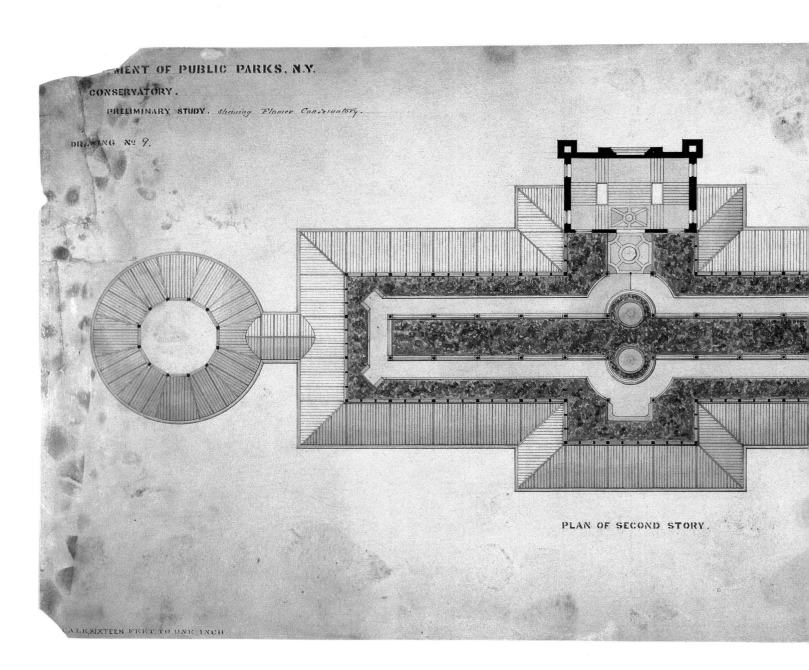

MENT OF PUBLIC PARKS, N.Y.

CONSERVATORY.

PRELIMINARY STUDY. *shewing Flower Conservatory.*

DRAWING No 9.

PLAN OF SECOND STORY.

SCALE SIXTEEN FEET TO ONE INCH.

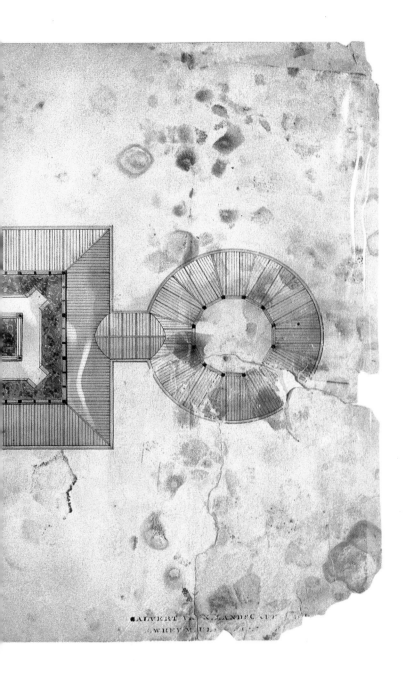

These European glass houses had their counterparts across the Atlantic. However, even though New York's Crystal Palace was impressive and more elaborate than its London parent, the erection of similar public buildings for plants did not proceed in America with the tornado-like momentum evident in Europe. This is attributable to the slow growth of the American urban public park; in the 1850s, America was much more interested in taming the wilderness and securing its borders west of the Mississippi than in creating urban gardens.

Although Boston's Public Garden, established in 1839, had two successive glass camellia houses prior to 1850, it was not until 1859 that New York followed with its own public park. It took the galvanizing rhetoric of A. J. Downing, several articles in *The Horticulturist*, and some enlightened disciples to persuade the city commissioners to form a Central Park for New York. Downing, in essence, had outlined specifications for its conservatory: *winter gardens of glass, like the great Crystal Palace, where the whole people could luxuriate in groves of the palms and spice trees of the tropics, at the same moment that sleighing parties glided swiftly and noiselessly over the snow-covered surface of the country-like avenues of the wintery park without.*[1]

The social influence of a public park was equally paramount in his plan: *The thoughtful denizen of the town would go out there in the morning, to hold converse with the whispering trees, and the weary tradesmen in the evening, to enjoy an hour of happiness by mingling in the open space with all the world ... how all over France and Germany, the whole population of the cities pass their afternoons and evenings together.*[2] The strongest model for his park was a cross between Kew and Chatsworth, both of which Downing had visited in 1850. *I left Kew with the feeling, that a national garden in America might not only be a beautiful, but a most useful and popular establishment.*[3]

In April 1858, a site in the centre of Manhattan was chosen; the designers were a young landscape architect farming on Staten Island, Frederick Law Olmsted, and his partner, Calvert Vaux, an English-trained architect whom Downing had brought to America in 1850 to be his associate. The conservatory was eventually planned for a site near a large baroque pool called 'Conservatory Water'.

The proposed 'Flower Conservatory' can be seen from a beautifully executed drawing[4] signed by Calvert Vaux and his assistant, Jacob Wrey Mould, *c.* 1860. The drawing indicates a typical cruciform central hall with side pavilions and hyphens in between, 370 feet in length. Judging from the drawing, one can speculate that the roof-line may have resembled the double curved outlines of Kew's Palm House, rising to a long rectangular lantern with pivotal windows for ventilation. If Vaux's supple design had been adopted, the American preference for interconnecting rectilinear buildings might not have dominated conservatory design to the degree it did in the last century. A large conservatory for palms and exotics was finally built in Central Park between 104th and 106th Streets in 1899, but was torn down in 1934.

The first iron and glass building in America for the sole purpose of displaying plants had to wait until the Philadelphia Centennial Exposition of 1876. H. J. Schwarzmann, the architect for the Horticultural Hall, departed from the conventional simple jewel box of the 1850s and 1860s and produced a grand Victorian building littered with ornamentation, from Gothic tracery and lancet windows to Moorish horseshoe arches and brilliant coloration. The smallest of the five principal buildings, it was the largest conservatory ever built at that time. The central conservatory, rising on its Saracenic embellishments, was flanked on its north and south aisles by four pillow-like propagating houses, and on its east and west ends were pavilions for restaurants, offices, and exhibition spaces for the latest in garden technology.

The colourful central conservatory, 230 feet long by 80 feet wide by 55 feet high, was another fairyland of multiple experiences, more richly embroidered than its antecedents. Victorian parterres, a sunken garden, marble fountains, medicinal plants and elaborate displays of exotics were theatrically lit by crystal chandeliers.[5] Once described as *the most spectacular garden under glass*, Horticultural Hall continued its reign as an integral part of Fairmount Park until 1955 when it was demolished.

The centennial commemoration of the construction of Baltimore's conservatory in Druid Hill Park has provoked its restoration. Planned in the early 1870s by the chairman of the park commission, John H. B. Latrobe and architect George Frederick, for financial reasons it was not built until 1887–88. This small, elegant, self-contained building with federal details rises 55 feet and is painted a creamy yellow with green trim. An 'H' plan addition to the conservatory, reminiscent of Loudon's earlier curvilinear house, is part of a major revitalization of Druid Hill Park.

A rainbow of conservatory building soon followed. The confidence of the age and a flurry of philanthropic activity encouraged the founding of many public institutions for art and education, of libraries and public parks. At Allegheny and Pittsburgh, the public park conservatories were a gift of the philanthropist Henry Phipps. Other mid-western cities soon followed in the establishment of their public palaces: Cleveland, Chicago, Detroit and Saint Paul, to name a few. Yet none was to surpass the great conservatory built in New York's Bronx Park at the end of the century.

The majestic Horticultural Hall, built for the Philadelphia Centennial Exposition in 1876. An astonishing variety of decoration was possible by using moulded cast iron for this popular glass house.

The conservatory at Druid Hill Park, Baltimore, 1887–88, bears a striking comparison to the cast-iron Palm House built for the 1873 Vienna World's Exhibition.
The new William Donald Schaefer Conservatory is designed by the Washington architects Cass & Pinnell, whose expansion succeeds in complementing the older and much smaller building. Construction is scheduled to start early in 1988.

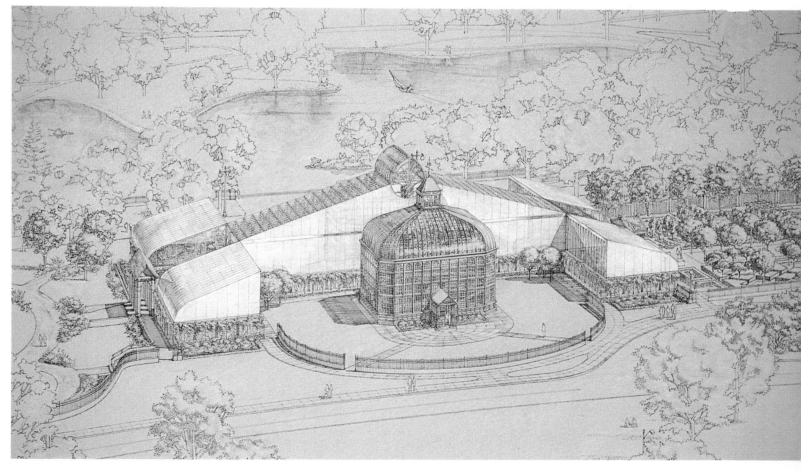

In 1899 the New York architect William R. Cobb was chosen to design New York's version of Kew, and Hitchings and Company was its builder. As in England, there was a long list of greenhouse manufacturers, of which Lord and Burnham and Hitchings and Company were the most famous. Because of a short-lived merger between these two, from 1905 to 1906, the building of the conservatory has often been misattributed to Lord and Burnham. It was, however, the pride of Hitchings and Company, and often featured in their magazine advertisements during the first decade of the twentieth century. The conservatory and Palm Court were completed in 1902; a glass, iron and steel structure of eleven houses covering an acre of ground, it is the largest and most beautiful of its kind in America.

This once richly ornamented building suffered from natural decay and two unsympathetic restorations in 1938 and again in 1952, when much of its elaborate decoration was removed. After a further passage of time it was in danger of total decay, but through sympathetic restoration the old dowager has been brought back to life, reclaiming her position as the premier botanical conservatory in America.

The Enid A. Haupt Conservatory, New York Botanical Garden, Bronx Park was completed in 1902. Originally inspired by the visit of two young botanists, Dr Nathaniel Lord Britton and his wife, to Kew Gardens in 1889, its construction was financed by such luminaries as J. P. Morgan, Cornelius Vanderbilt II and Andrew Carnegie.

While Queen Victoria was too preoccupied with government and her family to take a serious interest in an indoor garden, some of her royal cousins and counterparts in Europe found glass houses irresistible. The Princess Mathilde de Buonoparte had a large winter garden attached to her house in Paris, in the form of a wide gallery along the façade, connecting the principal apartments. From a description written in a magazine in 1869, it was clearly not so much a hot-house for plants as a reception room decorated with tree ferns, palms and climbing plants. There were Turkish, Persian and Afghan rugs, priceless pieces of Venetian glass, exquisite furniture from China and Japan, and dragons on the cast-iron columns.

If the glass house is a jewel by day, so much more is it by night, when the star-like lamps glitter between the green leaves ... One would imagine that The Decameron was transported from Florence to Paris. Suddenly there is a general hush; music has its say. One steps closer so as not to miss any of the concert. Leading performers consider themselves lucky to sing here, to play here ... Now and then, when the social gathering has reached its peak and the glitter and the diamonds are shining at their brightest, a more pallid bluish beam enters through the crystal roof of the glass house and spreads its gleaming drops on the broad leaves of exotic plants — it is the moon, which uninvited but feeling at home in this forest, weaves its silvery threads into the Smyrna carpeting.[6]

Princess Mathilde's winter garden was perhaps more of a social paradise, just a little more splendid and exotic than many a grand *hôtel* in Paris. Others were worlds of pure fantasy. Eccentric monarchs seized the chance to create strange scenes of enchantment to which they frequently escaped; none more so than King Ludwig II of Bavaria. Ludwig's Residenz in Munich already had one winter garden, but in 1867 Ludwig commissioned August von Voit to construct a second on the roof. It was another glass and iron combination with a barrel roof, and landscaped with quantities of soil and trees and a lake. Not unexpectedly, the lake leaked into the rooms below, and the apprentice cooks who slept there had to go to bed under umbrellas, but they never complained. The weight of the garden and its contents were far beyond the pressures for which the supporting walls had been built, so it was demolished after King Ludwig's death in 1886.

In Ludwig's lifetime, the garden was a magic valley in Kashmir. On the lake floated a Swan Knight in a gilded boat, and there were bridges, a grotto, a murmuring waterfall, winding paths, a well, and the peaks of the Himalayas painted on the west wall in perfect perspective. The garden was planted with giant palms and lush tropical vegetation. Across the 'valley' drifted music, played by invisible musicians hidden in a shrubbery.

The only entrance to this secret paradise was through the king's private apartments, and invitations from Ludwig were very rare, even for members of the royal family. Precisely because it was so private, everyone was desperate to see it, and, in the words of

The winter garden at the Royal Palace of Laeken, Belgium. Designed by Auguste Balat, and built of iron in 1876, it is an interesting contrast with its exact contemporary, the Horticultural Hall in Philadelphia, illustrated on page 150, and with the glass houses in Florence, on page 146, Copenhagen and Lyons.

Winfried Ranke, *eminent men dressed themselves as gardener's assistants in order to look at the splendour of the winter garden forbidden to them ...*[7]

There is a breath-taking description of it by the Spanish Infanta Maria de la Paz, bride of Prince Ludwig Ferdinand of Bohemia. They were invited to dine by King Ludwig in 1883: *We went on a simple wooden bridge over a floodlit lake and saw between chestnut trees an Indian city in front of us ... We came to a blue silk tent covered with roses. In it was a chair supported by two carved elephants, and in front of it lay a lionskin ... The dinner had been laid out in an attached round pavilion behind a Moorish arch. The king showed me to the place of honour and gently rang a bell. Out of the hidden recess there immediately appeared a lackey, bowing deeply. This man was to be seen only when serving and removing the food, and when the king summoned him. From my seat I saw beyond the arch splendid plants lit by different-coloured lights while invisible choirs sang softly. Suddenly a rainbow appeared. 'My God', I exclaimed involuntarily, 'This is indeed a dream ...'*[8]

For a royal botanical collection, for architectural diversity, for sheer quantity of glass houses, nothing can match the glass houses at the royal palace of Laeken in Belgium. They were the much loved

hobby of King Leopold II, who came to the throne in 1865 at the age of thirty. There was already an orangery, and also a round hot-house with a crown on top built at Laeken in 1859 for the prized *Victoria amazonica*; this has since been moved to the botanic garden at Meise. Leopold continued the gardening tradition, both inside and out, by extending the gardens, and started on a glass-house building programme of staggering proportions. By the time he was finished the area under glass totalled nearly five acres, and the length of paths and passageways through the maze of buildings reached one mile. Care of this abundant collection was entrusted to the head gardener, Mr Knight, formerly of Floors Castle in Roxburghshire.

The layout is a labyrinth of flower corridors and stairs that link the orangery, a dining room and tiny theatre, the winter garden, the Congo House, and specialist houses for camellias, rhododendrons, azaleas, palms, orchids, ferns and so on. Leopold's interest in such plants is partly explained by his travels before he became king. Just as English gentlemen had found inspiration for things European on the Grand Tour, Leopold had travelled through north Africa, India and China, where he had seen many of these flowers growing naturally. He had also invested in the Congo in central Africa, to the extent that the country was virtually his private colony. He financed the tropical gardens with his immense revenues from the Congo, which also supplied a harvest of plants.

Most of the buildings at Laeken are curvilinear or have curving roofs above straight glass walls. The main palm house is dominated by a huge projecting rotunda; nearby is the *serre chapelle,* a round glass chapel, with a dome surrounded by eight attendant side chapels; this was built in 1886 and was used for religious services, until converted to a swimming pool in the twentieth century by Leopold III. The passages led past the smaller specialist houses to the sizeable Congo House, through the palm corridor and on to the winter garden. This was, and still is, the most handsome of all the glass houses, and was used for court entertainments. It was designed by Auguste Balat, the Belgian state architect, and built in 1876. The diameter measures some 222 feet, 76 feet wider than the Kibble Palace, and the height is 111 feet. Like the Kibble Palace, it is a three-tiered glass dome with clerestories between the tiers; the outline is completed by a crown. Unlike Kibble's building, however, there are no internal columns, since the entire structure is supported by wrought-iron roof trusses, pierced and decorated with flowing scrolls to make a pleasing mix of strength with beauty. Twin adjacent chimneys look like minarets.

King Leopold enjoyed the peace of the conservatories. He built a small pavilion at the end of the long flowered corridors and repaired there eagerly when morning audiences were over. It was there that he died in 1909.

The royal glass houses at Laeken are beautifully maintained; they house a magnificent collection of plants and include the famed flower corridors, ablaze with climbing geraniums. They are open to the public once a year in May.

Flower passages at the Royal Palace of Laeken link the main glass houses, and here pale pink flowers of a pair of medinillas are offset by the subtle green of the paintwork.

Private Pleasure Domes

From the 1850s onwards, private conservatories were a normal part of upper- and middle-class life. They were usually attached to the house, except in a few spectacular cases such as Enville Hall in Staffordshire, and they always had glass roofs. Most were kept at a temperature of between 45 and 55° F in winter, although of course on sunny days they rapidly heated up to the seventies, losing heat quickly as soon as the sun disappeared. They were either supplied by the growing number of professional conservatory manufacturers, or designed by an architect to blend with the house. Examples of architects' conservatories are much more prolific between 1850 and 1870 than in the following decades, when manufacturers took over the lion's share of the market.

Flintham Hall in Nottinghamshire has a good example of an architect-designed conservatory. It was designed by T. C. Hine and built in 1853 for T. B. Thoroton Hildyard, great-grandfather of the present owner. Built of stone, the dominant influence is Italian, but the cast-iron and glass barrel roof, 30 feet high, is a clear reminder of the Crystal Palace. Inside is a small, highly decorated Italianate balcony, leading from the upper floor of the library. Climbers and a mimosa tree occupy the full height of the building.

The most enticing approach is from the library, from which a marble fountain is seen through three arched windows and an arched door. Green leaves of every hue and every shape grow here now, amongst trailing geraniums, agapanthus and plumbago, mimosa and *Tecoma stans,* and brilliant bird of paradise flowers, *Strelitzia reginae.* In spite of minimal heat in winter – the temperature is now kept only just above freezing and it is doubtful if it was ever much hotter because of the great height – the conservatory is colourful at all seasons and exciting in its jungly way.

On a much grander scale was the winter garden at Somerleyton Hall in Suffolk. The term winter garden had crept into English from the French and German, but was much less used than the word conservatory, particularly in the private context. The building at Somerleyton was, however, grand by any standards, and doubtless justified a more pretentious name. It had been built for Morton Peto, a Victorian industrialist who had made his fortune building railways. Peto, a colleague of Joseph Paxton, was a member of parliament and was created a baronet in 1855. A young architect called John Thomas was employed to remodel the house from 1846 onwards, and Thomas is generally thought to have been responsible for the winter garden too. It was a remarkable Italianate building, in keeping with Thomas's alterations to the house, with arched windows in a richly decorated stone façade. The glass roof was made up of curved ridges and dominated by a soaring dome. No expense was spared in contents and effects, since Sir Morton was naturally extravagant. Eventually this extravagance caught up with him, and in 1861 he was forced to sell Somerleyton. A catalogue prepared for a proposed auction of the house and estate contains a

The barrel-roofed conservatory at Kilruddery Castle, Ireland, was built c.1850. It follows the tradition of centuries in displaying sculpture as well as plants.

glowing description of the winter garden: *a magnificent structure, unsurpassed by anything of its kind in Europe. A crystal building in the Renaissance style with mosque dome.*

Another account of it in 1872 describes the interior as having a pool some 50 feet wide, with a dolphin fountain that threw water 50 feet up into the dome. *Cool-house ferns ornament the base of this tasteful display of waterworks ... The roof of this wintergarden is supported by light iron columns, all of which are covered with climbers, such as Passifloras, Kennedyas, Fuchsias, Tecomas, Lapagerias, Tacsonias, Mandevillas, &c; trellises along the sides of the house in front of the glass, and also the rafters, are covered with the same elegant drapery. From the roof are suspended ornamental wire-baskets filled with plants of a suitable character.*[9]

There was also a palm house at Somerleyton, which was kept at a higher temperature of 65° F or more, with tropical palms and bananas and yet more climbing plants. These included thunbergias, hoyas and allamandas, trained on trellises so that they hung down in graceful festoons. Both the winter garden and palm house were heated by just one boiler, which apparently never broke down. Like the Great Conservatory at Chatsworth, the winter garden could not survive the effects of war, and it was demolished in 1915.

The other special feature of Somerleyton is the range of ridge and furrow greenhouses designed by Joseph Paxton for the walled kitchen garden. A rare remaining example of Paxton's idea, these are in excellent condition, and used for vines and white peaches.

The winter garden at Somerleyton, built about 1850 and demolished in 1915. The Italianate exterior was decorated with many devices, while the interior was packed with exotic flowers. Curved glass vaulting was appropriately chosen for the roof surrounding the giant dome.

Ferneries were becoming popular at this time. One of the earliest purpose-built ferneries, still standing, is at Tatton Park in Cheshire. It has high brick walls and a glass roof, and is thought to have been designed by Joseph Paxton for the Egerton family, and built in 1859. Their cousins, the Egertons of Ashridge Park in Hertfordshire, had a fernery designed by Matthew Digby Wyatt and built in 1864. It is a remarkable and attractive building, newly restored. In America, a fine example of a fernery can still be seen at the Morris Arboretum of the University of Pennsylvania, built in 1899 to the design of John Morris, in consultation with J. and W. Birkenhead of Manchester, England.

Lutyens's orangery at Hestercombe, which dates from 1910, is a step backwards in time to the end of the seventeenth century. It is much more elaborate, with rusticated stonework, blank niches and medallions and a much smaller ratio of glass to wall than its contemporaries. The final word came from Clough Williams-Ellis, in a greenhouse built at Plas Brondanw in Wales, in 1914. Short in length but tall, it is immensely solid, built of local rough-hewn stone with three arched windows, above which is an upper floor with three small oval windows, and another octagon window in the hipped roof. This is a garden ornament in the eighteenth-century tradition, set in a terraced garden flavoured with Renaissance Italy, and built by an eccentric architect as war was about to overtake Europe.

Lutyens built this orangery at Hestercombe in 1910, one of the last of a long distinguished line.

Matthew Digby Wyatt's fernery at Ashridge Park was built in 1864, and has recently undergone a total restoration. Whether called fernery, orangery or conservatory, this style of stone and glass building was highly fashionable in the 1850s–1870s. Other examples are at Holkham Hall, Wimpole Hall and Westonbirt.

A twisting path in the fernery at Tatton Park, built in 1859.

The alternative to employing an architect to design a conservatory was to buy one of the products of conservatory manufacturers. Conservatories were so fashionable that a growing band of companies was entering an expanding, highly competitive market. Gray, Ormson and Brown, Cottam and Hallen, J. Weeks, J. Watts, Boulton and Paul, T. C. Messenger, Cranstons, James Boyd, W. H. Lascelles, MacFarlanes of Glasgow, Richardsons of Darlington, and Mackenzie and Moncur were the major companies that advertised in gardening journals; the only one to survive the shattering effects of two wars has been Richardsons of Darlington, which now trades under the name of Amdega.

Messrs Gray and Ormson (Brown had already departed) were responsible for the most original of mid-Victorian conservatories at Enville Hall in Staffordshire. It was built for the Earl and Countess of Stamford and Warrington, and was completed by 1864. Enville Hall had an enormous and elaborate garden, and this was its most astonishing feature. A mad confusion of Gothic windows, pinnacled towers and Saracenic domes separated by low, barrelled arches reminiscent of railway stations, it was a magnificent, even monstrous plant folly which unhappily no longer exists.

Up to the end of the century, cast iron was in greater demand than timber. The Victorians' compulsive passion for decoration was well met by mass-produced moulded metal. Elegance was more important than price, nor did upkeep influence people in favour of wood. Iron requires more maintenance than wood, since moist air corrodes metal fast, and the chemical fertilizers of today compound the problem; glass is broken by the expansion and contraction of a metal frame; and being a good conductor of heat, metal loses more heat than timber. About the turn of the century, wood was used more frequently in conjunction with metal, or else used on its own with cast-iron trimmings.

As far as hot-houses in kitchen gardens were concerned, wood was always the preferred material. The length and extent of these ranges in private ownership on both sides of the Atlantic were often amazing. They were built to control nature, to hoodwink plants into producing fruit when normally they would be resting or dormant. From them were supplied grapes for the table for eight months of the year, cut flowers such as roses and carnations for the house in winter, bedding plants and regular stock for the garden and conservatory, as well as vegetables and tropical fruit.

The extravagance of the Victorian age was astonishing. Lord Egremont described how his grandfather had a stove house built to grow bananas, purely because a friend said that the fruit tasted much better if eaten straight from the tree. *The banana tree was splendid. My grandfather took a lively interest in its progress until, lo and behold, it fructified. 'I will have that banana for dinner tonight', he said as soon as the banana was ripe. And so he did — amid a deathly hush. All were agog. The head gardener himself, controlling a great department of the estate, was not too proud to be there, concealed behind a screen between the dining room and the serving room. Even the groom of the chambers broke the habit of a lifetime and turned up sober to watch the event.*

The banana was brought in on a lordly dish. My grandfather peeled it with a golden knife. He then cut a sliver off and, with a golden fork, put it in his mouth and carefully tasted it. Whereupon he flung dish, plate, knife, fork and banana on to the floor and shouted, 'Oh God, it tastes just like any other damn banana!' Banana tree and all were ordered to be destroyed. My famous old gardener, Mr. Fred Streeter, told me that the banana cost my grandfather some £3,000.[10]

The conservatory at Broughton Hall, built for Sir Charles Tempest in 1854 by Andrews and Delauney, is attached to the house and projects into pleasure grounds landscaped by W. A. Nesfield.

A conservatory designed by Ormson and exhibited in 1862. Apart from cast-iron decoration applied by the yard like lace, its swivelling curved windows are an interesting feature.

The conservatory at Glenbervie House is set above a kitchen garden and protected by a shelter-belt of trees. In the central pavilion, which has a staged arrangement of flowering plants, is a little garden seat surrounded by cascades of plumbago and mimosa.

In addition to private individuals, manufacturers also supplied to parks departments, and to the nurserymen in the horticultural industry; then, as the therapeutic value of warm sunlight and flowers, especially in a northern climate, was established, the demand came from hotels and hydropathics, from sanitoriums and asylums. More surprisingly, winter gardens were exported to Durban in South Africa and Lahore in India. It was all big business.

The manufacturers were working on a few basic window shapes and units, which were simply adapted to suit customers' require-

ments. The basic formula did not change much between 1850 and 1920, except that brick bases, between two and three feet high, became more common at the end of the century. Curves were still in favour, principally for the roof. Domes that curved down to the ground were outmoded by the turn of the century, because this usually meant using curved glass, which was tiresome to replace when broken. In the 1870s companies such as Cranstons made a positive attempt to give the curved look with flat glass, by hanging panes in their sash bars on a circular tiered frame, as in the camellia house at Nettlecomb in Somerset. The effect was not nearly as graceful as with curved glass, but flat glass was a good selling point. MacFarlanes made a particular point of showing how they could construct in flat glass a cast-iron dome, half-dome or barrel roof, by scalloping each small pane of glass.

By the early twentieth century most companies had given up curved roofs except in domes; straight roofs, with opening lights for ventilation, were embellished with lantern ridges and topped with cast-iron cresting in a variety of patterns. Moncrieffs of Edinburgh offered a most attractive cresting of thistles interspersed with stars, which can still be seen at the conservatory at Glenbervie House in Kincardineshire. Because the outline shape was more simple, more angular, cresting and brackets and any other cast-iron trimmings became more elaborate. One late example of a restrained curved roof was at Fairlawne in Kent; Mackenzie and Moncur supplied a barrelled roof with lantern for a stone façade.

There was also a tendency, such as at Enville Hall, to mix architectural shapes and styles. In a large building the mixture might be carried off successfully, but many a small private conservatory ended up as an architectural House of Horrors. Richardsons of Darlington was responsible for one of the worst examples, with eight different shapes and sizes of glass, set in wood, within a façade some 18 feet wide. There were other disasters, such as the lean-to conservatory built at Swarland Hall in Northumberland for John Woods, where the glazed roof was built around the columns of the portico, a glass carbuncle on the face of an elegant Georgian house.

Reading the brochures of the major manufacturers, one is tempted to think that in late Victorian and Edwardian days the country must have been half-covered with glass houses. These brochures are fascinating social documents, since each company named a selection of its clients, a list which reads like an extract from *Who's Who*. Over a period of many years Richardsons of Darlington built up a client list of well over six hundred names. It started with Her Majesty's Government, followed by HRH Princess Louise at Osborne, Isle of Wight, eight dukes, twenty-four earls, twenty-three town corporations, dozens of colonels and rectors, and finished with a Mrs Wynne of Ystrad Cottage in Denbigh.[11]

The conservatory at Sennowe Park, built as a ballroom by Messenger and Co. in 1907.

I love a still conservatory
That's full of giant, breathless palms,
Azaleas, clematis and vines
Whose quietness great Trees becalms
Filling the air with foliage,
A curved and dreamy statuary . . .

Still as a great jewel is the air
With boughs and leaves smooth-carved in it,
And rocks and trees and giant ferns,
And blooms with inner radiance lit,
And naked water like a nymph
That dances tireless, slim and bare.

W. J. Turner, 'Magic', 1916

The Victorian conservatory or winter garden, in Britain and America, was part of the house; it was crammed with plants, just as the drawing room was crammed with furniture. Hardy species, such as roses, lilac and clematis, were planted in pots and forced to flower in winter and early spring, and in the autumn cyclamen and huge-headed chrysanthemums took pride of place. It was a jewel casket of brilliant hues, where biggest or rarest was thought to be best. Frequently the combinations were gaudy and tasteless, especially where bedding plants were concerned. James Shirley Hibberd, writing in 1875, observed that *the less we see of bedding plants in the conservatory the better.*[12] Hibberd also advised that *mere display is above all things to be avoided, for the mind needs food of a better sort than colour simply, however strong in tone and perfect in combinations.*

To this vibrant array of foliage and flowers, the Victorians added further decoration. Pots for flowers were carved or glazed, and elegant *étagères* were filled with rows of showy blooms. Flagstones, as used in greenhouses for two hundred years, were overlaid with tiles, sometimes arranged in two alternate colours but more often in elaborate Italian or Moorish patterns. Cast-iron grilles covering hot-water pipes were stamped with swirls and squares; cast-iron columns were twisted, grooved, garlanded or made classical with capitals; flowery baskets hung from curling brackets; fountains and statues completed the decoration.

Skilled labour was plentiful, and so was time. Any plant that was not successful was removed, and replaced with an alternative from the greenhouse or hot-house; no wonder that the specimens in old photographs look strong and healthy. At Woodhall in Lanarkshire the gardener was scolded if there were not more than a thousand blooms out at once on a venerable old double white camellia.

The day started early in the conservatory and winter gardens, since watering, spraying and general care had to be completed before the master and his family came downstairs. Everything had to be made perfect, and by invisible hands. Kenneth Lemmon described how gardening magazines proposed hidden doors for the gardener, so that he could disappear rapidly should a member of the family appear; a trap door was also suggested. Lemmon continued: *One can imagine the scene — abandon ship, her Ladyship approaches — and the gardener and his boy, who were busy watering and tending to the plants, do a reverse of Venus rising from the waves as they sink through the ferns.*[13]

The secret of success lay partly in good ventilation. The Victorian glass house always had opening flaps near ground level and plenty of opening lights in the roof, as well as several doors, so that there was a flow of air through the building on hot days. Robert Thompson advised that architects should always consult with cultivators, in order to avoid *a vegetable charnel house.* Roof ventilation was particularly important, since without it the temperature *quickly*

RE-POTTING.

rises to a dangerous and exciting degree, when comes the scalding and consequent disfigurement.[14] Shading with canvas or roller-blinds helped to reduce high temperatures, and shade was also supplied by planting tall, sun-tolerant trees, such as yuccas, palms and araucarias, under which other plants could nestle.

It is one of the paradoxes of many a Victorian conservatory that a building designed to catch the sun was turned into a gloomy place by dense planting. A thick canopy of overhead foliage certainly helped to give both shade and the jungle atmosphere, but denied the attraction of sunlight. The darkness, however, brought its own excitement. The very lushness of the vegetation, the dimness of the shadows, the warm heavy-scented air, and the twisting, turning paths were ideal for romance. Proposals of marriage – and perhaps others too – were thought appropriately made in the conservatory, a sensuous haven in the strict Victorian household. How propitious the big conservatories must have been for amorous young men; and how understandable that young ladies should discover a sudden, overpowering interest in botany.

His Majesty King Edward VII at Eastwell House, 2 July 1904.
Back row, from the left: Lady Norreys, Hon. Mrs George Keppel, Mr L. de Rothschild, Hon. H. Milner, Hon. H. Legge, Sir Ernest Cassel.
2nd row: Mrs L. de Rothschild, Lord Gerard, Marquis de Soveril, Countess Mar and Kellie, Earl of Mar and Kellie, Hon. Mrs Lowther.
Centre: Baroness de Forest, His Majesty King Edward VII (centre), Lady Gerard, Lord Charles Montague.
Front row: Baron de Forest, Master A. Lowther, Master Edmonstone, Miss Gosselin, Count Mensdorff, Lady Maud Warrender.

If romance is associated with conservatories, afternoon tea is synonymous with them. For much of the year, when the garden was too chilly, the conservatory was used for that very English pastime of eating cucumber sandwiches, buttered scones and sponge cake while drinking China tea. The 6th Earl of Harrowby recalled that when he was a small boy at the turn of the century, tea was always served in the conservatory at Sandon Hall in Staffordshire on Sunday afternoons in winter. *My mother and the other ladies dressed for it as if they were in the tropics, in long spotted muslins with flowing ribbons. The conservatory was kept so hot because it was full of exotic plants, strong scented crotons, beautifully coloured tropical flowers (no camellias then, it was too hot), bananas and oranges (though these only fruited occasionally) and palms.*[15]

The typical Victorian and Edwardian conservatories were confident and usually well ordered, whatever their size, cherished with devotion and hard cash, and conformed to an accepted pattern. A notable, eccentric exception was the crystal cavern, under ground and under water, at Lea Park in Surrey, built in 1895 for Whitaker Wright, a financier who invested, appropriately, in mining companies. *On the lawn, by the lake side, is to be seen a little erection sheltering the head of a spiral staircase. Descending the stairs one comes to a subway, 400 feet long, lighted by rows of electric lamps. The passage, which is wide enough for four people to walk abreast, leads into a great chamber of glass 80 feet in height — a beautiful conservatory with a wondrous mosaic floor, settees and chairs, palms and little tables.*

It is a wonderful place — a fairy palace. In summer it is delightfully cool — in winter delightfully warm, for the temperature is always fairly even. Outside the clear crystal glass is a curtain of green water — deep, beautiful green at the bottom, fading away to the palest, faintest green at the top, where little white wavelets ripple. Goldfish come and press their faces against the glass, peering at you with strangely magnified eyes. On summer nights one looks through the green water at the stars and the moon, which appear extraordinarily bright and large, for they are magnified quite ten times by the curved glass and the water.

This submerged fairy-room with appendages cost fully £20,000. It was built, of course, with the utmost care — for if one of the square panes of three-inch glass should break, the place would be filled with water in five minutes.[16]

Whitaker Wright did not enjoy his magic cavern for long. He was arrested on charges of fraud, tried, found guilty and sentenced to prison, but swallowed cyanide before leaving the courtroom. The house, renamed Witley Park, has since been demolished, but the underwater conservatory is still intact, a tribute to an unknown architect and structural engineer.

In the Conservatory *by Edouard Manet (1832–83)*

President and People

Americans were urged by many writers to enjoy the refreshing pleasure of conservatories, which were *probably the most important garden structures used in ornamental gardening,* according to the garden architect R. B. Leuchars in 1851.[17] *A conservatory is to be considered an absolute necessity in connection with the 'Home of Taste',* wrote James Shirley Hibberd in 1856. For A. J. Downing, the conservatory was a necessity for the plant lover, enabling him to enjoy an endless chain of bloom from autumn to spring.

The much read Gervase Wheeler in his *Rural Homes* of 1851–52 advocated the design of *a little gem of a room — if octagonal, or oval, or quaintly cornered, so much the better — for the lady of the house . . . let it have the sunniest aspect — the most charming prospect . . . a plant cabinet or ombra.* Designed for contemplation, relaxation or recreation, the conservatory was undeniably ornamental, either through construction or by the elegant arrangement of plants within its glass walls. Throughout the nineteenth century cautionary or catchy phrases such as Frank Fawkes's maxim: *Ornament the construction, never construct the ornament,* indicated that the dictum of good taste was not being followed by the builders of conservatories.

Americans could also follow the example of the White House. *Of all the rooms in the White House which possess an interest to strangers there is none in which a pleasant hour may be spent to better advantage than in Miss Lane's conservatory,* reported Frank Leslie in his *Illustrated Newspaper* of 1858. Built by President Buchanan for his niece and official hostess, Harriet Lane, this conservatory communicated directly with the long entrance hall and with the formal dining room. Its contents and impressions invariably echoed the fashionable trends at mid-century: orange and lemon trees, prickly cactus plants, aloes, camellias, spireas, South American pitcher plants, and wandering vines crawling along the wooden rafters, breaking the rigidity of this long simple building, and all bathed in the *penetrating fragrance of some South American island.* For state occasions the conservatory would be thrown open, creating an enchanting vista. One of the three gardeners of the conservatories was often called upon to arrange a special floral piece from the bounty under glass; such arrangements might be a *goddess of liberty* for the judiciary or a *ship of state* for the diplomats.

By 1890 the western side of the White House was completely obscured by more and more conservatories built by successive first ladies. So inspired was Mrs Harrison, an avid orchid grower, that

she engaged the architect Fred D. Owen to redesign a conservatory which stretched across the south lawn, paralleling and indeed hiding the garden front of the White House. Thankfully this cyclopean project was never realized, and all the greenhouses were demolished at the turn of the century as part of Stanford White's infamous renovation of the executive mansion.

A striking contrast with Miss Lane's pleasant yet predictable conservatory was the flamboyant edifice of Samuel Colt. Soon after Colt purchased land in 1854 for his mill along the Connecticut River south of Hartford, he began developing his suburban estate, named Armsmear. On it were greenhouses totalling 2,634 feet in length which produced pineapples, strawberries, bananas and every other kind of exotic fruit in profusion, and a long grapery interrupted by octagonal pavilions with decorative coloured glass panels and Victorian garden benches and chairs inside. The most striking architectural feature of Mr Colt's property was, however, the glass and iron Moorish conservatory overlooking the garden.

Originally erected on the front side of the house, this intricate feathery structure was incorporated into a much bolder statement at the back. A sweeping verandah began on the east side, wrapping

Miss Lane's Conservatory, The White House, 1858. Judging from contemporary impressions, the colourful prize plants from all over the globe more than compensated for the plainness of the structure.

Armsmear, home of the inventor of the Colt revolver, Samuel Colt. The house and its highly ornate conservatory are a bizarre mixture of Italian and Moorish influences.

Mark Twain's Conservatory at Hartford was sketched by the American Impressionist painter, Childe Hassam, in 1896.

itself around the octagonal tower with its open filigree ogee dome, and ended on the west side of the much larger Italianate observatory. Six-foot plate glass panels were set into a façade of cast-iron frames of Moorish arches, minarets and pinnacles; a central circular bay crowned by another ogee arch dome and a golden pineapple shielded the Triton fountain, whose sprays of water emitted a rainbow of colour. The iron tracery was painted in brilliant colours, red, yellow and purple-blue, an idea Colt may have gleaned from the two Crystal Palaces at which he exhibited in 1851 and 1853. Sunlight and temperature were controlled by blinds and underground flues, and in the evening the conservatory was lit by chandeliers sprouting from porcelain flowers. The impression must have been of a scene from the *Arabian Nights*.

Not far from Armsmear is a smaller but no less authentic nineteenth-century conservatory attached to the house that Samuel Clemens (Mark Twain) built in 1874 at Nook Farm on the western edge of Hartford. The New York architect Edward Tuckerman Potter, who also worked for Colt, designed a multi-faceted and bracketed Victorian mansion in the 'brick and stick' style. In keeping with the accepted tenets of Downing and Vaux, he included a polygonal conservatory off the library; it was entered through double sliding doors *fitted with slightly ornamental glass, so as to decrease the monotony of effect that would otherwise occur, while enough clear glass is left to give a good view of flowers.*[18]

Its ambience captivated both writers and artists. William Dean Howells, editor of *The Atlantic Monthly* and frequent visitor to Nook Farm, wrote: *The plants are set in the ground, and the flowering vines climbed up the sides and overhung the roof above the silent spray of a fountain companied by callas and other water-loving lilies. There, while we breakfasted, Patrick came in from the barn and sprinkled the pretty bower, which poured out its responsive perfume in the delicate accents of its varied blossoms ... In the midst of these luxuriant exotics ... and under the glass ceilings hangs a large cage in which a pair of California quail of brilliant plumage spend a brief period of happy captivity.* Childe Hassam also visited the house and chose to sketch the conservatory; a record of his impression appeared in *Harper's Monthly* in May 1896.

The lure of exotica was to capture the imaginations of two men of business whose glass conservatories stand today as symbols of an era and of the frontier achievements which helped to construct them. The Conservatory of Flowers, which is now part of Golden Gate Park in San Francisco, was originally one of two large conservatories ordered by the wealthy entrepreneur, James Lick, before 1876. Lick died that year before the glass, wood and iron structures could be built. Under the terms of an intricate trust, the California Academy of Science and the Society of California Pioneers received its residual property, which included crates containing the greenhouses. These in turn were sold to a group of wealthy city fathers and were then offered to the city of San Francisco. Frederick Lord, founder of Lord and Burnham, was engaged to erect the jigsaw puzzle, which he finished in 1879. Legend states that the greenhouses were ordered from England and shipped around Cape Horn in a chartered vessel, but the identity of the manufacturer or designer has not surfaced; identification was further complicated by a fire in January 1883, which caused alterations to be made to the building and the raising of the dome on to a taller drum.

Unique features of the conservatory are the projecting gables on its central curvilinear roof, stained-glass windows along the first-storey cornice, square Gothic corner towers and Oriental roof-line. The second conservatory found its way to the Crocker family who assembled it on their Sacramento estate. Similar in design to its sibling in San Francisco, it also resembles the tall Palm House in Druid Hill Park, Baltimore, built a few years later. It is no longer standing.

The origin of the first conservatory and greenhouse at Lyndhurst, designed in the popular 'E' layout, has also perplexed scholars. In 1864 a successful New York merchant, George Merritt, purchased a small Pointed Gothic villa on the Hudson River, designed in 1838 by A. J. Davis, whom he called upon to enlarge the house in 1865. By 1870, Merritt had built a large conservatory in the curvilinear style, with its wooden frames rising from low sash windows. The central conservatory was distinguished by a Moorish watch tower, capped by a ribbon onion dome in glass, not unlike the blue and gold starred Saracenic dome guarding Colt's mill at Armsmear. Merritt died in 1873, and his tremendous collection of exotica was sold at auction, a common practice in the nineteenth century. After several years the estate was purchased by the railroad tycoon and plant enthusiast, Jay Gould, who proceeded to revitalize Mr Merritt's 'folly'. Unfortunately the Merritt conservatory and greenhouses were destroyed by fire in December 1880.

On the same site and following the foundations of the older houses, Gould immediately began to reconstruct a new conservatory with the help of an architect, possibly J. W. Walter of Pugin and Walter, and the ubiquitous Lord and Burnham. According to Lord and Burnham in a later catalogue, this was the first time they had substituted cast-iron gutters and sills and iron framing for wood. The 376-foot-long conservatory was painted a pale yellow with chocolate brown trim, similar to the colour chosen for the Druid Hill Park Palm House. It stands today, glassless and bare-ribbed.

One of the most collectable of greenhouse plants at this time was the night blooming cereus, and those at Lyndhurst were the pride of Gould's heiress daughter, Helen Gould. A feature article on Lyndhurst in *The New York Tribune* Sunday supplement of 15 June 1902 described the reporter's own encounter with the cereus. Whereas in the previous year the cereus bore over 400 blossoms, 120 opening in one night alone, that June only four blossoms had appeared. Knowing that guests were due the same evening, the gardener ignored Miss Gould's order to cut two of her choicest blooms for the photographer and reporter. Her reprimand was so strong that he hastily returned to the greenhouse and cut the flowers. The journalist also recorded the Lyndhurst collections of orchids, carnations, ferns and other exotica as well as its alligators lounging in the water basin in the centre of the main house.

Lyndhurst is the archetypal example of the American country house which bridges two periods and two philosophies in the development of the American country estate in the second half of the nineteenth century. On the one hand, it was a country suburban retreat built on the precepts of Downing and Davis, a Gothic villa in a picturesque landscape. On the other hand, Lyndhurst introduces the golden age grandeur of American estate building. Beaux-arts palaces replace Gothic villas, huge winter gardens and grander greenhouses replace the quaint conservatories and show houses of the Civil War, and the contemplation of nature is to be observed from the gold-encrusted drawing rooms of the new rich, not from those rustic adornments quietly hidden among groves of specimen trees.

The first conservatory at Lyndhurst, known as Merritt's Folly, was built of wood in 1870 and destroyed by fire in 1880. Its unique central onion dome tower was not replaced when Jay Gould employed Lord and Burnham to build its cast-iron replacement, illustrated below. During the winter months when Mr Gould was alive, hundreds of orchids from the new greenhouse were sent down to his New York townhouse. Now in a ruinous state, its restoration is planned.

There was no larger family of country-house builders than the Vanderbilts, no better example of a late nineteenth-century baronial seat than Biltmore in North Carolina, and no comparable area of the country where these estates were concentrated than New York's Long Island. During a period which lasted only one generation, from the Gay Nineties to the outbreak of the First World War, the new and not so new industrial barons built Beaux-arts châteaux, Italian Renaissance palazzi, Tudor manors and Georgian mansions along America's 'Gold Coasts'. Whether summer retreats, sporting lodges or suburban residences, their would-be 'English' country estates had the inevitable ranges of conservatories, palm houses and greenhouses; and incorporated into the floor plan of the palazzo would be at least one room set aside for exotic plants, palms or seasonal potted treasures from the greenhouses.

Upon the death of Commodore Vanderbilt in 1877, the bulk of his fortune – the largest in America – was inherited by his fifty-six-year-old son, William Henry Vanderbilt, with smaller legacies bequeathed to William Henry's sons: Cornelius II, William Kissam I, Frederick William and George Washington II. No sooner had the old patriarch surrendered his well-guarded wealth and control of the Penn Central railroad than William Henry began planning his new mansion at 640 Fifth Avenue between 51st and 52nd Streets, planned by the popular New York firm of interior designers, Herter Brothers, and assisted by the architect J. B. Snook. Begun in December 1879, this masterpiece of opulence and splendour, at whose heart was a richly decorated atrium, was completed in January 1882.

Not unlike Mark Twain's more modest conservatory, there were steps down from the picture gallery to a room ornamented in an oriental style: lanterns hung from a ceiling of clear and coloured glass, and a brightly patterned tessera floor was edged with potted palms and exotics. The overall effect of this grandiose plan must have made a lasting impression on his sons, as they were all quick to emulate their father.

The architect who enjoyed the patronage of these superlatively rich brothers was Richard Morris Hunt. Hunt, dubbed 'the Vanderbilt architect', was the first American to study at the Ecole des Beaux-Arts in Paris, where he was enrolled for almost eight years from 1846 to 1854. Among his many student projects was a beautiful series of eleven designs for a square winter garden; it was enclosed in a shell of glass and iron, with semicircular apses on three sides and a long baroque masonry vestibule on the fourth. The influence of the Crystal Palace, which Hunt had visited a few months before, was unmistakable, and these designs anticipated the inclusion of similar structures in his later commissions. Hunt returned to New York in 1855, setting up his own atelier which could design buildings in a polyglot of styles. His reputation soared.

From 1876 onwards, Hunt's Vanderbilt commissions included town and country houses for William Kissam I and The Breakers in Newport, Rhode Island, for Cornelius II. Yet Hunt's most important work must be the country estate he designed for their brother, George Washington Vanderbilt II, at Biltmore.

The youngest and perhaps the most intellectual, George was also the only Vanderbilt brother who grew up in the splendours of 640 Fifth Avenue. At the age of twenty-five, he engaged Hunt to design his baronial estate, not in Newport or even Long Island, but on a precipice overlooking the Great Smoky Mountains in Western North Carolina, a spot he may have chosen to benefit his fragile health. Guiding him in his venture were Hunt and the equally sagacious Frederick Law Olmsted.

Biltmore was officially christened on Christmas Eve 1895, but several years passed before it was finished. At the core of this Loire valley château is an octagonal winter garden, sunk below an open gallery, from which radiate the billiard room, the banqueting hall, family dining room, morning salon and music room. Even the vista from the library and tapestry gallery on the other side of the entrance hall terminates with the winter garden. Delicate ferns, palms and potted seasonal flowers, French bamboo furniture and the graceful Karl Bidder sculpture fountain are in sharp contrast to the medieval hammer-beam rafters. Rising from the limestone piers of the gallery and the heavy timber mullions is a tall, double-tiered glass roof, with ventilator sashes in the upper tier, giving an even loftier feeling to this princely space. The tubs and plants are brought into the winter garden by a trap door in the marble floor – as advised in gardening magazines – to avoid the need for gardeners to pass through the principal reception rooms.

Below the terrace, with its magnificent view to the Smoky Mountains, are the shrub garden, walled garden and rose garden, the end of which is dominated by a red brick conservatory and adjoining greenhouses. From Biltmore's extensive archive of plans and correspondence, it appears that much of the technical work on these greenhouses and other nursery buildings on the estate was carried out by both Hitchings and Lord and Burnham. Olmsted's plan evokes an English baroque garden scheme, crowned by an orangery of the William and Mary type. This, however, having a glass roof, is a palm and exotic house, behind which are the greenhouses which supply it and the winter garden.

Though Biltmore soon became a financial albatross and was virtually abandoned by George Washington Vanderbilt after 1903, it epitomized at the time the golden age of American estate building. As Olmsted's son wrote in 1895, *Whether we think with some that it and the whole estate are un-American and out of accord with our nineteenth century feeling and civilization, or whether we think with others that this marks the beginning of an era of great American country places and country houses, we must at least accept it as a great Work of Art … At all events it stands as the best work ever done by the leading architect of the country,*[19] encouraged and aided by the consummate landscape architect of his day.

Previous page:
George Washington Vanderbilt's octagonal
Wintergarden at Biltmore, completed 1895.

The conservatory at Pembroke, Captain
DeLamar's estate on Long Island, was a
tropical extravaganza under glass. The gazebo
island was set in a swimming pool and
surrounded by a horticultural museum. One
of the last great glass fantasies, it was demolished
in 1968, fifty years after its completion.

Indeed, Biltmore was just the beginning. No area of the country was more attractive or susceptible to the footprints of the entrepreneurial élite than the white sandy shores and flat Dutch farmlands of Long Island – conducive to sailing, riding, polo and, of course, to gardening.

In April of 1899, flames besieged William Kissam Vanderbilt I's country house at Oakdale, Idlehour, where his daughter Consuelo and her husband, the Duke of Marlborough, had spent their honeymoon a few years before. Plans for its replacement were immediately drafted by Hunt's son, Richard Howland Hunt. The design was for a modern Carolinian brick and stone house with one distinguishing feature: a large conservatory attached at right angles to one corner of an inner cloister. It was a rectangular building with apsidal projections defined by decorative masonry pillars and bays of long slender sheets of glass in lunar windows. Paradoxically, it evokes a building of architectonic substance delicately faceted with crystals. Contemporary photographs show a conventional

interior with palms and ferns, large Oriental hanging lanterns and bamboo furniture, not unlike other Vanderbilt arrangements.

Yet another Vanderbilt estate, William Kissam Jr's Deepdale on the North Shore, had a large range of greenhouses which in design resemble the work of another major manufacturer, the American Greenhouse Manufacturing Company. This same company built the large Palm House at the United States Botanic Garden in Washington, DC, which still stands on the Mall below the Capitol.

These vast botanical complexes were familiar features at two of Stanford White's most successful country estates, designed at the turn of the century. One was The Orchards, a Mount Vernon-inspired country estate for James Breese, in which White converted a wide covered passageway into a trellised conservatory, and the other was Harbor Hill, the restrained seventeenth-century Norman château for Clarence Mackay, in which an enormous stone room doubled as a conservatory-like loggia. Another architect, John Russell Pope, who designed greenhouses for Marshall Field at his Caumsett estate, was also the designer of the Jefferson Monument and the National Gallery of Art, Washington. The major architectural firms of the wealthy, Warren and Wetmore, Carrere and Hastings, Walker and Gillette, all followed similar patterns, as did another architect trained at the Beaux-Arts, C. P. H. Gilbert.

Many of Gilbert's town houses, often incorporating conservatories, are still extant. Following the fashionable style of a French Renaissance château, he designed the Fletcher house of 1899 on 79th Street and the Thorne mansion of 1902 at 84th Street, both on Fifth Avenue. Both still possess their small glass conservatories perched like ornaments on a second-floor corner and entered from the dining room. For Augustus Paine's town house on East 69th Street, Gilbert adopted a similar plan, with one exception: the second-floor conservatory next to the dining room connected with a roof garden, which was surrounded by a pergola extending to 70th Street. Below the roof garden was Mr Paine's service building and garage. This rare instance of a 'block through lot' with all its components stands today and is now the Austrian Consulate.

Gilbert's mansions on Long Island also bore this familiar stamp. At F. W. Woolworth's Winfield at Glen Cove, the dining room extended beyond a pair of bronze gates to a palm court with elaborate bronze tracery outlining panes of glass. For William D. Guthrie, a Rockefeller lawyer, he built Meudon further up the shore in Locust Valley, and again placed a palm court in the same position. Here a fountain was encircled by great palms, Boston ferns were set on a marble floor, and treillage ornamented the walls. From the drives up to these ornate gleaming palaces could be seen huge Lord and Burnham greenhouses.

The millionaire mining and shipping magnate, Captain Joseph R. DeLamar, also hired Gilbert to design a grand, expansive palace at Glen Cove, to which he added the most extraordinary conservatory ever built; *a most unusual horticultural museum,* reported the *American Architect* soon after Pembroke's completion. A gentleman

of exquisite taste, Captain DeLamar also exhibited a well-developed interest in rare and beautiful plants, for which he built a glass mansion the size of his house. The plans which Gilbert drew up in 1913, and which were greatly enlarged by Lord and Burnham, survive today at the New York Botanical Garden Library. The original plan was for a not insubstantial cruciform tropical house wing, connected by a one-storey corridor leading to the house; however, this was very quickly expanded to the east by a long curvilinear house, making the entire Long Island Sound frontage over 400 feet long. Another 72-foot Australian House extended perpendicular to the central cruciform towards the landscaped park on the entrance side of the house. The interior was as theatrical as the exterior was monumental.

The main focal point of the Tropical House was a large circular swimming pool, lined with decorative tiles and encircled by planters and a tall iron-columned open screen. On a central pedestal was an octagonal gazebo of intricately patterned grilles and columns on which rested a fish-scaled iron and glass canopy. An ornamental bridge connected the gazebo with the 'mainland', and above was a double-tiered glass roof. At one end was a grotto with a cascade flowing into a stream that meandered through all parts of the conservatory. Palms up to 35 feet high, mature grapefruit and orange trees and banana plants were set in tubs and hidden beneath three feet of soil. At night an elaborate electrical system, controlled from one of the many rooms under this massive building, illuminated the house and pool, adding another dramatic dimension to Captain DeLamar's Shangri-la. King Ludwig II of Bavaria and Whitaker Wright of Surrey would surely have revelled in this extraordinary scene.

As was so often the case, the patron enjoyed his creation for only a few months. The captain died in 1918, and Pembroke was purchased by the movie mogul, Arthur Loew, who created a movie picture gallery in one of the rooms below the conservatory. The house was closed in the 1950s, and a bulldozer crushed DeLamar's dream palace in 1968, a fate which, alas, befell too many fine *fin de siècle* buildings.

All these mansions, like those on the Hudson River and elsewhere, were private residences enjoyed by their owners and their guests. Fabulous parties there were, but people were admitted by invitation only. Occasionally, journalists were permitted to describe the treasures within, but Mr Vanderbilt's railroads brought no thronging masses through the gates, no crowds like those at Chatsworth. The British tradition of the public visiting other people's houses never took hold in America.

Frank Lloyd Wright's conservatory of 1904–6 for Darwin D. Martin was featured in House & Garden *in October 1915.*

The East Conservatory at Longwood – the epitome of a great garden under glass. In the many conservatories at Longwood, the interior landscapes are enhanced by the changing seasonal displays of plants, always of superior quality.

Great Gardens Under Glass

The real delight of the greenhouse comes with finding that it is not so much a greenhouse as a garden under glass,[1] remarked F. F. Rockwell, a prolific garden writer, in 1924. To him, the secret pleasure in greenhouse gardening was creating a make-believe, miniature landscape under a sky of glass. This vision surely permeated the creation of Longwood Gardens in Pennsylvania.

While William Dick in 1904 was telling *Country Life in America* readers how to build a *hundred dollar greenhouse* to satisfy a *working man's hobby* at a cost of $25 a year, Pierre Samuel du Pont, great-grandson of the founder of the E.I. du Pont chemical company, was about to satisfy his childhood dream of creating his own conservatory, *maintained solely for pleasure* but on a scale somewhat less humble than that suggested by Mr Dick.

Unlike many industrial giants of his day, Mr du Pont's keen interest in botany and horticulture stemmed from a well-founded family passion, developed before the first du Pont crossed the Atlantic in 1800. Pierre Samuel's work on Longwood succeeded that of other members of his family who had created and developed gardens on a magnificent scale: Henry Francis du Pont at Winterthur and Alfred Irenée du Pont at Nemours. All three are open to the public today.

The first conservatory at Longwood was constructed in 1914, but a much larger one was soon envisaged; after two abortive attempts in 1917 and 1919, Pierre Samuel du Pont enlisted the aid of J. Walter Cope, an architect for du Pont Company. Cope's plan was accepted, and the conservatories were begun in 1919 and completed in 1921. Even though du Pont engaged architects, engineers and horticulturalists to design his gardens, it is evident from the

CONSERVATORIES FOR THE MODERN · HOUSE

Frank Lloyd Wright, architect

beginning that the creative and engineering masterplans were greatly influenced by du Pont himself.

The focus of Longwood's many richly adorned conservatories is the T-shaped main conservatory built in 1921: an orangery in the crossbar and an exhibition hall in the stem. Conceived as an arcaded Georgian building with a strong Lutyens influence, the conservatory now displays spectacular seasonal plantings changed gradually throughout the year: chrysanthemums in the autumn, poinsettias at Christmas, bulbs in the spring and lilies at Easter.

Adjacent to the main conservatory is the East Conservatory, built between 1969 and 1973 by the firm of Richard Phillips Fox, which replaced an earlier building. It was constructed to show off superbly designed landscape settings; the large uninterrupted expanse, 106 by 220 feet, gives one the feeling of being in a real garden. One of the building's most interesting features is the roof construction: rising 50 feet above the landscape, this 'Lammella Arch' roof is formed by steel 'I' beams, bolted together in a diamond pattern in which are placed 2,500 individual plates of slightly curved prismatic lucite. This specially manufactured acrylic material does not require shading in summer.

In front of the main conservatory – which with its attendant buildings now covers nearly four acres under glass – is an immense five-acre fountain garden, where numerous jets of water play in canals surrounded by carved stonework and *allées* of clipped Norway maples. Mr du Pont ensured that all the senses would be called upon to enjoy fully the many splendours of his hobby. Longwood Gardens may truly be called a *house of many blooms*, a phrase which also identifies another mystical garden under glass, the Duke Gardens of Somerville, New Jersey.

Originally built at the turn of the century by Lord and Burnham for James B. Duke, a North Carolina tobacco magnate, the gardens were renovated and extended by Miss Doris Duke from 1959 onwards. There is now a total of eleven interconnecting gardens under glass, depicting major garden traditions and styles throughout the world: a novel concept, *a Disney World for horticulturalists*.[2]

The central conservatory, laid out in the turn-of-the-century 'grand manner', introduces the visitor's kaleidoscopic passage through time and space from one garden to another. The path begins with the Italian Renaissance garden, and leads to the colonial garden, then the Edwardian garden, and from there to the large French parterre garden with its trellised walls and seasonal plantings; the English topiary and knot garden and the desert garden lead to the exotic gardens of the Orient. The Chinese garden, with its pagoda and winding pool beneath a footbridge, culminates with a bonsai room; a meditative Japanese garden with its own tea-house leads into a long three-tiered Persian garden with rose parterres, fountains and a canal. A semi-tropical rain forest concludes the journey. Although each garden is kept at the peak of perfection all the year round, limited viewing is offered, by appointment only, by the Duke Gardens Foundation.

Into the Twentieth Century

New approaches to the use of glass have been formulated in the twentieth century, with Frank Lloyd Wright as one of the most innovative pundits in America. He succeeded in adapting A. J. Downing's nineteenth-century theories to a more mobile and frenzied twentieth century, and then transposing them from the Hudson to the great prairies of the Mississippi valley. *A building should appear to grow easily from its site, shaped to harmonize with its surroundings;*[3] as an organic structure, the house should grow from within.

Important in all Wright's designs from the beginning was fluidity of movement. This was expressed by many features, including broad bulbous bay windows with continuous walls of glass, so often becoming a haven for plants. It was this desire to extend the wall out into the same horizontal landscape that inspired Wright to design one of the most expressive architectural statements in conservatory design.

Wright was commissioned to build a house in Buffalo, New York, for Darwin D. Martin, an executive with the Larkin Company. This led to a number of pivotal commissions, including a new administrative building for Larkin, and Martin's own house, built between 1904 and 1906. In the latter Wright expanded the centrifugal floor plan to include a long pergola stretching 100 feet beyond the core of the house to a terminus of green and light, enclosed by ribbons of glass. The pergola, placed dramatically in line with the entrance, not only unified the plan, but had other more practical functions: it divided the kitchen garden from the drying yards, and it also contained a basement passage for a large conduit for steam pipes coming from the furnace in the garage.

The conservatory was planned as a 'T', the stem offering sanctuary from the non-glazed pergola, and the crossbar providing a link between the garage and the house. Flowers and ferns were contained in large cement planters along the periphery of the walls, and at the end Wright placed a marble replica of his favourite classical statue, the Victory of Samothrace. Although Wright would interpret the pergola and conservatory many times, never again would the two be used with such dramatic effect.

After the war, Americans lost interest in conservatories and decorative ranges of greenhouses, even though countless books and articles would indicate the contrary. When built at all, the conservatory was a functional single-span or lean-to addition to the back of a house or service building, or a cookie-cutter variation of the manufactured variety at the turn of the century. In more recent times, the conservatory has taken on the appearance of a solarium, an enclosed passageway, or what is called a garden room, its primary usage being a sitting room rather than a room for exotic plants.

Sharing a similar philosophy of architecture with Frank Lloyd Wright is Paul Rudolph. An architect with a visionary perception of modular planning, Rudolph was commissioned in 1968 to design a country residence on a grassy plateau in north-eastern

Pennsylvania. It was conceived as a building made up of three long fold-out modular boxes, 12 feet by 60 feet; the sides tip out to become floors and ceiling, the ends open out to become windows and clerestories. Between the first and second module of periscopic windows and cantilevered planes grows a 20-foot glass and aluminium conservatory. Designed simply as a triangle between two living spaces, the conservatory is actually divided into three different horizontal spatial areas. The first and second levels are individual plant-growing environments, while the third is an open-air attic across which is suspended a footbridge connecting the guest wing and the living room.

Although only 1,400 square feet, this weekend house evokes an illusion of being much larger – all due, according to Rudolph, to the conservatory, which he planned at the instruction of his client, a keen gardener. Viewed from the meadow, the conservatory's pointed diagonal roof-line carries the eye upward, away from the horizontality of the modular forms, while from the interior its openness dissolves the constraints of the smaller rooms, by creating vistas downwards, upwards and outwards. The concept of intermingling open and closed areas is not new, but never has it been so successfully designed. To this day, the architect has sustained his enthusiasm for this plan he devised over twenty years ago.

The Green House, designed by Paul Rudolph in 1968. This cross-section shows a multi-level conservatory at the centre of the house.

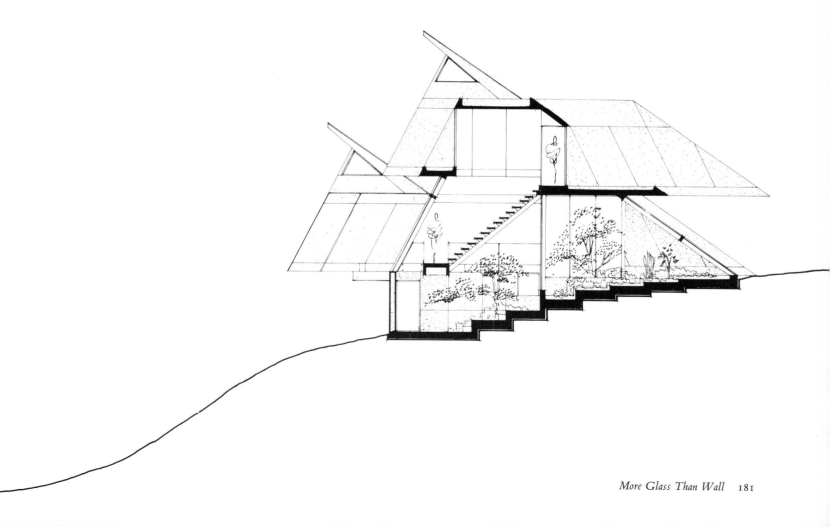

Climatron, designed for the Missouri Botanical Garden in 1959, heralded the new age in glass house building. This was the first time the geodesic dome was used for a botanical structure and the first time that climate control was a primary goal.

New Botanical Conservatories

The refreshing influence of nature on man, of plants on people, is evident in the use of atriums in modern buildings. New skyscraper hotels, whether in the centre of New York or on a Hawaiian island, invariably possess at their hearts an atrium, an indoor botanical garden. The favourite features of the nineteenth century are still there: waterfalls, statuary, birds and streams, perhaps with modern interpretation. Leisure complexes boast conservatory restaurants too, and swimming pools are surrounded with palm trees and bananas.

The atriums of commercial buildings are less romantic, more dramatic, with the emphasis on bold-leafed trees and palms. Here the choice of plants is intended to complement the architecture, yet also to provide a sympathetic environment for people in the challenging world of work. In the Opryland Hotel in Nashville, Tennessee, the Ford Foundation in New York, the Winter Garden at the World Financial Center, Battery Park City, New York, and in London at the Barbican and the new Lloyd's Building, plants are a major feature.

The most original buildings purely for plants are still to be found in the botanical gardens. Current design patterns in public glass house construction have shifted from the ceaseless interpretations of the curvilinear form to a new age of hemispheres and domes, pyramids and cones, hexagons and crystals.

In the vanguard of the new glass house design has been St Louis, Missouri. To celebrate the hundredth birthday of the Missouri Botanical Garden in 1959, the director, Dr Fritz Went, advocated the replacement of the older greenhouses with a building which would symbolize the newest technology and design. The key factors of combining a variety of climates for conservation and research as well as public display were incorporated into plans by the firm of Murphy and Mackey in the spring of 1959. The monumental geodesic dome, based on the principles of R. Buckminster Fuller, was named Climatron, in recognition of its attribute of climate control.

Climatron is 70 feet high at the centre and 175 feet in diameter and covers half an acre of ground. Unusually, the protective transparent skin is suspended from an exterior skeletal framework. The geodesic framework of aluminium tubing rests on five concrete piers, spaced equidistantly along the circular base; arches are formed as the five points curve down to meet the piers, and provide spaces for vents, openings and machinery stores. Also arranged in a hexagonal pattern are 3,625 triangular panes of quarter-inch plexiglass, which after twenty-eight years of changing seasons will shortly be replaced. The original intention of simulating four climates has been modified to two, one for lowland and the other for mountainous tropical flora.

In 1961 the architects won the coveted international R. S. Reynolds Memorial Award for architectural design; and in 1976

Climatron was selected in a survey conducted by the American Institute of Architects as one of the 260 most significant architectural achievements of America's two hundred years.

A landmark in design and technology, Climatron's greatest contribution may be in its bold statement that not all conservatories or greenhouses must be crystal boxes. Milwaukee, Wisconsin, soon followed the example of St Louis by constructing in Mitchell Park three smaller conservatories with geodesic domes, and in Switzerland three plastic domes have been built at the University of Zurich's botanic garden. At the Royal Botanic Gardens in Sydney, Australia, a triodetic frame greenhouse was introduced in 1972, a pyramid designed to be at the centre of a future cluster of conservatories.

Following Climatron came another new concept, the clustering of crystals that could provide varying climates within the whole. For the New York Botanical Garden, Edward Larabee Barnes was asked in 1975 to devise a structure encompassing climate zones from all over the world, as organic as the collection it would contain. The proposed Plants and Man Building is founded on the simple crystal; a hexagonal module which grows by duplicating itself, forming a visual pattern as quietly pleasing as a honeycomb, or as energetic as the Giant's Causeway formations in Northern Ireland. Each hexagonal chamber is independent of the other, and is supported by a system of slender pipe columns, tubular beams and diagonal tension rods. Each glass chamber may have its own climate, or incorporate itself with any number of cells, since the inner glass walls are mere partitions.

To accommodate ever-growing trees, Barnes created a system by which the height of any chamber may be increased by lifting the roof, extending the pipe columns, and putting the roof back in place like a bonnet. Each roof is divided into two semi-hexagons, sloping like a leaf downward to a central gutter, which connects with the pipe column. This doubles as a downspout, a technique used by Wyatville at Wollaton in 1823 and advocated by Downing in the 1840s.

This imaginative cluster of glass houses remains a dream that has not been realized.

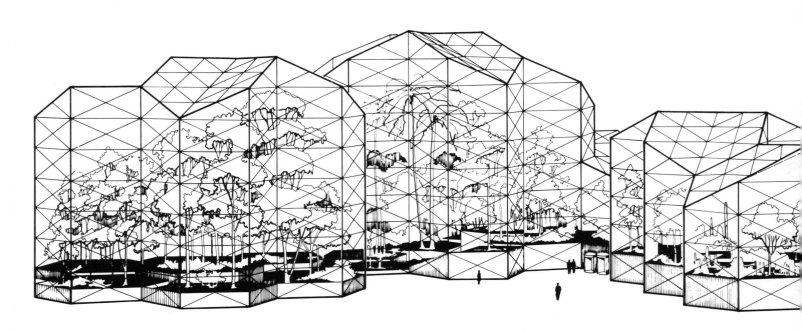

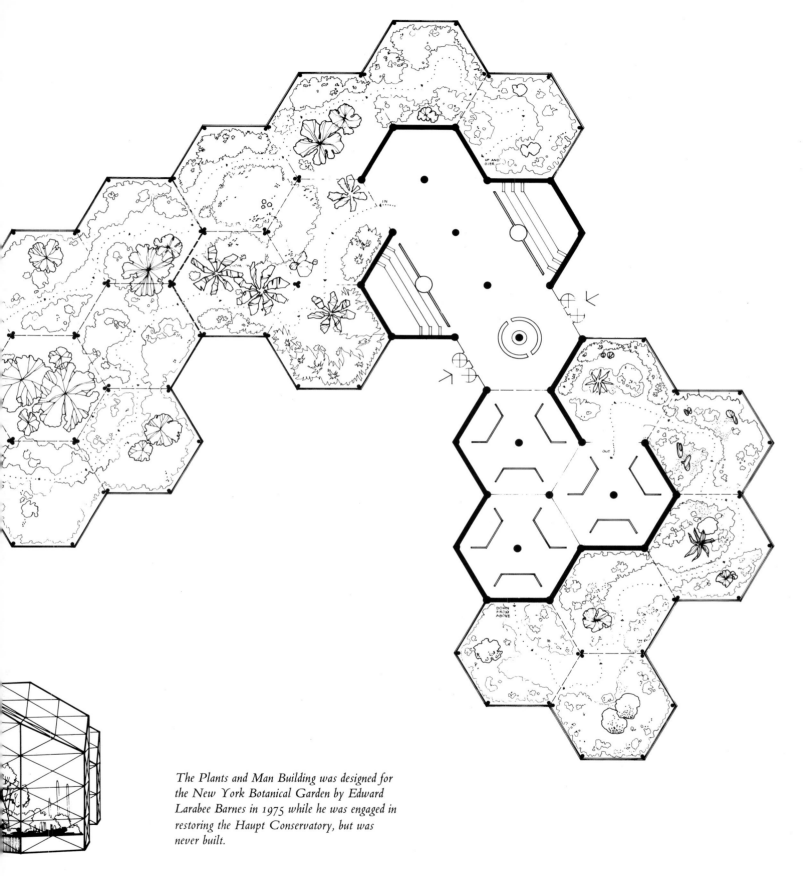

The Plants and Man Building was designed for the New York Botanical Garden by Edward Larabee Barnes in 1975 while he was engaged in restoring the Haupt Conservatory, but was never built.

The Lucille Halsell Conservatory at the San
Antonio Botanical Garden, completed in 1988.
To counteract the San Antonio climate, the
architect Emilio Ambasz has evolved new
forms, sunk into earth berms for insulation.

Nowhere is the play of geometric forms in and on a landscape more poetically profound than at the San Antonio Botanical Garden's new Lucille Halsell Conservatory. This was designed by Emilio Ambasz, a New York-based architect from the Argentine who won a 'Progressive Architecture' award in 1985 for this innovative building.

Faced with an entirely different set of requirements in San Antonio from those at St Louis, Mr Ambasz's challenge was the reverse of those for a northern greenhouse. Located in a dry, hot climate, this new building must protect its plants from the sun, excessive temperatures, and strong winds that sweep down from the Great Plains. In addition, San Antonio often experiences freak temperature changes which are equally detrimental to plant growth. Ambasz's solution incorporates one of his favourite landscape and architectural devices: the earth berm. Here earth becomes the container, the protector, the natural insulator. The playful glazing forms act as giant hats, which vary in size, shape and surface area proportionally to the size of the plant material and growing conditions.

In its plan and design, the San Antonio environment evokes a mysterious primordial order of life: the visitor approaches an amphitheatre of steps and descends to a circular entrance. What is to follow is a botanical play in many acts. For Ambasz, the visitor is not only the spectator, but a principal participant in the garden's hierarchy of natural and man-made experiences.

German architects of today have continued the great tradition of their predecessors in the nineteenth century in the interplay of glass and metal for botanic houses. Six flat-topped interconnecting hexagons at the University of Tübingen contrast sharply with the angular skeleton that supports six climates at the Hamburg Botanical Garden, while the latest addition is at Frankfurt. Completed in two stages, the Tropicarium North was opened in 1984 and the Tropicarium South in 1987.

The architect of the Tropicarium at Frankfurt, Hermann Blomeier, was inspired by seeing a cross-section of a cereus cactus. The structure that grew from a botanical form is composed of seven principal star-like octagons, varying in height from 23 feet to 50 feet, with three smaller octagons attached. It is a highly complex and sophisticated building on the forefront of new technology, and cost DM 50 million (£16.6 million). Among many novel features is the heating system; hot-water pipes are built into the frame, and contain 10 tons of water circulating up and round the structure at any one time, which explains the solidity of the building. Not only is the air heated, but the soil in planting beds is warmed as well. Rainwater storage tanks are located under the building – a common custom in the nineteenth century, for example, in the Palm House at Kew and in the Paxton greenhouses at Somerleyton in Suffolk – but at Frankfurt the rainwater is automatically heated to the right temperature for watering the plants. The Tropicarium is also computer-linked with the Meteorological Station at Frankfurt, so that the computer controlling the internal temperature can take account of anticipated changes in the weather.

The new Princess of Wales Conservatory at Kew is yet another version of the multi-climate house. It was conceived early in the 1970s, built between 1983 and 1985 at a cost of £4.75 million, and opened in 1987 by the Princess of Wales. For Gordon Wilson, the architect, the challenge was to create a structure of some significance, appropriate to Kew, yet within the necessary financial constraints and capable of housing the entire contents of the old 'T' range of glass houses and ferneries.

The crisp outline, a series of integrated overlapping ridges that stretch wide on either side, is reminiscent of the glass houses it replaced, yet it is a fresh, original interpretation of the familiar span-roofed house. With operational costs in mind, energy-saving devices have been incorporated: as at San Antonio, an earth berm insulates the building, since it is sunk into the ground to roof level, and winter sun is caught by all the south-facing vertical surfaces. The result is a marriage of the aesthetic and the practical, in which the prime needs of plants have been met by the architect and structural engineers.

The house contains ten separate climates, carefully landscaped to display plants to their best advantage. There are rare succulents from the deserts, orchids from the tropics, and an aquarium in which *Victoria amazonica* blooms and spreads its giant leaves in summer. The walkways lead the visitor round and up and down through these different worlds, always with the prospect of another continent's climate through the glass. It is an exciting living exhibition, and at the same time a vital contribution to the conservation of endangered species of the world.

Glass plant environments are complicated to control. Not only are they affected by sun and wind and external temperatures, but the plants themselves also influence the atmosphere. A newly planted glass house will need a changing balance of heat and moisture, ventilation and shading as the vegetation develops, and at Kew computers control each separate environment to keep the balance right at all times. The technology is proven, and works well. Diffused glass provides some shading, but it also concentrates the eye on the plants within, rather than those in the gardens beyond. Equally, the frame, brickwork, paving and concrete columns are as simple as possible to avoid distraction; a far cry from the ambience of Victorian conservatories. The age-old problem of maintenance has been tackled by flame-spraying the pre-drilled steel frame with aluminium; it was then finished with rubberized paint, inside and out, which has water-dispensing qualities and can even be reapplied when the building is in use.

The Princess of Wales Conservatory complements the other great glass buildings at Kew, both botanically and architecturally; it embodies the technology and the spirit of the late twentieth century, as the others have done in their own time. It looks forward to the future, continuing the great tradition of the Royal Botanic Gardens.

*The Tropicarium at the Palmengarten der
Stadt Frankfurt was designed by Hermann
Blomeier and completed in 1987.*

Kew's latest glass house, the Princess of Wales Conservatory, was designed by Gordon Wilson and opened in 1987.

Private Decline and Fall

The Great War was disastrous for the private glass house in Britain, as young and able-bodied gardeners went off to fight, and the tragic loss of life meant that garden staffs were permanently depleted. Many families suffered financially too, and funds had to be kept for more important items than the repairing and heating of glass houses. The Great Conservatory at Chatsworth was deliberately blown up, and many others were allowed to fall gently into ruin, leaking and overgrown; few were maintained as magnificently as before. In the conservatory at Sandon Hall in Shropshire, as in many others, the heat was turned down to keep the temperature just above freezing, and the beds replanted with more resilient specimens.

J.G. Farrell's description of the old Majestic Hotel's Palm Court in *Troubles*[4] paints a picture of the conservatory in decline: *The Palm Court proved to be a vast, shadowy cavern in which dusty white chairs stood in silent empty groups, just visible here and there amid the gloomy foliage. For the palms had completely run riot, shooting out of their wooden tubs (some of which had cracked open to trickle little cones of black soil on to the tiled floor) towards the distant murky skylight, hammering and interweaving themselves against the greenish glass that sullenly glowed overhead. Because of the dense vegetation, a standard lamp throttled by a snake of greenery that had circled up its slender metal stem needed to be turned on in mid-afternoon. It was a morbid place, dirty and neglected, probably a riot of pests, but still with a hint of the elegance of Edwardian days.*

Since these great glass houses could no longer be kept to the same high standard, necessity brought about a swing away from them, a swing against their very artificiality. Over-heated palm houses simply went out of fashion as people preferred genuine fresh air to mock jungles from the tropics. Attached conservatories were replaced with open loggias and verandahs; pergolas were built for wisteria and clematis; roses took the place of passion flowers glimpsed through the drawing-room window; geraniums and lobelia supplanted more tender hoyas in hanging baskets.

In 1932 the gardening writer Beverley Nichols described how owning even a practical hot-house seemed a wicked extravagance: *'This is folly ... this is reckless squandering ...' so my subconscious mind tells me. It is to no avail that my conscious mind reassures me that the expense of the hot-house for a whole winter is not as great as that of a single dinner at the Savoy. The feeling of alarm remains. I feel as though I had invested in a yacht, with a huge crew, and an appalling bill to foot every week. All because I was told by my mother that 'hot-houses' were 'terribly expensive'.*[5]

The conservatory manufacturing companies that had enjoyed an unbroken heyday for over sixty years found times very hard, and many were forced to diversify or close. Mackenzie and Moncur of Edinburgh and Richardsons of Darlington concentrated on supplying greenhouses for the kitchen garden, or modest conservatories for middle-class houses.

The Second World War brought further destruction, as income and labour again dwindled. Viscount Boyne's conservatory at Burwarton House in Shropshire was, however, dismantled for a different reason. The present Viscount recalls: *My grandfather had his sisters living here, one of whom was convinced that Hitler would see the reflection from the glass and would bomb us! In the cause of domestic peace, he eventually removed the glass, and of course it was then impossible to maintain.*

Of new glass houses built since the war, the conservatory at Glenveagh, County Donegal, in Northern Ireland is one of the most attractive. Built in 1958 for the late Henry McIlhenny of Philadelphia, it is a new interpretation of old ideas. It has a wide lantern along the roof ridge in the Victorian tradition, with Gothic glazing bars and a crenellated cresting to echo the crenellations on the wall behind.

The 11th Duke of Devonshire has continued tradition at Chatsworth with a modern aluminium display house, built in 1970 and designed by George A. H. Pearce. The Chatsworth greenhouse is similar to George Pearce's design for the Botanic Gardens in Edinburgh. It is divided into three climates, tropical, Mediterranean and temperate, the latter housing plants that could thrive outside in milder areas of Britain. The spiky structure could hardly offer a greater contrast to the smooth curves of the demolished Great Conservatory, but these very contradictions emphasize the extraordinary variety of original forms that can be made from metal, wood and glass.

7 The Conservatory Today

Fortunately, enough of the eighteenth- and nineteenth-century glass houses have survived to show the wealth of the glass house inheritance. The rich diversity of form and materials can be enjoyed by students of architecture, and the sound horticultural principles that influenced their design can be adapted to conservatories today.

Today's American greenhouse and conservatory manufacturers offer glass living space additions that complement the stark lines of modern houses. Frequently made of aluminium rather than wood, they are as likely to contain a hot tub as a hoya, and resilient members of the ficus family rather than delicate climbers. Plants may often be a decorative feature, but not the prime purpose. Extremes of climate in North America mean that the range of plants is more limited than in temperate northern Europe, except for the dedicated enthusiast who puts plants before people; since summer temperatures are so high, most plants have to be moved outside for several months in the year. The rise in oil prices in the late 1970s and, to a certain extent, the boom in growing organic vegetables, gave birth to a new type of glass house in the United States, the solar greenhouse. This is a well-insulated, south-facing lean-to house addition designed to catch winter sun. The balance of purpose is often tipped in favour of horticulture, with flowers and vegetables grown in beds as well as in pots, particularly during winter and spring. Its angular appearance, with windows sloped to take maximum advantage of winter sun, is practical rather than aesthetic, and its popularity has risen and declined in line with energy costs.

A revival of interest in conservatories in Britain started in the early 1970s and has gained pace rapidly in the 1980s. Architects are creating novel structures which embrace two floors, or which unite a house rather than appearing as an addition. A wealth of companies has leapt into this expanding market – Amdega, Alexander Bartholomew, Machin, Marston and Langinger, Room Outside, Town and Country Conservatories, and scores more. Except for those who use aluminium, British conservatory manufacturers lean heavily on Victorian tradition. The brick base, the arched windows, the lantern ridges, the cast-iron braces, cresting and finials – all are derived from the past. The plainer versions, too, with squared frames that can be adapted for differing styles of domestic architecture, could have been taken from early plans by Decimus Burton or by Humphry Repton and his sons; while the far earlier Gothic ogee arch has been transposed from window to roof by another manufacturer.

Maintenance has been revolutionized by new materials and new coatings. With thermal breaks to reduce heat loss through conductivity, aluminium structures now bypass the old problems of cast iron, and are claimed to be maintenance free. Seasoned timber is impregnated with preservatives, while paint technologists develop coatings that will last longer, although regular attention still has to be paid to wooden buildings. Some conservatory manufacturers combine the two materials, using wood for aesthetic reasons for the vertical plane, and aluminium in the roof where its advantages are most beneficial. The most interesting developments are in glass technology and glass substitutes, an area in which yet more energy-efficient products are constantly appearing. Architects and conservatory manufacturers will be able to advise on the latest products, and on whether double or even triple glazing is cost-effective, dependent on climate and intended winter use.

The location of the glass house depends on many individual factors and needs. Accessibility and visibility are important considerations. Even if barely heated in winter, it can still give great pleasure if visible from another room or a staircase; cyclamen and spring bulbs will add a bright splash of colour, and will last much longer than in a warmer room. Whatever its location, whether on the rooftop or as part of the living space on the ground floor, it need not always have three glazed walls, and may often be more attractive and comfortable with only two of glass. Since there is no heat gain through a north-facing wall, that is an obvious choice for a solid

Made of a plastic polycarbonate, the solar heated 'Growth Accelerator' was designed recently by the Missouri architect Michael Jantzen as a new option for the greenhouse grower. Architecturally and sculpturally bewitching, this small 40-foot modular structure with a sliding roof can be expanded, or dismantled easily for transportation.

A conservatory designed by Francis Machin, with its distinctive ogee arched roof. This is a mixture of old and new, hardwood for the uprights and aluminium for the curved glazing bars of the roof, glass for vertical glazing and PVC for the curved roof. The finials are made of fibreglass.

A modern version of a grotto, by Arnold Machin. Water trickles down a stepped cascade in the centre, and there are other little waterfalls on either side. A collection of moisture-loving plants, Nephrolepsis exaltata, Rhoicissus rhomboidea, Ficus pumila *and* Pandanus veitchi, *are fast adapting to their warm locations.*

Glazed swimming pools are the latest glass house fashion in unreliable climates. Rather than collections of small plants, it is more appropriate to use large palm trees and climbing plants, such as passion flowers, hoyas and stephanotis.

wall. A cold prevailing wind in winter is another factor that might influence replacement of glass by brick for one wall, since wind will cool a single glazed room rapidly. Double glazing and blinds pulled down at night will help to preserve heat in this situation, and chilly blasts can be diverted by a screen of trees or a wall.

One of the advantages of an attached conservatory is that it insulates the adjoining room, even if the conservatory is unheated; the insulation benefit increases with the temperature level. Natural sunlight will warm the conservatory rapidly, even in winter – and, of course, the room next door. There is thus a compensating factor to the cost of building an adjoining conservatory. One of the possible disadvantages lies in the reduction of light in the room it adjoins. When blinds are pulled down there is a consequent loss of light in the inner room. This can be counteracted in part by enlarging the glazed area between the two rooms, and by choosing light colours for the floor and paintwork in the conservatory. While a slight

Mackenzie and Moncur's conservatory at Letham Grange Hotel, built in the 1890s and recently modernized. Its old Victorian air has been swept away by removing a frieze of coloured glass, and cladding the frame with huge panels of tinted plastic glazing.

reduction in light is unavoidable, it will only occur during the three or four months when shading is essential, and that coincides with the season for being in the conservatory or in the garden.

Would that equal attention were paid today to the ventilation systems of the last century as is paid to Victorian decoration. Robert Thompson's advice that the architect should consult the cultivator in order to avoid a *vegetable charnel house* is as relevant now as it was in 1878. Without good ventilation it is virtually impossible to keep plants alive, since the 'greenhouse effect' results in temperatures rocketing to well over 100° F in a sunny summer day. Such heat is beyond human comfort too, so there is every reason to insist on adequate ventilation. Ignoring this aspect of design is a mistake that is exceedingly hard to rectify at a later date.

In Victorian days there were gardeners to open and close the windows and lights, morning and evening, whereas now it is usually the owner who must take heed of the weather forecast and its likely effect on the glass house. Nowadays, security provisions complicate the issue further, since ventilators must be burglar-proof when the house is empty; windows and doors should not be the basis of ventilation. A secure system must therefore be built into the design, with opening roof-lights and further ventilation low in the wall to ensure a constant flow of air. The rule of thumb for the ratio of roof light to floor area is that the surface area of the opening should be one-eighth of the floor area. Low ventilation can be built into a brick base with a cavity wall by placing a cast-iron grille in the outer wall and a louvred wooden panel in the inner wall. If the walls are glazed to the ground, louvred glass panels can be placed discreetly in corners. Two or more low ventilators will allow cool air to be drawn in at floor level, while hot air escapes through the roof.

Charles Morris's design of 1986 for a garden room. With an understanding of the need for ventilation, Morris has used louvred windows beside the door and in the lantern to ensure a continual flow of air. For another client, he has given a conservatory an oriental look by using louvred columns, narrow louvres set into pairs of uprights. Louvres have many advantages: security, adjustability, flexibility of width, height and location, and they can be operated by remote control via a thermostat. While a modern device, they are reminiscent of the overlapping panes of the late eighteenth century.

Shading is invaluable, especially where ventilation is imperfect; without shading, the temperature will be intolerable for both people and plants. There are various possibilities, at various prices. Exterior cedar chain lathe blinds – thin strips of cedar joined by copper clips and rings – have been popular for many years with horticulturalists because some sunlight comes through but not enough to scorch; the wooden slats cast a pleasing shadow inside but do not interfere with internal climbing plants, and sections can be cut out to allow roof lights to open freely. Internal blinds come in a range of materials, some heat reflectant, some insulated, some made of fine spills of wood sewn together, and they can be an attractive feature as well as a means of protection from the sun. A vine provides lovely dappled shade in summer, as sunlight streams through the leaves. Blinds, external and internal, are also useful in winter as an insulator, particularly when wind combines with low temperatures.

There is a maze of different heating systems available, covering a wide variety of capital and running costs, from electric fans to balanced-flue heaters to underfloor hot-water pipes. Two factors to bear in mind when selecting a system are first, the need for heat in the conservatory at night when the rest of the house may be unheated; and secondly, the extent to which the room is likely to be used as living space as well as for plants. It will be cost-effective to install an expensive system, such as hot-water radiators or underfloor heating, if the conservatory is used regularly by people or contains tropical or sub-tropical plants; if the aim is merely to keep the frost out, a simpler electric or gas appliance will be adequate. Any system should be thermostatically controlled to keep the temperature constant. Climate has an obvious bearing on choice, so with all these variables and an array of products from which to select, the advice of a local heating engineer will be invaluable.

The interior decoration of the conservatory depends to a certain extent on the number of plants it will contain – a few token plants will make little difference to the furnishings. If, however, there are large climbing plants and collections of others in pots, all of which will require spraying in summer, the floor will need to be water tolerant. It is wiser not to use fibre floor covering or wood, since it has to be said that drips and leaks are not unknown in most glass houses. Ceramic and quarry tiles and stone paving are ideal, with the entire floor sloping to a drain; in winter, when roof lights are closed and plants kept drier, the floor can be covered with matting or rugs for greater comfort and warmth.

Traditional conservatory furniture is made of cane and wicker, for good reason, since they do not warp in heat and are not affected by damp; cast iron and hardwood are also appropriate. All will need a generous quantity of cushions, which may need to be removed in winter if there is no or little heat and humidity levels rise.

For non-gardeners, there are two excellent ways of covering a masonry wall besides using climbing plants. The first is trellis or treillage, an ideal decoration, especially the *trompe l'œil* versions. With a clever design, a flat wall can be given depth, and an impression of space can be created even in a small room. Painted in a rich dark green, trellis can be a good substitute for foliage, while paler shades of green are more restful; a blue-grey trellis against white is cool and sophisticated.

Another possibility is a mural, perhaps a painted profusion of blossom if living specimens are too much trouble. Classicists might favour ancient ruins, as there were at Shugborough; garden history lovers could indulge in a Renaissance scene: a cascade or a grotto, or an orange grove behind a pair of living orange trees, a landscaped park, or perhaps a romantic waterfall. Non-traditional escapist scenes could be even more imaginative. A world of fantasy lies here, potentially as dazzling as King Ludwig's valley in Kashmir.

Statues are still a favourite decoration in conservatories, and porcelain and pottery plates are ideal replacements for pictures on the walls. But perhaps the most attractive feature is a fountain. Fountains can be free-standing if space permits, or sunk into the floor, or mounted on a wall; a small electric pump will have to be concealed nearby. As well as the soothing sound as they trickle and gurgle, they have the beneficial effect of raising the humidity level in summer, which helps to cool the air a little. Since the humidity level should be low in winter, the fountain should be emptied of water and filled instead with flowering or foliage plants.

A conservatory is often the most inviting room in the house, a quiet place to read, far from the invasive television, and a pleasant room in which to entertain. Sunlight is free and cheering to the spirit; even on a dull day a glass room feels bright. To be surrounded by plants and flowers gives constant pleasure, especially for the gardener who enjoys watching new shoots develop and buds unfold. At night it is even more magical. Candlelight and moonlight add an unexpectedly hypnotic beauty, regardless of the weather outside. A plumbago dripping with clusters of pale blue blossom or a wall gleaming with trailing pink geraniums is twice as effective at night. Add to this the exquisite scent of orange blossom and lilies, and the vision is complete.

The shape of a conservatory is always governed by the construction of the roof, and by the walls to which it is attached; a lean-to conservatory cannot be built against a wall with low windows on an upper floor. Thus, for practical as well as aesthetic reasons, a pair of hipped roofs has been devised here by the Peter Tigg partnership, in collaboration with Josephine Marston.

Paul Avis devised this roof, with projecting bays at either end, for a large conservatory to house a swimming pool.

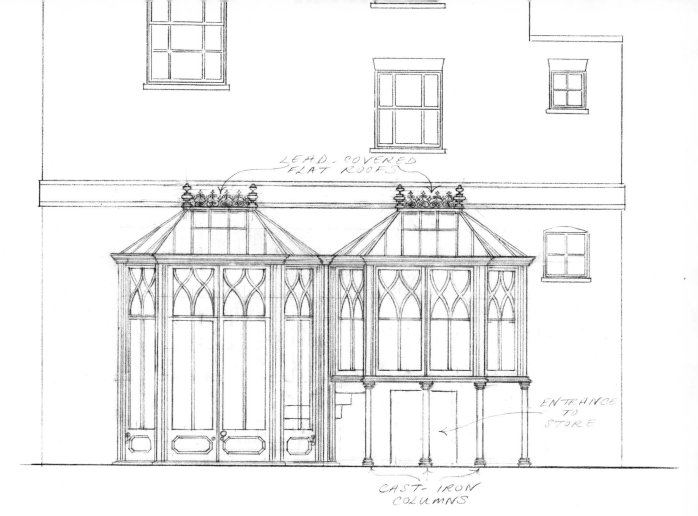

LEAD-COVERED
FLAT ROOFS

ENTRANCE
TO
STORE

CAST-IRON
COLUMNS

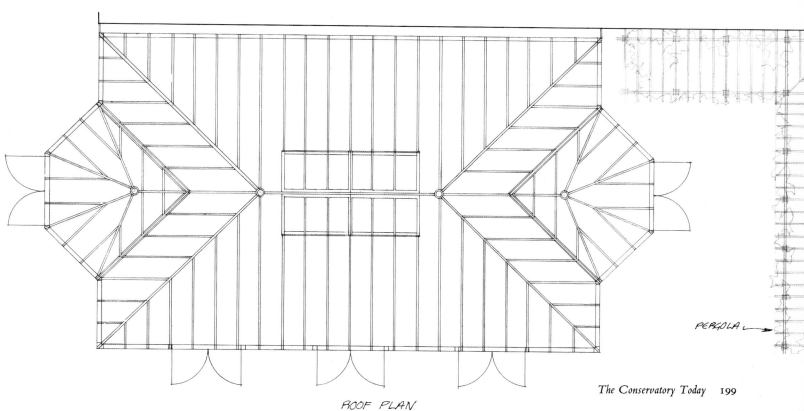

PERGOLA

ROOF PLAN

The interior and exterior of a conservatory designed by Jeffrey Gold. Bright and spacious inside, from the outside it nestles snugly beside the house, adding a certain unity through repetition of triangular gables.

Caring for Plants

The frequency of watering and quantity needed vary so much from one plant to another that it is dangerous to generalize. One basic piece of advice, however, is to feel the compost frequently, and if that is moist there is no need to water. The weight of the pot is another good guide to the moisture content, since the surface may look and feel dry when there is moisture an inch or two below. Most plants prefer a good drink followed by a rest to allow the moisture to be absorbed, rather than a regular trickle; frequency of watering should therefore be reduced in winter when the plant will be using less water. Plants are killed just as easily by over-watering as by lack of water, and, with the exception of those that grow naturally in bogs, they must not be allowed to become waterlogged. There is a danger that a china cachepot or planter can hide a stagnant puddle. A handful of fine pebbles inside the cachepot will provide a draining base, but in any case the pot should be checked regularly.

There are two alternatives to daily watering in summer, which may be particularly useful during long hot weekends or vacations. The first is capilliary matting. This is fed from a reservoir of water, so that when pots are placed on the matting it enables the roots to draw up exactly the amount of water they require. The second is an automatic watering device, a system of plastic tubing attached to a reservoir which will drip water into selected pots.

Another point to remember is that clay pots permit evaporation through the sides of the pot, whereas plastic ones do not; plants in plastic pots will therefore need a little less watering. Peat-based composts require more consistent watering than soil-based composts, since they dry out more quickly and are difficult to remoisten: the best way is to soak the pot in a bucket of water until it is completely wet through.

Watering should be done regularly, which means daily in hot sunny weather, every second day in duller weather, and always more frequently in early spring and through the summer than in the autumn, even in identical weather conditions. Hanging baskets may need water twice a day in hot weather, since there is little soil to retain moisture and they usually contain a thirsty collection of plants. In summer, early morning or evening is the preferred time to water, but urgent first-aid supplies should be given if leaves are seen to be drooping, whatever the time of day. In winter, the lower the temperature, the less water should be given, as it is vital to keep the air and the plants as dry as possible to prevent fungal diseases.

Spraying or misting should not be done in bright sunlight, as the sun's heat is magnified in each drop of water and causes brown scorch marks; the early morning or the end of a hot day are the correct times for spraying. Generally, leaves rather than flowers should be sprayed. Avoid spraying white or very pale flowers, as even tiny particles of water can spoil delicate petals. Plants with hairy leaves do not require spraying often, whilst those with smooth shiny leaves will benefit most. Cyclamen should never be sprayed and should only be watered from below, so that water never comes in direct contact with the corm.

There is much debate about the varying quality of water, and the preference for rain water to tap or faucet water. In hard water areas, rhododendrons and azaleas will require rain water to give of their best, but generally tap water is satisfactory. In summer it is preferable to rain water from an open tank which may be rife with disease.

Ideally the temperature of the water should be the same or slightly higher than the soil in which the plants are growing. An internal water storage tank is obviously the answer in a practical greenhouse, but is not so easy to disguise in a small conservatory. A mixture of cold water with a little from the hot tap will solve the problem, and if both taps are located in the conservatory, the watering process will be easier and quicker.

Most plants need to be repotted once a year in spring, or when they grow too large for their pots, which might be two or three times in the growing season. A large plant which would be hard to move can have the top layer of soil carefully removed without damaging the roots, and fresh soil applied.

A top dressing can also be given to planting beds. If in doubt about whether to use a soil-based compost or a peat-based compost, it is advisable to repeat the mixture as before, unless it has proved unsatisfactory; generally, growers use the most appropriate compost.

Fertilizers should be applied to all but newly potted plants, since the latter will have sufficient supplies for the first six to ten weeks. They should be given at the very start of the growing season and continue till flowers fade or new shoots cease to form, which will be spring to autumn for many plants, but may be autumn or winter for others, such as cyclamen, azaleas and jasmine.

Hygiene in the greenhouse is vitally important. Mould and fungus will develop in cold damp conditions, and will eventually damage the paintwork as well as making it look dirty. Apart from regular cleaning, inside walls and paintwork should be washed once a year with soft soap, and the glass cleaned thoroughly inside and out. It is especially important to clean out all the nooks and crannies, because pests will quickly find secluded corners in which to settle and breed. Any dead plant material should always be picked off and removed from the conservatory, and emptied pots washed before storage, as these can be breeding grounds for undesirable creatures. All these measures will help to prevent the spread of disease and proliferation of pests, and will save time in the long run.

The best natural defence against pests and disease is good health; however, pests are always a problem in an enclosed environment which natural predators rarely enter. Plants should be examined carefully for signs of pests before purchase, and an infected plant isolated elsewhere until pests are eradicated. It pays dividends to deal with them as soon as signs appear, either by simply removing the offensive creatures by hand, or with chemical products or by biological control, preferably the latter if appropriate predator insects are available. Predators are effective provided the temperature is kept at or above the recommended level, since cold will kill them off; suppliers' instructions on other matters should be followed carefully too. Names of suppliers can be found in the small advertisements columns of gardening magazines.

Disease is a more difficult subject for general advice; the conservatory is no place for sickly plants, and the best motto for the amateur is 'when in doubt, throw out'.

The Choice of Plants

Today's glass house gardener is likely to be an amateur with many other activities to occupy his or her time, so the plants must give pleasure without being too much trouble. All the plants mentioned in the following pages should survive with reasonable care, provided they have the required degree of heat, and should be reasonably easy to obtain. There are many other more temperamental species, such as certain orchids, to which the specialist may devote his time, but these are not for the busy amateur. Precise advice is impossible, and depends so much on the individual situation; these pages are intended to give the reader a simple understanding of a glass environment plus inspiration for what to grow.

The choice of plants depends on many factors, such as the location and orientation of the conservatory, heating, shading, ventilation, humidity and the amount of attention that will be given. There are many encyclopedias that list essential requirements for plants in glass houses, and staff at garden centres will often give sound advice for specific circumstances. Generally speaking, flowering plants need more sunlight than foliage plants, and plants with variegated leaves need more light than their plain-leafed cousins. If the Royal Botanic Gardens at Kew needs ten different computer-controlled climates for its tropical plants alone, plus other houses for plants from other climates, it is not surprising that any one private conservatory is unsuited for all the plants that fill the flower shops. Beguiling as a stephanotis might be, it should be enjoyed for its blossoms and perfume while they last, and its subsequent demise need not be taken as a personal failure.

In deciding which plants to choose, it is imperative to ascertain the minimum winter temperature and select accordingly. The winter minimum will be raised naturally on sunny days, and can be raised artificially for several days without harming plants, whereas an instant fall in temperature, damp and cold draughts will be damaging; an open door on a very cold day could be disastrous. Many plants will survive a short spell of a temperature lower than the recommended level without adverse effects, but will suffer if kept permanently below the ideal winter minimum. An unheated conservatory partly sheltered by the adjacent house, where the temperature may fall a few degrees below freezing for short periods, can be home to bay trees, ceanothus and some silver-leafed species that succumb to long hard frost. If the winter temperature is maintained

at 65° F or more, non-tropical plants should be moved to a cooler location for a month or two, in order to give them a period of rest.

One lesson to be learned from the nineteenth century is the value of planting beds. Most plants in beds grow better than those in pots, because their roots have room to spread in search of moisture and nutrients. An adequate level of moisture is easier to maintain in a bed, and the growth therefore is more luxuriant; it is much quicker and easier to create an atmosphere of lush profusion with two or three healthy climbing plants than with rows of plants in pots.

Apart from the visual delight, a quantity of vegetation helps to deaden sound. A conservatory is a glass box with little fabric to absorb sound, and if two or three people are talking at once the noise level is surprisingly high. Climbing plants are one solution, internal blinds are another, but the two cannot be used together unless the climbers are constantly pruned to avoid growing into the blind. Hanging baskets also help to muffle sound.

Planting beds need be only nine or twelve inches wide, but they should be two or three feet deep, and drain away into the earth below. If adjacent to the house, the brickwork must be sealed from above the level of the bed to the bottom in order to prevent damp penetrating the wall. The wall above should be rendered and painted, but not plastered, since moisture from the foliage will eventually bring the plaster away from the wall. The bed should be filled with good, sterile compost, well tramped down and allowed to settle, with more compost added on top before planting. An alternative is a very large tub or trough, which in itself can be an attractive feature.

There are various climbing plants that can be recommended for a conservatory that is kept at about 40° F in winter, and no hotter than 95° F in summer and maintains average humidity: jasmine, plumbago, passion flowers and trailing geraniums are the usual favourites; vines, dripping with grapes in late summer, can be planted outside if temperatures permit, and the stem brought through a small aperture in the brickwork. If higher winter temperatures are maintained, the choices are increased to include bougainvillea, allamanda and many other more exotic species.

In planning the arrangement of the room, its furniture and plant material, one or two carefully selected taller plants or trees will be invaluable; smaller ones can be grouped together in large bowls, several of the same kind for maximum effect. Colour can be an important theme too – dramatic or subtle, according to taste. Contrasting foliage plants give rise to unusual colour combinations, rich in endless shades of green, tinged with red, or edged with white. If there is a good variety of plants, it is wise to let them dominate the room, without distracting the eye to a multitude of coloured cache-pots. Terracotta pots and saucers are traditional and ideal, and white pottery and porcelain pots will not detract from the plants.

Sweet-scented flowers give great pleasure in the conservatory, since their perfume is intensified in the enclosed atmosphere. Apart from hyacinths and narcissi brought on to bloom in the dullest months in winter and white jasmine flowers in early spring, fragrant lilies can be planted in successive months in winter to ensure flowers in late spring and summer. Citrus flowers have one of the most delightful scents; the Earl of Chesterfield enthused about the joys of orange blossom indoors in the seventeenth century with good reason. The fragrant rhododendrons bloom in spring too, and can be followed by daturas in summer, then myrtles and belladonna lilies in late summer. Autumn-scented flowers include the gardenia, but this may be difficult to bring into flower in succeeding years.

As far as orientation is concerned, there is no orientation for a conservatory that is unsuitable for plants; it is simply a matter of selecting plants that will flourish in any given quantity of light. A north-facing conservatory can be filled with graceful ferns, and a south-facing one that has no shading and a forgetful gardener will be suitable for succulents and cacti. The range of plants in between these two extremes is vast.

Selection and care of plants can give great pleasure both to the gardener and to the visitor. It is the whole ambience, the combination of flowers and foliage, furnishings and design, which makes the glass house a continual challenge and a unique source of delight.

Notes

Introduction

1. John Hix, *The Glass House*, Cambridge, Mass., MIT, 1974; Stefan Koppelkamm, *Glass Houses and Wintergardens of the Nineteenth Century*, London, Granada Publishing, 1982; Georg Kohlmaier and Barna von Sartory, *Houses of Glass*, Cambridge, Mass. and London, MIT, 1986.

Chapter 1: The Innovators

1. Kenneth Lemmon, *The Covered Garden*, London, Museum Press, 1962, p.14.
2. Giovanni Boccaccio, *The Decameron*, The Third Day (Introduction), trans. G.H. McWilliam, London, Penguin, 1972, p.232.
3. Calendar of State Papers Domestic, SP 12, Vol. XXII, Item 22.
4. Ibid., Item 52.
5. John Gerard, *Catalogus arborum, fruticum ac plantarum*, London, 1599.
6. William Harrison, *The Description of England*, London, 1587, Book II, p.322.
7. *Biographia Britannia*, London, 1760, p.3467.
8. Calendar of State Papers Domestic, SP 12, Vol. XXII, Item 22.
9. Surrey Archaeological Collections, Vol. XXXI.
10. Surrey County Record Office, 281/2/22.
11. Ibid., 2152/1 Earl of Warwick's Accounts.
12. J. Gibson, *London Gardens, 1691*, published in *Archaeologica*, Vol. 12, and in W.C. Hazlitt's *Gleanings in Old Garden Literature*, Elliot Stock, 1887.
13. Paxton's *Magazine of Botany*, Vol. 1, 1834, p.90.
14. Prudence Leith-Ross, *The John Tradescants*, London, Peter Owen, 1984.
15. In the National Library of Wales, Aberystwyth.
16. Wynnstay MS 167, f.510.
17. Ibid., f.55.

Chapter 2: The Fashion for 'Exoticks'

1. See Pierre Patel's bird's-eye view of Versailles of 1668.
2. There are six manuscript versions of the *Manière de Montrer les Jardins de Versailles* from between 1689 and 1705.
3. Letter to the Earl of Sandwich, August 1668, *The Diary and Correspondence of John Evelyn*, ed. Bray, London, Henry Bohn, 1859, Vol. 3, p.205.
4. Gibson, *London Gardens*, 1691; and Stephen Switzer in *Iconographia Rustica*, 1718, Vol. I, p.60.
5. Manuscript *History of Derbyshire* written in 1712 by J. Wolley and printed in S. Glover's *History and Gazetteer of the County of Derby*, 1833, p.158.
6. British Library, Department of MSS, Sloane 3569.
7. Joan Johnson, *Excellent Cassandra*, Gloucester, A.J. Sutton, 1981, p.69.
8. Gibson, *London Gardens*, 1691.
9. *Aubrey's Brief Lives*, ed. Oliver Lawson Dick, London, Secker and Warburg, 1949, p.145.
10. Philip Miller and Thomas Martyn, *The Gardener's and Botanist's Dictionary*, London, 1807, under 'Stoves'.
11. Thomas Faulkner, *An Historical and Topographical Description of Chelsea and its Environs*, London, 1829.
12. British Library, Department of MSS, Add. MS 15,889, f.45.
13. Switzer, *Iconographia Rustica*, 1718, Vol. I, p.61.
14. William Camden, *Britannia*, London, 1722, Vol. I, Middlesex, p.368.
15. *A Tour Through the Whole Island of Britain*, London, 1742, Vol. II, p.159.
16. A selection of these paintings has been edited by Gloria Cottesloe and Doris Hunt and published as *The Duchess of Beaufort's Flowers*, Exeter, Webb & Bower, 1983.

17. Switzer, *Iconographia Rustica*, 1718, Vol. III, pp.115–17.
18. Ibid., Vol. I, p.77.
19. David Green, *Gardener to Queen Anne*, London, Oxford University Press, 1956, p.112.
20. *Powis Castle Guidebook*, London, The National Trust, 1987, p.38.

Chapter 3: The Golden Age of the Greenhouse

1. Horace Walpole, *The History of Modern Taste in Gardening*, facsimile reprint, New York and London, Garland Publishing, 1982, p.268.
2. Peter Martin, *The Gardening World of Alexander Pope*, Hamden, Archon Books, 1984, p.72.
3. Defoe, *A. Tour Through the Whole Island of Britain*, 1742, Vol. I, pp.114–15.
4. Terry Friedman, *Garden History Society Journal*, Vol. 7, no.3.
5. N. Gauger, *Fires Improv'd*, trans. Dr Desaguliers, 1715. This is a book for house architects, not for greenhouse gardeners, and it contains diagrams for fireplaces that will draw better, smoke less and throw more heat into the room.
6. *The Curious and Profitable Gardener*, London, 1730.
7. In the possession of the Marchioness of Cholomondeley; copies at Ham House and elsewhere.
8. Thomas Martyn in the revised edition of Philip Miller's *Gardener's and Botanist's Dictionary*, London, 1807.
9. Tilleman Bobart of the Oxford Physic Garden, see Leith-Ross, *The John Tradescants*, 1984.
10. Philip Miller's *Dictionary*, 1731 edition.
11. Elizabeth Hall, *Garden History Society Journal*, Vol. 14, no.1.
12. Lord Dunmore was appointed Governor of New York and Virginia in 1770, where he subsequently made some grave errors of judgement.
13. Sir George Clutton and Colin Mackay, *Garden History Society*, Occasional Paper 2.
14. Alastair Rowan, *Garden Buildings*, Feltham, Country Life, 1968.
15. Robert Beverly, *The History and Present State of Virginia*, 1705, ed. Louis B. Wright, Chapel Hill, University of North Carolina Press, 1947, p.15.
16. Alice G.B. Lockwood (ed.), *Gardens of Colony and State: Gardens and Gardeners of the American Colonies and of the Republic before 1840*, Vol. II, New York, Charles Scribner's Sons, 1934, p.95.
17. Peter Martin, '"Long and Assiduous Endeavours": Gardening in Early Eighteenth Century Virginia', *British and American Gardens in the Eighteenth Century*, ed. Robert P. Maccubbin and Peter Martin, Williamsburg, The Colonial Williamsburg Foundation, 1985, p.113.
18. E.G. Swem, *Brothers of the Spade*, Barre, Massachusetts, Barre Gazette, 1957, p.50.
19. John Bartram Association, *Bartram's Garden*, Philadelphia, John Joseph McVey, 1970, p.10.
20. Kathryn S. Taylor, *Winterflowers in the Sun Heated Pit*, New York, Charles Scribner's Sons, 1941, p.10.
21. J.C. Loudon, *Encyclopaedia of Gardening*, London, 1822, p.44.
22. David Watkin, *Athenian Stuart*, London, Allen & Unwin, 1982.
23. *Country Life*, 25 Feb, 4–11 Mar, 15–22 Apr, 1954.
24. British Library, Department of MSS, Add. MS 48218.
25. William Watkins, *A Treatise on Forest-Trees*, 1753.
26. Mutual Assurance Policy of 1803: Mount Airy. Collection of The Virginia State Library, Richmond.
27. Several years after Wye's completion, Jane Tayloe, Elizabeth Lloyd's younger sister, and her husband Robert Beverly built an orangery in 1805. Now called Dumbarton Oaks, this seven-bay orangery is clearly a hybrid of Wye and Mount Airy.
28. Michael F. Trostel, AIA, *Mount Clare, Being an Account of the Seat of Charles Carroll, Barrister, upon his Lands at Patapsco*, Baltimore, The National Society of Colonial Dames in America in the State of Maryland, 1981, pp.47–8.

29. Ibid., p.77.
30. Elizabeth Kellam deForest, *Gardens and Grounds at Mount Vernon*, Mount Vernon, Virginia, Mount Vernon Ladies Association of the Union, 1982, p.67.
31. Bensing J. Lossing, *The Two Spies, Nathan Hale and John André*, 2nd ed., New York, D. Appleton and Co., 1897.
32. Lockwood (ed.), *Gardens of Colony and State*, Vol. I, 1931, p.338.
33. Edwin Morris Betts (ed.), *Thomas Jefferson's Garden Book 1766–1824, with Relevant Extracts from his Other Writings*, Philadelphia, The American Philosophical Society, 1944, p.323.
34. Elizabeth McLean, 'Town and Country Gardens in Eighteenth Century Philadelphia', *British and American Gardens in the Eighteenth Century*, 1985, p.144.
35. Unsigned review of *Memoirs of John Bartram and Humphrey Marshall* by William Darlington, *The Horticulturist*, Vol. IV, no.7, Jan 1850, p.326.

Chapter 4: Glass Roofs and Graceful Curves

1. William Speechly, *A Treatise on the Culture of the Pineapple and the Management of the Hot-House*, York, 1779.
2. Charles M'Intosh, *The Greenhouse, Hot House and Stove*, London, 1838.
3. Sir John Soane Museum, Drawings Collection, 8/3/22 and 8/3/46.
4. J.C. Loudon, *Gardener's Magazine*, Vol. II, p.481.
5. There are two versions of Siberecht's painting, one in the possession of Lord Middleton and one in the Mellon Center at Yale.
6. Humphry Repton, *Observations on the Theory and Practice of Landscape Gardening*, London, 1803.
7. George Tod, *Plans, Elevations and Sections of Hot-Houses, Greenhouses*, York, 1807.
8. Mrs Philip Lybbe Powys, *Passages from the Diaries of Mrs. P. L. Powys, 1756–1808*, ed. E.J. Cleminson, London, Longmans, 1899, p.368.
9. Walter Nicol, *The Gardener's Kalendar*, Edinburgh, 1810, p.541.
10. G. Richardson, *New Vitruvius Britannicus*, Vol. I, 1802.
11. Warwick Castle archives.
12. Ibid.
13. R. Warner, *A Tour Through the Northern Counties of England*, 1802, p.255.
14. Ibid., p.181.
15. J.B. Papworth, *Rural Residences*, London, 1818.
16. Other examples were at Peper Harow in Surrey, Westport in Co. Mayo and Castle Coole in Fermanagh.
17. RIBA Drawings Collection, Wy Je [1] 220, 223, 234, 240, 241.
18. *Gardener's Magazine*, Vol. XII, p.291.
19. *Transactions of the Horticultural Society*, Vol. II, p.171.
20. *Gardener's Magazine*, Vol. V, 1828.
21. Ibid., Vol. VII, 1831, p.652.
22. Storch's description of 1802 in *The Encyclopaedia of Gardening*, 1822. The greenhouse was built *c.* 1780 and Prince Potemkin died in 1791.
23. Ibid., 1850, ed. Mrs Loudon, p.600.
24. Paxton's *Magazine of Botany*, Vol. II, 1836, p.105.
25. The Chatsworth Account Books are the property of the Trustees of the Chatsworth Settlement.
26. The Duke of Devonshire's Handbook.
27. Violet Markham, *Paxton and the Bachelor Duke*, London, Hodder and Stoughton, 1935, p.129.
28. *Director's Report*, 1895.
29. *Encyclopaedia of Gardening*, 1850, p.122.
30. Mrs Philip Lybbe Powys, *Diaries*, pp.288–9.
31. *Victoria regia* was subsequently renamed *Victoria amazonica*.
32. Storch's description, *Encyclopaedia of Gardening*, 1822.
33. J.C. Loudon, *The Greenhouse Companion and the Natural Arrangement of Greenhouse Plants*, London, 1824, preface.
34. William Cobbett, *The English Gardener*, London, 1833, p.39.
35. *Gardener's Magazine*, Vol. XII, 1836, p.293.

36. Christine Chapman Robbins, *David Hosack, Citizen of New York*, Philadelphia, The American Philosophical Society Memoirs, 1964, pp. 64–5.
37. Betts (ed.), *Thomas Jefferson's Garden Book*, 1944, p.323. Jefferson was referring to Hamilton's *Albizzia julibrissin*.
38. Andrew Jackson Downing, *A Treatise on the Theory and Practice of Landscape Gardening*, 9th ed., New York, Orange Judd Company, 1875, p.391.
39. Roger Hale Newton, *Town and Davis, Architects*, New York, Columbia University Press, 1942, p.109.
40. Letter from Robert Donaldson to Alexander Jackson Davis, 'Sylvania', 13 Mar 1854. Collection of the Avery Library, Columbia University.
41. 'Clinton Point', *The Horticulturist*, Vol. IV, no.4, Oct 1849, pp.178–80.
42. Constance Grieff, *John Notman, Architect, 1810–1865*, Philadephia, The Athenaeum of Philadelphia, 1979, p.119.

Chapter 5: The Victorian Glass House

1. Andrew Jackson Downing, *Rural Essays*, New York, George P. Putnam, 1853, p.150.
2. Ibid., pp.150–1.
3. Ibid., p.489.
4. Preliminary Study: Drawing No. 9 showing Flower Conservatory.
5. James R. Buckler, 'Victorian Horticulture: The Smithsonian Approach', *Nineteenth Century*, Vol. 7, no.1, spring 1981, p.54.
6. *Uber Land und Meer*, 1869, II, Vol. 22.
7. Winfried Banke in G. Kohlmaier and B. Von Sartory, *Houses of Glass*, Cambridge, Mass. and London, MIT, 1986, p.33.
8. Infanta Maria de la Paz in Kohlmaier and Von Sartory, *Houses of Glass*, p.33.
9. *The Garden*, 20 April 1872, p.189.
10. Lord Egremont, *Wyndham and Children First*, London, Macmillan, 1968, pp.57–8.
11. The brochure is undated, possibly printed shortly before the First World War, but more likely produced after the war to stimulate business.
12. James Shirley Hibberd, *The Amateur's Greenhouse and Conservatory*, London, Groombridge, 1875, pp.217–18.
13. Kenneth Lemmon, *The Covered Garden*, London, Museum Press, 1962, p.145.
14. Robert Thompson, *The Gardeners Assistant*, London, Blackie, 1878, p.809.
15. Elizabeth Dickson, *The English Garden Room*, London, Weidenfeld & Nicolson, 1986, p.25.
16. *The Royal Magazine*, 1903.
17. R.B. Leuchars, *Practical Treatise on the Construction, Heating and Ventilation of Hot-Houses*, Boston, John P. Jewett, 1851. This is the first American publication devoted totally to the greenhouse.
18. Calvert Vaux, *Villas and Cottages*, reprint of 1857 edition, New York, Dover Publications, 1970, p.81.
19. Susanne Brendel-Pandich, 'Biltmore in Asheville, North Carolina', *The Magazine of Antiques*, Vol. CXVII, no.4, Apr 1980, p.864.

Chapter 6: More Glass Than Wall

1. F.F. Rockwell, 'The Greenhouse Garden', *House and Garden*, XLVI, Oct 1924, p.88.
2. Informal discussion in November 1986 with Charles Anzalone, The Horticultural Society of New York.
3. Frank Lloyd Wright, *The Work of Frank Lloyd Wright*, facsimile of 'Wendingen' edition, New York, Horizon Press, 1965, p.11.
4. J.G. Farrell, *Troubles*, Harmondsworth, Penguin, 1982, p.17.
5. Beverley Nichols, *Down the Garden Path*, London, Cape, 1932, pp.209–10.

Select Bibliography

Abercrombie, J., *The Hot House Gardener*, London, 1789.
American Architect.
American Florist.
American Gardener's Magazine.
American Greenhouse Manufacturing Company, *American Greenhouses*, Chicago, n.d.
American Institute of Architects Journal.
American Society of Landscape Architects, *Colonial Gardens: The Landscape of George Washington's Time*, Washington, D.C., United States George Washington Bicentennial Commission, c. 1932.
Andrews, Wayne, *The Vanderbilt Legend: The Story of the Vanderbilt Family, 1794–1940*, New York, Harcourt Brace, 1941.
Androuet du Cerceau, J., *Les Plus Excellents Bastiments de la France*, pub. in English as *French Châteaux and Gardens in the XVIth Century*, ed. W.H. Ward, London, Batsford, 1909.
Angus, William, *The Seats of the Nobility and Gentry in Great Britain and Wales*, London, 1787.
Architectural Forum.
Architectural Record.
Architectural Review.
Architecture.
Architecture Australia.
Art Journal.
Aubrey, John, *Brief Lives*, ed. Oliver Lawson Dick, London, Secker and Warburg, 1949.
—*Natural History and Antiquities of Surrey*, London, 1718.

Bacon, Sir Francis, *Of Gardens*, London, Oxford University Press, 1958.
Badeslade and Rocque, *Vitruvius Britannicus*, London, 1739.
Baker, John Cordis (ed.), *American Country Homes and Their Gardens*, Philadelphia, The John C. Winston Company for *House and Garden*, 1906.
Barnard, Henry (ed.), *Armsmear: The Home and the Armoury of Samuel Colt*, New York, 1866.
John Bartram Association, *Bartram's Garden*, Philadelphia, John Joseph McVey, 1907.
Beekman, Abraham J., *History of Part of the Beekman Family*, Babylon, Long Island, 1885.
Beekman Family Papers, New York Public Library, Genealogy and History File.
Beeton, S., *The Book of Garden Management*, London, Ward, Lock and Tyler, 1870, 1871.
Betts, Edwin Morris (ed.), *Thomas Jefferson's Garden Book 1766–1824*, Philadelphia, The American Philosophical Society, 1944.
Beveridge, Charles E., and Schuyler, David (eds), *The Papers of Frederick Law Olmsted*, Vol. III, *Creating Central Park*, Baltimore, The Johns Hopkins University Press, 1983.
Beverly, Robert, *The History and Present State of Virginia, 1705*, ed. Louis B. Wright, Chapel Hill, University of North Carolina Press, 1947.
Bird, Anthony, *Paxton's Palace*, London, Cassell, 1976.
Bishop, Isabella Lucy Bird, *The Englishwoman in America*, London, J. Murray, 1856.
Blomfield, Reginald, *The Formal Garden in England*, London, Macmillan, 1901.
Boccaccio, Giovanni, *The Decameron*, trans. G.H. McWilliam, London, Penguin, 1972.
Boniface, Priscilla, *The Garden Room*, London, HMSO, 1982.
Bowle, John, *John Evelyn and his World*, London, Routledge and Kegan Paul, 1981.
Bradley, Dr Richard, *A General Treatise of Husbandry and Gardening*, London, 1724.
—*The Gentleman and Gardener's Kalendar*, London, 1718.
Bremen, Paul, *Guide to Vitruvius Britannicus*, New York, B. Blom, 1972.
Brendel, Susanne, 'A.J. Davis' Designs for Two Hudson River Estates: Montgomery Place and Edgewater', unpublished student paper, Avery Library, Columbia University, spring 1974.
—'Documentation of the Construction of Biltmore House through Drawings, Correspondence and Photographs', unpublished Master's thesis, Historic Preservation Program, Columbia University, 1978.
Britz, Billie S., *The Greenhouse at Lyndhurst* (Research on Historic Properties Occasional Papers, no. 1), Washington, D.C., National Trust for Historic Preservation, Preservation Press, 1977.
Burke's and Savill's Guides to Country Houses, London, Burke's Peerage, Vol. 2, ed. Peter Reid, 1980; Vol. 3, ed. J. Kenworthy-Browne, 1981.
Bush Brown, James and Louise, *Portraits of Philadelphia Gardens*, Philadelphia, Dorrance, 1929.

Camden, William, *Britannia*, ed. E. Gibson, 1722.
Campbell, Colen, *Vitruvius Britannicus or The British Architect*, Vol. I, 1715, Vol. II, 1717, Vol. III, 1725.
Carnegie Magazine.
Carter, George, Goode, Patrick, and Laurie, Kedrun, *Humphry Repton, Landscape Gardener*, Norwich, Sainsbury Centre for Visual Arts, 1982.
Casson, Hugh, *Victorian Architecture*, London, Art and Technics, 1948.
Cavendish, William, 6th Duke of Devonshire, *Handbook*, London, privately printed, 1844.
Cecil, Hon. Mrs Evelyn, *A History of Gardening in England*, London, Quaritch, 1895.
Chadwick, G. F., *The Works of Sir Joseph Paxton*, London, The Architectural Press, 1961.
Chambers, William, *Designs of Chinese Buildings*, London, 1757.
Chisling, Elliott, L., *Wye House, home of the Lloyds, Talbot County, Maryland*, The Monograph series, Vol. XVI, no. 5, New York, R.F. Whitehead, 1930.
Clutton, Sir George, and Mackay, Colin, *Lord Petre*, Garden History Society Occasional Paper 2.
Cobbett, William, *The English Gardener*, London, 1833.
Colvin, Howard, *A. Biographical Dictionary of British Architects*, London, John Murray, 1978.
Cooke, Robert, *West Country Houses*, Bristol, privately printed, 1957.
Coolidge, John, *Mill and Mansion*, New York, Russell and Russell, 1967.
Coppa and Avery Consultants, *Botanical Gardens, Arboretums and Greenhouses: A Bibliography*, Architectural Series A-1191, Monticello, Illinois, Vance Bibliographies, 1984.
Cottesloe, Gloria, and Hunt, Doris, *The Duchess of Beaufort's Flowers*, Exeter, Webb and Bower, 1983.
Country Life.
Country Life in America.
Cowell, F.R., *The Garden as a Fine Art*, London, Weidenfeld and Nicolson, 1978.
Cowell, J., *The Curious and Profitable Gardener*, London, 1730.
Cox, E.H.M., *A History of Gardening in Scotland*, London, Chatto and Windus, 1935.
Cruikshank, Dan, *Georgian Buildings of Britain and Ireland*, London, Weidenfeld and Nicolson for the National Trust and the Irish Georgian Society, 1985.
Croly, William, *Houses for Town and Country*, New York, Duffield, 1907.

Darbee, Henry (ed.), *Mark Twain's House*, Hartford, The Mark Twain Memorial, 1977.
Davies, R., *The Greatest House at Chelsey*, London, John Lane, 1914.
Davies, Terence, *The Gothic Taste*, Newton Abbot, David and Charles, 1974.
Defoe, Daniel, *A Tour Through the Whole Island of Great Britain*, London, 1742.
deForest, Elizabeth Kellam, *Gardens and Grounds at Mount Vernon*, Mount Vernon, Virginia, Mount Vernon Ladies Association of the Union, 1982.
Delderfield, Eric, *West Country Historic Houses and their Families*, Newton Abbot, David and Charles, 1968–73.
Demorest's Family Magazine.
de Serres, Olivier, *Le Théâtre d'Agriculture*, Paris, 1600.
Desaguliers, Dr, *see* E. Gauger.

Desmond, Ray, *Bibliography of British Gardens*, Winchester, St Paul's Bibliographies, 1984.
—'Who Designed the Palm House in Kew Gardens?', *Kew Bulletin*, Vol. 27(2), 1972.
Dickson, Elizabeth (ed.), *The English Garden Room*, London, Weidenfeld and Nicolson, 1986.
Diestelkamp, Edward, 'The Conservatories and Hot-Houses of Richard Turner', pub. in *Historic Greenhouses and Kew*, Kew, Royal Botanic Gardens, 1982.
—'The Design and Building of the Palm House, Royal Botanic Gardens, Kew', *Journal of Garden History*, 2(3).
Donaldson, Robert, unpublished letter to A.J. Davis from 'Sylvania', 13 March 1854, New York, Avery Collection, 2–4A.
Douglas, R.W., and Frank, S., *A History of Glassmaking*, Foulis, 1972.
Downing, Andrew Jackson, *Cottage Residences*, 2nd ed., New York and London, Wiley and Putnam, 1844.
—*Rural Essays*, New York, Putnam, 1853.
—*The Architecture of Country Houses*, New York, D. Appleton, 1854.
—*A Treatise on the Theory and Practice of Landscape Gardening*, 2nd and 7th eds, New York, Orange Judd, 1844, 1865.

Eberlein, Harold Donaldson, *The Manors and Historic Homes of the Hudson Valley*, Philadelphia, J.B. Lippincott, 1924.
—*The Practical Book of Garden Structure and Design*, Philadelphia, J.B. Lippincott, 1937.
Egremont, Lord, *Wyndham and Children First*, London, Macmillan, 1968.
Elliott, Dr Brent, *Victorian Gardens*, London, Batsford, 1986.
Evans, John, *Richmond and Its Vicinity*, Richmond, 1824.
Evelyn, John, *The Diary and Correspondence of John Evelyn*, ed. William Bray, London, Henry Bohn, 1859.
—*Directions for the Gardiner at Says-Court*, ed. Geoffrey Keynes, London, Nonsuch Press, 1932.
—*Kalendarium Hortense or the Gard'ners Almanac*, London, 1664 and 1691.
Ewan, Joseph and Nesta, *John Banister and his Natural History of Virginia, 1678–1692*, Urbana, University of Illinois Press, 1970.

Fairchild, Thomas, *The City Gardener*, London, 1722.
Farrell, J.G., *Troubles*, London, Cape, 1970.
Faulkner, Thomas, *An Historical and Topographical Description of Chelsea*, London, 1829.
Favretti, Rudy, J., and Putnam, Joy, *Landscapes and Gardens for Historic Buildings*, Nashville, American Association for State and Local History, 1978.
Fawkes, Frank A., *Horticultural Buildings, their Construction, Heating, Interiors, Fittings, etc.*, London, 1881.
Ferre, Barr, *American Estates and Gardens*, New York, Munn, 1904.
Fiennes, Celia, *The Illustrated Journeys of Celia Fiennes*, ed. Christopher Morris, London, Macdonald, 1984.
Fleming, Laurence, and Gore, Alan, *The English Garden*, London, Michael Joseph, 1976.
Frank Leslie's Illustrated Newspaper.
Friedman, Terry, 'Galilei's Greenhouse', *Garden History Society Journal*, Vol. 7, no. 3.

Galpine, J.K., *The Georgian Garden*, intr. by John Harvey, Wimborne, Dovecote Press, 1983.
Garden Club of America Bulletin.
The Gardener's Chronicle and Agricultural Gazette.
Gardeners Magazine, ed. J.C. Loudon.
Gauger, N., *Fires Improv'd*, trans. Dr Desaguliers, London, 1715.
Gerard, John, *Catalogus arborum fruiticum ac plantarum tam indigenarum, quam exoticarum in horto Johannis Gerardi … nascentium*, London, 1599.
—*Herball*, London, 1597.
Gibbs, James, *A Book of Architecture*, London, 1728.

Gibson, J., 'A Short Account of Several Gardens near London in December, 1691', pub. in *Archaeologia*, Vol. 12, London, Society of Antiquaries, 1794, and in W.C. Hazlitt, *Gleanings in Old Garden Literature*, London, Elliot Stock, 1887.
Giles, John, *A Treatise on the Pineapple*, London, 1767.
Girouard, Mark, *Life in the English Country House*, New Haven, London, Yale University Press, 1978.
—*The Victorian Country House*, Oxford, Clarendon Press, 1971.
Gloag, John, *Mr. Loudon's England*, Newcastle-upon-Tyne, Oriel Press, 1970.
— and Bridgewater, Derek, *A History of Cast Iron in Architecture*, London, Allen and Unwin, 1948.
Glover, S., *History and Gazetteer of the County of Derby*, Derby, 1833.
Gothein, Marie Luise, *A History of Garden Art*, London, Dent, 1928.
Green, David, *Gardener to Queen Anne*, London, Oxford University Press, 1956.
Grieff, Constance, *John Notman, Architect 1810–1865*, Philadelphia, The Athenaeum of Philadelphia, 1979.
Gunther, R.T., *Oxford Gardens*, Oxford, Parker, 1922.

Hadfield, Miles, *A History of British Gardening*, London, Hutchinson, 1960; Penguin, 1985.
Halfpenny, William and John, *Chinese and Gothic Architecture Properly Ornamented*, London, 1752.
—*Rural Architecture in the Chinese Taste*, London, 1752.
Hall, Elizabeth, 'Plant Collections of an Eighteenth Century Virtuoso', *Garden History Society Journal*, Vol. 14:1.
Hamlin, Talbot, *Greek Revival Architecture in America*, New York, Dover Publications, 1964.
Hanmer, Sir Thomas, *The Garden Book*, MS of 1659, London, Gerald Howe, 1933.
Harris, John, *The Artist and the Country House*, London, Philip Wilson for Sotheby Parke Bernet, 1979.
Harris, Leslie, *Robert Adam and Kedleston*, London, The National Trust, 1987.
Harrison, William, *The Description of England*, Holinshed's Chronicles, Vol. II, 1587.
Harvey, John, *Early Gardening Catalogues*, London and Chichester, Phillimore, 1972.
Hazlitt, W.C., *Gleanings in Old Garden Literature*, London, Elliot Stock, 1887.
Henrey, Blanche, *British Botanical and Horticultural Literature before 1800*, London, Oxford University Press, 1975.
Hibberd, James Shirley, *The Amateur's Greenhouse and Conservatory*, London, Croombridge and Sons, 1875.
—*The Fern Garden*, London, 1870.
—*Rustic Adornments for Homes of Taste*, London, Driffield, 1856.
Hibbert, Christopher, *The Rise and Fall of the House of Medici*, Harmondsworth, Penguin Books, 1979.
Hierneis, Theodor, *The Monarch Dines: Reminiscences of Life in the Royal Kitchens at the Court of King Ludwig the Second of Bavaria*, London, Werner Laurie, 1954.
Higham, G.S., *Wimbledon Manor House under the Cecils*, London, Longman, 1962.
Hill, Sir John, *The Gardener's New Kalendar*, London, 1758.
Historic American Buildings Survey, National Park Service, Department of the Interior, *Virginia Catalog*, compiled by the Virginia Historic Landmarks Commission, Charlottesville, University Press of Virginia, 1976.
Historic Preservation.
Hitchings and Company, various catalogues, Elizabeth, N.J., 1905–27.
Hix, John, *The Glass House*, London, Phaidon, 1974.
The Horticulturist and Journal of Rural Art and Rural Taste.
House and Garden.
Hyams, Edward, *Capability Brown and Humphry Repton*, London, Dent, 1971.

Jacques, David, *Georgian Gardens: the Reign of Nature*, London, Batsford, 1983.
Jekyll, Gertrude, *Garden Ornament*, London, Country Life and George Newnes, 1918.

Johnson, J., *Excellent Cassandra: The Life and Times of the Duchess of Chandos*, Gloucester, A.J. Sutton, 1981.
Jones, Barbara, *Follies and Grottoes*, London, Constable, 1953.
Journal of the Society of Architectural Historians.

Kimball, Fiske, *Mr. Samuel McIntire, Carver; The Architect of Salem*, Portland, Maine, The Southworth-Anthoensen Press, 1940.
—*Thomas Jefferson, Architect*, reprint of 1916 ed., intr. by Frederick Nichols, New York, 1968.
Kohlmaier, G., and Von Sartory, B., *Houses of Glass*, Cambridge, Mass. and London, MIT Press, 1986.
Koppelkamm, Stefan, *Glasshouses and Wintergardens of the Nineteenth Century*, St Albans, Granada, 1981.

Lambton, Lucinda, *Vanishing Victoriana*, Oxford, Phaidon, 1976.
Langley, Betty, *Gothic Architecture Improved*, London, 1742.
Lees-Milne, James, *The Earls of Creation*, London, Century Hutchinson, 1986.
Leighton, Ann, *American Gardens in the Eighteenth Century, 'For Use or for Delight'*, Amherst, The University of Massachusetts Press, 1986.
—*Early American Gardens, 'For Meate or Medicine'*, Boston, Houghton Mifflin, 1970.
Leith-Ross, Prudence, *The John Tradescants*, London, Peter Owen, 1984.
Lemmon, Kenneth, *The Covered Garden*, London, Museum Press, 1962.
Leuchars, Robert B., *A Practical Treatise on the Construction, Heating and Ventilation of Hot-houses, etc.*, Boston, John P. Jewett and Company, 1851.
Linstrum, D., *Sir Jeffry Wyatville: Architect to the King*, Oxford, Clarendon Press, 1972.
Little, Bryan, *Sir Christopher Wren*, London, Robert Hale, 1975.
Lockwood, Alice G.B. (ed.), *Gardens of Colony and State: Gardens and Gardeners of the America Colonies and of the Republic before 1840*, 2 vols, New York, Charles Scribner's Sons, 1931, 1934.
Lockwood, Charles, *Bricks and Brownstones, The New York Row House, 1783–1929*, New York, McGraw-Hill, 1972.
Lord and Burnham, various catalogues, Irvington-on-Hudson, N.Y., 1893–1976.
Lossing, Benson J., *The Two Spies: Nathan Hale and John André*, 2nd ed., New York, D. Appleton, 1897.
Loth, Calder (ed.), *The Virginia Landmarks Register*, 3rd ed., published for the Virginia Historic Landmarks Commission, Charlottesville, University Press of Virginia, 1986.
Loudon, J.C., *The Encyclopaedia of Gardening*, London, 1822 and 1850.
—*The Greenhouse Companion*, London, 1824.
—*Sketches of Curvilinear Hothouses*, London, 1818.

Macartney, Mervyn, *English Houses and Gardens in the 17th and 18th Centuries*, London, Batsford, 1908.
Maccubbin, Robert P., and Martin, Peter (eds), *British and American Gardens in the Eighteenth Century*, Williamsburg, Virginia, The Colonial Williamsburg Foundation, 1985.
MacDougall, Elizabeth B. (ed.), *John Claudius Loudon and the Early Nineteenth Century in Great Britain*, Dunbarton Oaks Colloquium on the History of Landscape Architecture, VI, Dunbarton Oaks, 1980.
McGrath, Raymond, and Frost, A.C., *Glass in Architecture and Decoration*, London, The Architectural Press, 1937.
M'Intosh, Charles, *The Book of the Garden*, Vol. II, Edinburgh, 1855.
—*The Greenhouse, Hot-house and Stove*, London, 1838.
Macky, J., *A Journey Through England*, London, 1714.
McKenzie, Sir George, Paper to the Horticultural Society, 1815, pub. in *Transactions of the Horticultural Society*, Vol. II, London, 1817.
Mackenzie and Moncur's *Catalogue*, Edinburgh, 1907.
M'Mahon, Bernard, *The American Gardener's Calendar*, Philadelphia, B. Graves, 1806.
Magazine of Antiques.
Magazine of Botany, ed. Joseph Paxton.

Manning and Bray, *History and Antiquities of the County of Surrey*, Vol. II, London, 1809.
Markham, Violet, *Paxton and the Bachelor Duke*, London, Hodder and Stoughton, 1935.
Martin, Peter, *The Gardening World of Alexander Pope*, Hamden, Archon Books, 1984.
Maryland Historical Magazine.
Masson, Georgina, *Italian Gardens*, London, Thames and Hudson, 1961.
Michell, Ronald, *The Carews of Beddington*, Sutton, London Borough of Sutton, 1981.
Miller, Philip, *Decimus Burton, A Guide to the Exhibition of his Work*, London, Building Centre Trust, 1981.
Miller, Philip, *Dictionary*, London, 1731–1807.
Milward, R.J., *Tudor Wimbledon*, Wimbledon, Milward, 1972.
Missouri Botanical Garden Bulletin.
Mitford, Nancy, *The Sun King*, London, Hamish Hamilton, 1966.
Moore, Patricia, *Margam Orangery*, Glamorgan, Glamorgan Archive Service, 1986.
Mount Vernon Ladies Association, 'Washington and Mount Vernon Archives'.
New York Journal, or the General Advertiser.

Newton, Roger Hale, *Town and Davis, Architects*, New York, Columbia University Press, 1942.
Nichols, Beverley, *Down the Garden Path*, London, Cape, 1932.
Nicol, Walter, *The Gardener's Kalendar*, Edinburgh, 1810.
Nineteenth Century.
Nygren, Edward, J., Robertson, Bruce, *et al.*, *Views and Visions: American Landscape Before 1830*, Washington, D.C., Corcoran Gallery of Art, 1986.

Old Time New England Journal.

Papworth, J.B., *Hints on Ornamental Gardening*, London, 1823.
—*Rural Residences*, London, 1818.
Parkinson, John, *Paradisi in Sole, Paradisus Terrestris*, London, 1629.
Paul, Jerry, *Original Drawings of Early Philadelphia*, Historical Society of Pennsylvania Collection, *c.* 1794.
Pennsylvania Magazine of History and Biography.
Pepys, Samuel, *Diary, 1660–69*, London, Dent, 1971.
Pevsner, Nikolaus *et al.*, county volumes in the series *The Buildings of England*, Harmondsworth, Penguin Books, 1951–87.
Pierson, William H., Jr, *American Buildings and their Architecture, Technology and the Picturesque*, Garden City, New York, Doubleday, 1978.
Platt, H., *The Garden of Eden*, London, 1653.
Plaw, John, *Sketches for Country Houses, Villas and Rural Dwellings*, London, 1800.
Plumb, J.H., *Georgian Delights*, London, Weidenfeld and Nicolson, 1980.
Plumptre, George, *Royal Gardens*, London, Collins, 1981.
Pomet, Pierre, *Compleat History of Drugs*, London, 1737.
Powys, Mrs Philip Lybbe, *Passages from the Diaries of Mrs. P. L. Powys, 1756–1808*, ed. E.J. Cleminson, London, Longmans, 1899.
Powys Castle Guidebook, London, The National Trust, 1987.
Progressive Architecture.
Prosser, G.F., *Select Illustrations of the County of Surrey*, London, 1828.
Putnam's Monthly Magazine of American Literature, Science and Art.

Randall, Colvin, L., 'Longwood, History of the Conservatories', unpublished material, 1987.
Randall, Monica, *The Mansions of Long Island's Gold Coast*, New York, Hastings House Publishers, 1979.
Read, Conyers, *Lord Burghley and Queen Elizabeth*, London, Cape, 1960.
Reader's Digest Encyclopaedia of Garden Plants and Flowers, London, Reader's Digest Association, 1978.
Reed, Henry Hope, and Duckworth, Sophia, *Central Park, A History and a Guide*, New York, C.N. Potter, 1972.

Repton, Humphry, *Designs for the Pavillon at Brighton*, London, 1803.
—*Fragments on the Theory and Practice of Landscape Gardening*, London, 1816.
—*Observations on the Theory and Practice of Landscape Gardening*, London, 1803.
—*Barton Seagrave,* Red Book, 1793.
Richardson, George, *The New Vitruvius Britannicus*, London, Vol. I, 1802; Vol. II, 1808.
Richardson & Co., Catalogue, n.d.
Riedesel, Baroness Fredericke (Mrs General), *Letters and Journals relating to the War of the American Revolution*, trans. William L. Stone, Albany, Joel Munsell, 1867.
Robbins, Christine Chapman, *David Hosack, Citizen of New York*, The American Philosophical Society, Memoirs, 1964.
Robinson, John Martin, *The Wyatts: An Architectural Dynasty*, London, Oxford University Press, 1979.
Roth, Leland, M., *McKim, Mead and White, Architects*, New York, Harper and Row, 1983.
Rowan, Alastair, *Garden Buildings*, Feltham, Country Life, 1968.
Rudder, Samuel, *A New History of Gloucestershire*, Cirencester, 1779.

Schuyler, David, 'Public Landscapes and American Urban Culture, 1800–1870', unpublished Doctoral dissertation, Columbia University, 1979.
Sclare, Liisa and Donald, *Beaux Arts Estates, A Guide to Long Island Architecture*, New York, Viking Press, 1979.
Seeley, J., *Stowe, A Description of the House and Gardens*, 1797.
Shell Gardens Book, ed. Peter Hunt, London, Phoenix House, 1964.
Soane, Sir John, *The Works of Sir John Soane*, ed. A.T. Bolton, London, Soane Museum Publications, 1924.
Speechly, William, *A Treatise on the Pine Apple*, York, 1779.
Stein, Susan R. (ed.), *The Architecture of Richard Morris Hunt*, Chicago and London, The University of Chicago Press, 1986.
Stephens, Ann Sophia, *Fashion and Famine*, New York, Bunce, 1854.
Stokes, I.N. Phelps, and Haskell, Daniel C., *American Historical Prints of American Cities, etc. 1497–1891*, New York, The New York Public Library, 1933.
Strahan, Edward, *Mr. Vanderbilt's House and Collection*, 2 vols, Boston, New York, Philadelphia, George Barrie, 1883–4.
Strong, Sir Roy, *The Renaissance Garden in England*, London, Thames and Hudson, 1979.
Stroud, Dorothy, *Capability Brown*, London, Country Life, 1950; Faber and Faber, 1957.
Summerson, Sir John, *The Life and Work of John Nash*, London, Allen and Unwin, 1980.
Surrey Archaeological Collections, Vols II, XXXI.
Swem, E.G., *Brothers of the Spade*, Barre, Massachusetts, Barre Gazette, 1957.
Switzer, Stephen, *Ichonographia Rustica*, Vols I, III, London, 1718.

Taft, Levi Rawson, *Greenhouse Construction, A Complete Manual*, New York, Orange Judd, 1894.
Tallack, J.C., *The Book of the Greenhouse*, New York and London, J. Lane, 1908.
Tanner, Ogden, *Garden Rooms: Greenhouse, Sunroom and Solarium Designs*, New York, Linden Press/Simon and Schuster, 1986.
Taylor, Adam, *A Treatise on the Anana*, Devizes, 1769.
Temple, Sir William, *Upon the Gardens of Epicurus*, London, Chatto and Windus, 1908.
Thacker, Christopher, *The History of Gardens*, London, Croom Helm, 1979.
Thompson, Francis, *Chatsworth: A Short History*, London, Country Life, 1951.
Thompson, Robert, *The Gardeners Assistant*, London, Blackie and Son, 1878.
Tod, George, *Plans, Elevations and Sections of Hot-Houses, Greenhouses, etc.*, York, 1807.
Town and Country.
Tressider, Jane, and Cliff, Stafford, *Living Under Glass*, London, Thames and Hudson, 1986.

Trevelyan, G.M., *English Social History*, London, Book Club Associates, 1973.
Trostel, Michael F., AIA, *Mount Clare, Being an Account of the Seat of Charles Carroll, Barrister, upon his Lands at Patapsco*, Baltimore, The National Society of Colonial Dames of America in the State of Maryland, 1981.
Turnor, Reginald, *The Smaller English House*, London, Batsford, 1952.

Van den Muijzenberg, Dr Erwin W.B., *A History of Greenhouses*, Wageningen, Institute for Agricultural Engineering, 1980.
Vance, Mary, *Garden Rooms and Greenhouses: A Bibliography*, Architectural Series A-1042, Monticello, Illinois, Vance Bibliographies, 1983.
Vaux, Calvert, *Villas and Cottages*, New York, Dover Publications, 1970.
Victoria County History, Warwickshire, Vol. VIII.

Walpole, Horace, *The History of the Modern Taste in Gardening*, New York, London, Garland Publishing Inc., 1982.
Walter Macfarlane, *Macfarlane's Architectural Ironwork*, Glasgow, 1922.
—*Macfarlane's Castings*, Vols I, II and *Examples Book*, n.d.
Walton, Guy, *Louis XIV's Versailles*, Harmondsworth, Viking, 1986.
Warner, R., *A Tour Through the Northern Counties of England*, Bath, 1802.
Watkin, David, *Athenian Stuart: Pioneer of the Greek Revival*, London, Allen and Unwin, 1982.
—*The Life and Work of C. R. Cockerell*, London, Zwemmer, 1974.
Watts, William, *The Seats of the Nobility and Gentry*, Chelsea, 1779.
Weitenkampf, Frank, *The Eno Collection of New York City Views*, New York, The New York Public Library, 1925.
Wheeler, Gervase, *Rural Homes; or Sketches of Houses Suited to American Country Life with Original Plans, Designs, &c.*, New York, Charles Scribner, 1851–2.
Whistler, Laurence, Gibbon, Michael, and Clarke, George, *Stowe: A Guide to the Gardens*, Stony Stratford, Hillier Design, 1974.
White House Gardens: A History and Pictorial Record, New York, Great American Editions, Ltd, 1973.
Whitehill, Alfred Muir, *Dunbarton Oaks 1800–1966*, Cambridge, Mass., Belknap Press of the Harvard University Press, 1967.
Wilkinson, Norman B., *E.I. du Pont, botaniste: The Beginning of a Tradition*, Charlottesville, University Press of Virginia, 1972.
Winterthur Portfolio.
Woodward, Frank, *Oxfordshire Parks*, Woodstock, Oxfordshire Museum Services, 1982.
Worrilow, William H., *James Lick (1796–1876) Pioneer and Adventurer*, New York, The Newcomen Society of England, American Branch, 1949.
Wright, Frank Lloyd, *Buildings, Plans and Designs*, reprint of Ernst Wasmuth's Berlin edition of 1910, New York, Horizon Press, 1963.
—*The Work of Frank Lloyd Wright*, facsimile of 'Wendingen edition, New York, Horizon Press, 1965.
—*The Natural House*, New York, New American Library, 1963.
—*Autobiography*, New York, Duell, Sloan and Pearce, 1943.
Wright, Louis B., *The First Gentlemen of Virginia*, Charlottesville, University Press of Virginia, 1964.

Index

Figures in italic refer to illustrations

Picture Acknowledgements

Note: Details of books which also appear in the bibliography may be found there in full.

Page 1 Photograph by Hugh Palmer. **2** Reproduced by courtesy of the Trustees of the British Museum, Sloane 4016, ff.5b/6. Marie Luise Gothein, *A History of Garden Art.* **6** Scala/Firenze. **8** Marie Luise Gothein, *A History of Garden Art.* **9** Androuet du Cerceau, *Les Plus Excellents Bastiments de la France.* By permission of the British Library. **11** National Portrait Gallery, London. **12, 13** J. B. Ferrarius, *Hesperides*, Rome, 1646. Royal Horticultural Society, Lindley Library. **14, 15** J. C. Loudon, *Encyclopaedia of Gardening.* **16, 17** Salomon de Caus, *Les Raisons des Forces Mouvants*, Paris, 1624. **18** Marie Luise Gothein, *A History of Garden Art.* **20** Reproduced by courtesy of the Trustees of the British Museum. **23** In a private collection. **24(t)** Jean de la Quintinye, *The Compleat Gard'ner*, trans. John Evelyn, 1693. **24(b)** Marie Luise Gothein, *A History of Garden Art.* **26** Statens Konstmuseer, Stockholm. **27** J. C. Volkamer, *Nurnbergische Hesperides*, Vol. I, 1708. RHS, Lindley Library. **28, 29** J. Commelyn, *Nederlantze Hesperides*, 1683. RHS, Lindley Library. **30** John Evelyn, *Kalendarium Hortense*, 1691. RHS, Lindley Library. **32** J. Commelyn, *Nederlantze Hesperides*, 1683. RHS, Lindley Library. **33** Reproduced by courtesy of the Trustees of the British Museum. **35** Badeslade and Rocque, *Vitruvius Britannicus*, 1739, from the British Architectural Library, RIBA, London. **37** Reproduced by courtesy of the Trustees of the British Museum. **38** Marie Luise Gothein, *A History of Garden Art.* **39** Photograph by May Woods, reproduced by gracious permission of Her Majesty The Queen. **40** Photograph by Michael Alexander, reproduced by courtesy of the Duke of Beaufort. **42** In the collection of May Woods. **43** Marie Luise Gothein, *A History of Garden Art.* **44** J. C. Volkamer, *Nurnbergische Hesperides*, Vol. II, 1714. RHS, Lindley Library. **45** J. B. Ferrarius, *Hesperides*, Rome, 1646. RHS, Lindley Library. **46** Reproduced by courtesy of the Vicomte de Sigalas. **47** J. C. Volkamer, *Nurnbergische Hesperides*, Vol. I, 1708. RHS, Lindley Library. **48, 49** Photograph by Hugh Palmer. **50** Pierre Pomet, *Compleat History of Drugs.* **52** In the collection of May Woods. **54** Badeslade and Rocque, *Vitruvius Britannicus*, 1739, from The British Architectural Library, RIBA, London. **55** Pierre Pomet, *Compleat History of Drugs.* **56, 57** Richard Bradley, *The Gentleman and Gardener's Kalendar.* **58** Mary Evans Picture Library. **59** John Cowell, *The Curious and Profitable Gardener.* **60** Pierre Pomet, *Compleat History of Drugs.* **62** Mary Evans Picture Library. **63** Photograph by Hugh Palmer. **64** Philip Miller, *Gardener's Dictionary*, 1731. RHS, Lindley Library. **65** Reproduced by courtesy of the Trustees of the British Museum. **66** In the collection of May Woods. **67** Photograph by Hugh Palmer. **69** Copyright of the Trustees of The Royal Botanic Gardens, Kew © 1987. **70** By courtesy of the Government Service for the Preservation of Monuments and Historic Buildings, Zeist, The Netherlands. **71** Photograph by Hugh Palmer. **72, 73** Photograph by May Woods. **74** In a private collection. **75** William Halfpenny, *Rural Architecture in the Chinese Taste*, from The British Architectural Library, RIBA, London. **77** Photographs by Hugh Palmer. **78** By courtesy of The National Trust. **79** Photograph by May Woods. **80** By courtesy of English Heritage, Historic Buildings and Monuments Commission for England. **80–1** Glamorgan Archive Service. **82, 83** Photographs by Arete Swartz Warren. **85** By courtesy of the Essex Institute, Salem, MA. **86** *The American Florist*, 15 February 1887. **87** The Historical Society of Pennsylvania, no.1000.5. **88, 89** Photographs by May Woods. **90** By courtesy of the Trustees of Sir John Soane's Museum. **91** Humphry Repton, *Fragments on the Theory and Practice of Landscape Gardening.* **92, 93** Humphry Repton, *Designs for the Royal Pavilion.* RHS, Lindley Library. **94** Photograph by May Woods. **95** Photograph by Hugh Palmer. **96–7** G. Richardson, *New Vitruvius Britannicus*, from the British Architectural Library, RIBA, London. **97(t, b)** The British Architectural Library, RIBA, London. **98** J. C. Loudon, *Encyclopaedia of Gardening.* **99** Photograph by Hugh Palmer. **100** By courtesy of the Victoria and Albert Museum. **102** By courtesy of the Ayr Public Library. **103** J. B. Papworth, *Rural Residences*, from the British Architectural Library, RIBA, London. **104–8** Photographs by Hugh Palmer. **109** The British Architectural Library, RIBA, London. **110** Photograph by Hugh Palmer. **111** *Gardeners Magazine*, Vol. II. RHS, Lindley Library. **112(t)** *Transactions of the Horticultural Society*, Vol. II. RHS, Lindley Library. **112(b)** *Gardeners Magazine*, Vol. V. RHS, Lindley Library. **113** Photograph by May Woods. **114, 115** Photographs by Hugh Palmer. **116** Photograph by Hugh Palmer by courtesy of English Heritage, Historic Buildings and Monuments Commission for England. **117** Nottingham City Council. **118, 119** Photographs by Hugh Palmer. **120** Royal Commission on the Historical Monuments of England. **121** Mary Evans Picture Library. **122** By courtesy of the Duke of Devonshire. **123** Photograph by Hugh Palmer. **124** Royal Commission on the Historical Monuments of England. **125** Photograph by Hugh Palmer. **126** Copyright of the Trustees of The Royal Botanic Gardens, Kew © 1987. **128** Mary Evans Picture Library. **129** *Illustrated London News.* **130** In a private collection. **131** Nationalbibliothek, Vienna. **132** J. C. Loudon, *Encyclopaedia of Gardening.* **133** Photograph by May Woods. **134** Eno Collection, no. 65, The New York Public Library. **135** Thomas Jefferson Memorial Foundation, photograph by Robert Llewellyn. **137** A. J. Davies Collection, Avery Architectural and Fine Arts Library, Columbia University. **139** Copyright © 1987, The Metropolitan Museum of Art, Harry Brisbane Dick Fund, 1924. **140** *The Horticulturist*, October 1847. **141** The Bettman Archive. **142** In the collection of May Woods. **144** Photograph by Hugh Palmer. **146** Photograph by May Woods. **147** Copyright of the Trustees of The Royal Botanic Gardens, Kew © 1987. **148** Collection of The Municipal Archives, City of New York. **150** The Bettman Archive. **151(t)** Photograph by Arete Swartz Warren. **151(b)** Cass & Pinell, architects. **152** Photograph by Arete Swartz Warren. **154** Gardeners Chronicle, Vol. 7, 1890. RHS, Lindley Library. **155** Photograph by Patricia Matthieu de Wynendaele. **156** Photograph by Hugh Palmer. **157** Royal Commission on the Historical Monuments of England. **158(t)** Photograph by Hugh Palmer. **158(b)** The British Architectural Library, RIBA, London. **159** Photograph by Hugh Palmer. **160** Photograph by Kay Sanecki. **161** Mary Evans Picture Library. **162, 163** Photographs by Hugh Palmer. **164** Mary Evans Picture Library. **165** By courtesy of English Heritage, Royal Commission on the Historical Monuments of England. **166** Staatliche Museen Preussischer Kulturbesitz, Nationalgalerie, West Berlin. Photograph by Jörg P. Anders. **168** By courtesy of the Library of Congress. **169** Collection of the Connecticut Historical Society. **170** Mark Twain Memorial, Hartford, CT. **172, 173** Lyndhurst, Tarrytown, NY. The National Trust for Historic Preservation. **175** By courtesy of Biltmore Estate, Asheville, NC. **176** By courtesy of the Library of Congress, Witteman Collection. **178** Longwood Gardens, Kennett Square, PA. Photograph by Larry Albee. **179** By courtesy of *House and Garden.* Copyright © 1915 (renewed 1943) by the Condé Nast Publication Inc. **181** Paul Rudolph, architect. **182, 183** Photographs by Arete Swartz Warren. **184, 185** Edward Larabee Barnes Associates. **186** Emilio Ambasz & Associates. **188** Palmengarten der Stadt Frankfurt. **189** Copyright of the Trustees of The Royal Botanic Gardens, Kew © 1987. **190** Photograph by Hugh Palmer. In a private collection. **192** Photograph by Michael Jantzen, architect. **193–6** Photographs by Hugh Palmer. **197** Charles Morris, FRICS. **199(t)** Marston and Langinger. **199(b)** Town and Country Conservatories. **200–1** Photographs by Stan Ribton for Town and Country Conservatories. **202** Robert Thompson, *The Gardeners Assistant.* **204** Photograph by May Woods.